CATHOLICS

AND

AMERICAN CULTURE

CATHOLICS
AND
AMERICAN CULTURE

Fulton Sheen, Dorothy Day,
and the Notre Dame Football Team

MARK S. MASSA

A Crossroad Book
The Crossroad Publishing Company
New York

The Crossroad Publishing Company
370 Lexington Avenue, New York, NY 10017

Printed in the United States of America

Library of Congress Cataloging-in-Publication Data
Massa, Mark Stephen.
    Catholics and American culture : Fulton Sheen, Dorothy Day, and the Notre Dame football team / Mark S. Massa.
        p.   cm.
    Includes bibliographical references and index.
    ISBN 0-8245-1537-4 (hardcover)
    1. Catholics – United States – History – 20th century. 2. Catholic Church – United States – History – 20th century. 3. Christianity and culture – Catholic Church – History – 20th century.   I. Title.
BX1406.2.M38 1999
305.6'2073 – dc21   98-31072

2   3   4   5   6   7   8   9   10   03   02   01   00   99

To Howard Gray, John Libens, and John O'Malley,
Members of the "Least Society"

"Hi Fide viverunt"

Contents

Acknowledgments

The project that evolved into this book began a number of years ago in Cambridge, Massachusetts, during a summer spent working with the exceptionally talented scholars who constituted the John Court- ney Murray Working Group. What is now the opening chapter in this book took shape in that group, and to them I owe a debt of gratitude both for it and for giving me the initial idea of the study that follows.

The article that resulted from that Cambridge summer — an ear- lier version of what is now chapter 1 — was published in the *Harvard Theological Review.* Likewise, an earlier version of chapter 2 was pub- lished in the *U.S. Catholic Historian,* and of chapter 6 in the *Journal of Church and State.* The editors of all three of these excellent jour- nals offered sage advice and helpful critiques in honing those chapters, and I gratefully acknowledge their help. Likewise, my editor at Cross- road, James LeGrys, offered consistently cheerful and infallibly correct suggestions in reshaping sections of the manuscript.

As is always the case with scholarly projects that evolve over time, a number of debts — both personal and academic — are incurred that cannot be repaid but only acknowledged. Such is certainly the case in this book: Gerard Reedy, S.J., and Joseph McShane, S.J., talented scholars as well as successive deans of Fordham College, supported this project through constant personal interest, research monies, and valuable release time from committee work and teach- ing. Dr. Robert Carrubba, Fordham's academic vice president, and Dr. Robert Himmelberg, dean of the Graduate School of Arts and Sciences, likewise offered consistent research support and a sabbatical during which much of the first draft of the manuscript was written. They likewise provided me with an invaluable graduate research assis- tant, Mark Newcomb, who cheerfully spent a mind-numbing amount of time trailing footnotes for me. Joseph Novak, S.J., rector of Ford- ham's Jesuit community, offered both *cura personalis* and the generous backing of the Jesuit community during my sabbatical. To all of these I can only acknowledge a debt that extends beyond the academic.

A number of my colleagues at Fordham, excellent scholars whom

I am lucky to count as friends, listened to and critiqued my ideas over myriad dinners and office chats: Mary Callaway, Elizabeth Johnson, and Robert Cornelison offered helpful suggestions and perceptive criticisms at important junctures in this project. Susan Simonaitis, an extremely talented and much-welcomed recent addition to Fordham's faculty, read most of the chapters in the final draft of this manuscript, offering insightful readings and superb suggestions to both content and form. Much of what "works" in the conclusion to this study is a result of her scholarly acumen and brilliant critical eye. Finally, this book is dedicated to three fellow members of the Society of Jesus who have served as mentors, models, and friends to me over the past thirty years: Howard Gray, John Libens, and John O'Malley. In manifold ways during my pilgrimage in St. Ignatius Loyola's "Least Society," they have provided guidance, support, and inspiration in ways that only they fully know. To them one can confidently apply the highest accolade of Holy Scripture: "These live by faith."

Introduction

"Oh, the Irony of It All"

"We Were Raised Different"

In April 1949, Boston's revered liberal printing house Beacon Press published the first edition of Paul Blanshard's *American Freedom and Catholic Power* — arguably the classic twentieth-century American statement of "progressive" fears of Catholic authoritarianism. Blanshard's call to arms almost immediately sold out at the bookstores, and Beacon Press printed eleven editions of the book within as many months. Unlike the crass "popular" classics of the anti-Catholic genre in the nineteenth century — works like Maria Monk's fanciful *Awful Disclosures of the Hotel Dieu Nunnery,* Rebecca Theresa Reed's deliciously salacious *Six Months in a Convent,* or Lyman Beecher's semi-hysterical *A Plea for the West* — Blanshard's book sought to eschew the shenanigans of escaped nuns, hooded patriots, and "mick-haters" entirely. Rather, Blanshard sought to present a rather dispassionate and closely reasoned philosophical and historical argument for his and other progressives' fears of the Church of Rome in America:

> Unfortunately the Catholic people of the United States are not citizens but *subjects* in their own religious commonwealth. The secular as well as the religious policies of their Church are made in Rome by an organization that is alien in spirit and control. …They are compelled by the very nature of their Church's authoritarian structure to accept nonreligious as well as religious policies that have been imposed upon them from abroad.[1]

Blanshard's classically liberal fears were thus centered on an image of basically loyal and intelligent American Catholics marching lockstep under compulsion to martial music played by leaders trained in Roman authoritarian ways and loyal to Rome's hegemonic designs on the free institutions of Protestant-inspired cultures like that of the United States. Blanshard's lucid exposition of fears widely shared in

1

the liberal Protestant "Establishment" in America clearly struck a deep nerve at the outset of a cold war between democratic and authoritarian cultural systems, and the huge success of his book testified to a widespread dis-ease with which many Americans viewed "Catholic culture" in America in the years immediately after the Second World War.[2]

Blanshard's fears of an anti-accommodationist, relentlessly authoritarian faith, however, much like the reports of Mark Twain's death, turned out to be somewhat exaggerated. Many American Catholics during the quarter century after the Second World War entered the American middle-class mainstream with an ease, and embraced middle-class values with an enthusiasm, that belied Protestant fears of a religiously undigestible "otherness" threatening the American way of life. Moreover, Blanshard's implied dichotomy between a Catholic leadership fanatically loyal to the authoritarian Roman Curia and the "masses" of good-willed but misled folks in the pews, "yearning to breathe free," also proved to be unduly simplistic: Catholic leaders in the style of New York City's Francis Cardinal Spellman proclaimed themselves, and were viewed by others, as chaplains to the nation's crusades. Indeed, in the case of Cardinal Spellman, this position was quite literal, as he was the official chaplain to the armed forces of the United States, traveling to the far-flung battlefields of Korea to bless with holy water the bayonets of servicemen fighting communism.

Perhaps the single most important long-term factor in abetting the move of a significant portion of American Catholics into the verdant and affluent pastures of middle-class acceptance and affluence between 1945 and 1970 was the movement out of the "Catholic ghetto" — a nurturing but confining subculture marked by membership in "our" institutions from cradle to grave — into the beckoning and pluralistic ranks of the American cultural mainstream. The years that define the following story saw the "peaking" and then gradual disappearance of much of the far-flung network of institutions, so painstakingly constructed in the nineteenth century, that indeed *was* American Catholic life for a century.

As Garry Wills, in his "Memories of a Catholic Boyhood," remembered it, the "ghetto mentality" that had defined American Catholicism from the mid-nineteenth until the mid-twentieth century was shaped by a quite distinct awareness that "we grew up different. There were some places we went, and others did not — the confessional box, for instance." This Catholicism that shaped the lives and memories of millions of children in the 1940s and 1950s was first experienced as "a vast set of intermeshed habits" that *was* the American world of religion. And the habits and memories of childhood, as Wills shows, are tenacious: "heads ducked in unison, crossings, chants, beads, incense; nuns in the classroom alternately too sweet and too severe; priests garbed in black on the street and brilliant at the altar; confession as intimidation and comfort (comfort, if nothing else, that the intimidation was survived)." Indeed, this American Catholic world was a "total experience" not unlike being Amish in Pennsylvania or Mormon in Utah, but stretching coast to coast:

> We spoke a different language from the rest of men — not only the actual Latin memorized when we learned to "serve Mass" as altar boys. We also had odd bits of Latinized English that were not parts of other six-year-olds' vocabulary — words like "contrition" and "transubstantiation." Surely no teenager but a Catholic ever called an opinion "temerarious." The words often came embedded in formulae ("imperfect contrition") ... and distinctions: mortal sin and venial sin, matter of sin and intention of sin.... To know the terms was to know the thing, to solve the problem. So we learned, and used, a vast terminology.[3]

This "Catholic speak" marked certain Americans as "ours," and others as "theirs": "One could tell, after a certain amount of talk with Senator Eugene McCarthy, that he was a Catholic, though theology had not formally been brought up or discussed." The initiate could tell that he used "giveaway phrases such as 'occasion of sin,' 'particular friendships,' and 'special dispensation.'" This special American language was shaped by the "parallel network" of American institutions that formed the memories of several generations of "cradle Catholics" — a parallel network that has been described by Charles Morris as a "Catholic ministate" within the larger culture: Catholic businessmen's clubs, medical societies, bar associations, teachers' guilds, youth organizations, historical, sociological, and economic associations, Catholic book clubs and literary guilds, and a flourishing national Catholic press.[4]

Further, this ministate had its own "liberals" questioning the stodginess and smugness of the status quo, although in this case that status quo was the local pastor more than Ike. Liberals within the American Catholic subculture in the 1930s through the 1950s crafted what has been termed "the theological equivalent of the higher patriotism," a higher churchiness, the style of a believing critic:

[The liberal] would be the *true* churchman of doctrine and liturgy — just as liberals throughout the country were the true
patriots, fighting McCarthy's caricature love of country and
"superpatriotism." He made ceremony less vulgar by making it
even more exotic. It was not Rome he disliked in his churches;
it was Peoria....While Paul Blanshard said that priests were
foreign agents, the liberal sensed the more horrible truth, that
they were aspiring nativists — heirs of their former persecutors,
the Know-Nothings (about whom, with typical lack of historical
perspective, Catholics knew nothing).[5]

American Catholic liberals of the 1940s and 1950s "outchurched
[their] own parish church," becoming more of "old world" Catholics
than their own parish priests by returning to a romantic past in order
to escape the cloddish present. Their local parish churches — clumsy
imitations of the European Gothic structures that had stirred the souls
of Henry Adams and George Santayana — were narrowly American,
"more easily stirred by a Father Coughlin or Senator Joe McCarthy
than by papal encyclicals." They thus rushed off to Monsignor Hellriegel's "liturgically correct" church in St. Louis, to see what *real*
ceremonies looked like. Each of these trips made their return to Main
Street more painful — the Latin prayers mumbled mindlessly, the pathetic choir's performance "exactly suited to its syrupy repertoire, the
stations of the cross both lugubrious and laughable."[6]

The Catholic liberal's fear of a pedestrian, Main Street religion,
producing Babbitts with crucifixes, was, of course, deliciously ironic,
as the very idea of a "Catholic liberal" in the America of the 1940s
and 1950s appeared risible to those who shared Paul Blanshard's profound misgivings about the authoritarian, anti-democratic nature of
Catholic culture: to the Protestant "progressive" keepers of the culture, the words "Catholic" and "liberal" seemed oxymoronic in the
same sentence. But the irony here goes considerably deeper; the Catholic liberals' fear of Mother Church's capitulation to mass culture was,
in retrospect, infallibly well-placed. The gates of the Catholic ministate
within American culture were being unlocked by a far larger group
than their local priests. The "unlocking" of those gates — achieved by
a congeries of sociological, theological, and political factors begun in
the 1930s and 1940s but accomplished with zeal in the twenty-five
years after World War II — was marked by a series of quite definite
and datable events: the "G.I. Bill," which allowed Catholic war veterans to attend both Catholic and secular colleges after 1946 ("when

Catholic lambs ate ivy" for the first time in significant numbers) and
so helped to produce a sizeable class of "professional" Catholics ready
and willing to share in the suburban American dream of tolerance and
affluence. Catholic participation and leadership in the domestic anti-
communist crusade in the early years of the Cold War — a crusade
publicized and led by an Irish Catholic senator from Wisconsin and
the cardinal archbishop of New York — appeared to proclaim Catholic
loyalty and devotion to the "American Way" when troubling fears of
a "Protestant loss of nerve" at the highest reaches of the government
haunted a culture fearful of subversion at home and abroad.[7]

Likewise, the emergence and success of national media personalities
like best-selling author/monk Thomas Merton and Bishop Fulton J.
Sheen — whose weekly program *Life Is Worth Living* became one
of the earliest hits in the new world of television — made Catholicism appear both benign and even helpful in addressing the exigencies
of the atomic-fueled "Age of Anxiety." The first Roman Catholic to
successfully run for the highest political office in the land was also
the proponent of what is arguably the strictest understanding of the
"wall of separation" between church and state ever outlined by a president in the twentieth century, so that many political pundits at the
time (and since) have referred to him as the "first completely secular
American President."[8]

A drive through the boroughs of Queens and Brooklyn in the postwar years — where American flags presided with "BVMs in a bathtub"
over well-trimmed lawns — revealed far more than landscape architecture: in a very real (and richly ironic) sense, in these areas of a
"second urban settlement" after the tenements of the Lower East Side
and Hell's Kitchen of Manhattan, the "outside" made loud and quite
conscious claims on being the "inside" in the years between the end of
World War II and the onset of the Vietnam era. That is, many Catholics moved (and sought to move) ecologically from the margins to the
mainstream of the culture, even making claims to being the "last, best
hope" of liberal democratic values in the "Redeemer Nation." This
move into the mainstream of the culture announced a dramatically
new identity for a significant portion of the Catholic community, a
new identity that would help to unleash a traumatic identity crisis for
American Catholics by the end of the twentieth century. The down-
turn in the fortunes of the "Catholic ministate" after John F. Kennedy's
election is often blamed on the "liberalizing," adaptationist impulses
blessed by Vatican II or on the negative impulses unleashed by *Hu-
manae Vitae,* the papal condemnation of birth control. But by the time

of the implementation of that ecumenical council's decrees (1965) and the publication of the birth control encyclical in 1968, the breakup of the old Catholic culture was well underway: "suburbanization was dispersing the urban Catholic village, and the social and educational advancement of Catholics was as fast as that of any other ethnic/ religious group except Jews."[9]

Jay Dolan, in his magisterial study of American Catholicism, dates the beginnings of the loss of the sense of community in many of the immigrant urban enclaves and the emergence of disorienting transitions in American Catholic social life to the years 1920 to 1960 — that is, considerably before the "fallout" from Vatican II. Likewise, sociologist Andrew Greeley has recorded a "profound modification" of American Catholic culture during these same years. Dino Cinel has estimated that between 1938 and 1961, 40 percent of Italian Catholics had left their old urban neighborhoods in San Francisco — "Little Italys" clustered around basilica-size parish churches — for the suburbs ringing the Bay area. Similarly, Douglas Miller and Marian Nowak place the beginnings of suburbanization (with the accompanying building of new parishes and parochial schools) in the Northeast and in the cities around the Great Lakes to the 1930s and 1940s.[10]

But even apart from this demographic reconfiguration underway during the second quarter of the twentieth century, the reasons for the headlong rush of many American Catholics to embrace the hitherto forbidden fruit of the affluent mainstream culture with renewed fervor in the decades after World War II have even older roots. Historically speaking, Catholics had sought some form of accommodation with American culture since the *Ark* and *Dove* brought the first group of English Catholics to the eastern shore of Maryland in the seventeenth century.

Both the "Whitemarsh Constitutions" of 1784, which had called for the congregational election of pastors and the lay control of parochial finances, and Bishop John England's Diocesan Constitution in the early nineteenth century, which set up "conventions" of popularly elected delegates in his diocese of Charleston, South Carolina, witnessed to an ongoing attraction to American democratic and egalitarian values on the part of a significant section of the Catholic community. Perhaps most famously, the "Americanist Crisis" that ended with the papal letter *Testem Benevolentiae* of 1899, which condemned the proposition that "the Church should adapt itself to modern culture" (a proposition labeled "Americanist" by its ultramontanist opponents in both Europe and North America), illustrated

the ongoing tension within the American Catholic community between two groups: the "ultramontanists," who saw the "real church"
as being in Rome, and who therefore sought an American Catholic
community which stood above and apart from the culture; and the
"Americanists," who sought a close accommodation between the ancient faith and the "first new nation." The centralizing tendencies of
the Roman hierarchy throughout the nineteenth century, however —
peaking in the declaration of papal infallibility in 1870 — favored
the ultramontanists in this battle and more than counterbalanced the
innate accommodationist impulses in the American church throughout the nineteenth and early twentieth centuries. But the centralizing
loyalties of the winning side in this accommodation debate notwithstanding, the "heroes" of the American Catholic story (at least as that
story has been told by historians of the American Catholic experience
for most of the twentieth century) have tended to be the "American-
izers" — those Catholics who called for a closer relationship to and in
the culture.[11]

But the years following the Second World War saw a dramatic rise
in the "Americanist" impulse that had defined the Catholic community's relation to American culture from its first appearance in the New
World. Contributing in significant ways to the enthusiasm of many of
the "major players" in mid-twentieth-century Catholicism's embrace
of American culture was its cultural "innocence."

Unlike the American Protestant mainstream, which had undergone
a series of traumatic identity crises during the first third of the twentieth century over its ability to remain the "cultural faith," American
Catholicism at mid-century has been described by William Halsey as
manifesting a "survival of innocence." That is, the Catholic community in America had weathered both the Great Depression and the
traumas of the world wars with its self-confidence and corporate es-
prit intact, proclaiming itself (and being viewed by others) as far more
self-assured, cohesive, and vibrant than the much larger and more established Protestant mainstream that had piped the cultural tune for
three centuries. To some extent this survival of innocence was due
to the intellectual success of the "Catholic Revival" that had drawn
American writer-converts like Alan Tate to the "Faith" in the first four
decades of the twentieth century because of Catholicism's promise of
epistemological and moral certitude, while the center was most assuredly not holding for many Protestant and secular intellectuals in
the interwar years. To some extent the optative mood of the Catholic
community at mid-century was due to its privileged "ambivalent" so-

ciological position of being *both* the largest religious group in the land while also being something of a distrusted outsider: it had no larger cultural obligation to make sense of the great intellectual and social crises of the twentieth century as it made no claims to speak for the culture as a whole. Its very identity as a "ghetto" and "subculture" preserved it from the internal debates that split American Protestants into "liberals," "evangelicals," and "Fundamentalists" over the high stakes of preserving the voluntary establishment of religion for the United States. While mainstream Protestants fought like theological cats and dogs over evolution, biblical criticism, and the uniqueness of Jesus as savior, American Catholics worried over who would speak at the next Communion breakfast and what Catholic team would win the city-wide parochial high school championship: its very marginality to sources of cultural power and prestige thus preserved it — to a large extent — from the ravages of the first half of the century.[12]

Likewise, economic factors also played an important part in preserving Catholic "innocence" until mid-century, as most Catholic Americans lived their lives in working-class enclaves defined by parochial institutions controlled by Holy Mother Church. While "lace curtain Irish" might claim residences on the eastern point of Long Island and Nob Hill, most American Catholics in the years before World War II could claim neither the financial nor social resources to take an active part in the intellectual and social debates of middle-class culture. The lures of affluence and intellectual sophistication — save for pockets of German Catholicism in the "German Triangle" formed by Cincinnati, St. Louis, and Milwaukee — were simply not a real option for most Catholic families until the mid-twentieth century.[13]

The one major exception to this cultural marginality was to be found in the rough-and-tumble world of urban politics, in which the Irish claimed victories by the second half of the nineteenth century in Boston, New York, Chicago, and San Francisco. But their very success in operating smooth-running "urban machines" and controlling both city hall and the police force helped to contribute to a middle-class Protestant caricature of "micks" double-dealing and bribing uneducated immigrants toward duplicitous ends. Ceding Tammany Hall to the Irish Catholics was viewed as an unfortunate but culturally irrelevant victory when "nice people" (meaning middle-class Protestants) no longer viewed urban politics as an acceptable career for gentlemen.[14]

Much of that would change in the years after World War II, however. Indeed, Catholic cultural marginality would be, by and large, transcended — for good and for ill — during the middle of the twentieth century precisely as the Catholic community made larger claims to speak to (and even for) the culture itself. With the hitherto clearly defined boundary between "inside" and "outside" blurred by incidents like that of the Boston Heresy Case, as a result of which Jesuit Leonard Feeney was excommunicated precisely for holding on to too strict an interpretation of the old dictum "outside the church there is no salvation," Catholics found themselves in a new and potentially confusing epistemological landscape — twenty years before the famous ecclesial revolution unleashed by the Second Vatican Council. The older "Catholic ministate," which had defined American Catholic identity for a century, was abandoned by many Catholics for a newer and more affluent culture religion, one which called for a denominational status modeled much more closely on that of the "seven sisters." The election of America's first Catholic president in 1960 on a platform which proclaimed that his Catholicism represented an essentially "private" set of beliefs that would not (and should not) interfere with the duties of public office — however problematic and even nonsensical such an interpretation appeared to Catholic theologians and church leaders — helped to define this Catholicism, along with Protestantism and Judaism, as one of the three "safe" ways of "being American." As Will Herberg and other critics of the putative "religious revival" of the postwar years noted, Catholicism's very "safeness" as a respectable American religion raised profoundly disturbing questions about its faithfulness to biblical faith, but nonetheless gained it access to the resources of affluent middle-class culture.[15]

Thus, by the end of the twentieth century the American Catholic adaptationist "culture religion" that had been cemented in the postwar years — what H. Richard Niebuhr labeled a "Christ of Culture" model of accommodation of the gospel to human culture, which had defined the halcyon days of the American Protestant mainstream — entered into a prolonged period of internal crises when the culture it had become so identified with underwent a series of nasty "shocks" as a result of the Vietnam conflict, the civil rights and feminist movements, and the theological repercussions of Vatican II. Quite ironically, as a result of their "arrival" on the mainstream stage, American Catholics entered a "critical period" analogous to that which had divided the evangelical Protestant mainstream a century before.[16]

Thus, it might be argued — and in the following pages it *will* be argued — that, far from accepting "secular as well as religious policies imposed on them from abroad" by an authoritarian and anti-American hierarchy, many Catholics embraced the liberal mainstream values of the postwar world with a fervor and devotion that were, if anything, far too uncritical and far too celebratory of American culture for the long-term health of their religious community.

It is the contention of this study that, as a result of the cultural embrace begun in the 1930s and 1940s but pursued with real fervor in the twenty-five years in the middle of the twentieth century, the "broad mainstream" in American Catholicism became the culture's loudest and most uncritical cheerleader, with (at best) ambivalent results for its explicitly religious mission by the final decade of the century. Blanshard's progressive fears of a totalitarian bulwark against popular democracy and modernity at the very heart of Western civilization's liberal culture now appear ironic, if not risible: a significant section of the American Catholic community all but fell over itself to be accepted into middle-class, affluent culture in the decades after 1945, in the process "backing" into modernity. This "backing into" modernity by uncritically but enthusiastically accepting American cultural values succeeded *sociologically* in making American Catholics all but indistinguishable as a group from their fellow citizens in terms of ethical values, social mores, and cultural tastes. *Theologically* speaking, however, American Catholicism's identity at the end of the century — in the wake of those halcyon years of acceptance as one of "America's established faiths" — raises profound questions about its vision and mission.[17]

The Irony of American History

The story of American Catholicism at mid-century is a complex one, layered with thickly textured sociological, economic, psychological, and theological impulses: for this very reason, the following "theological morality tale" focusing on American Catholicism between 1945 and 1970 attempts to balance methodological *pluralism* — very different social scientific approaches fitted to each chapter — with a *synthetic* narrative voice — the rich vein of "theological irony" mined by Reinhold Niebuhr in one of the classic twentieth-century interpretations of American history. Further, the following study makes no attempt to speak for the *entire* American Catholic community in the postwar years. Indeed, important tribes in that community — Hispanic Catholics of the Southwest, eastern European and Eastern Rite Catholics in the upper Midwest, pockets of Italian Catholics in the old Northeast, were far less involved in the "rush into the cultural limelight" than the figures/groups representing the broad mainstream of Catholics that forms the object of the following pages. To that extent, what follows is less a "master narrative" claiming total synthesis than "soundings" of representative figures and events that offer an important glimpse of "how we started there and ended up here."

Further, the different hermeneutical methods that structure each of the following chapters have been borrowed from the field of social science: "deviance theory" from sociologist Emile Durkheim and cultural anthropologist Mary Douglas; the "great man hypothesis" from social psychologist Erik Erikson; the "secularization" thesis offered by the seminal social theorist Peter Berger; the models of "Christ and Culture" advanced by arguably the most influential sociologist of American religion, H. Richard Niebuhr; Max Weber's famous theory of the "routinization of charisma," etc. The reason for this utilization of various social scientific methods in a work of religious history is threefold: first, as the project of studying American Catholicism in the mid-twentieth century unfolded, it struck me that no single theological, historical, or social scientific approach or method could do justice to the convoluted mid-century tale of Catholicism's "readjustment" to American culture as it moved from its older, ghetto style of religion to a newer, "culture religion" one. To attempt to force the story of American Catholicism at mid-century into any one model appeared more arbitrary and artificial than allowing each component of this mid-century history to "stand on its own." To that extent, interpretive synthesis in this study has been sought by means of methodological pluralism: each chapter in the following work utilizes a distinct and free-standing social scientific framework for considering the "tales" offered.

The second reason for the methodological pluralism in the following chapters has to do with how I spend my days. As the director of the American Studies Program at Fordham University for the past eight years — and therefore called on regularly to approach the study of American culture from a variety of interpretive stances — I have come to value the idea that the various academic disciplines (history, theology, sociology) can be enriched and even strengthened by means of conversation and engagement with each other. Thus, I would argue that theology and religious history have much to gain and little to fear from an interdisciplinary conversation about the "meaning of the past."

And finally, my use of various social scientific approaches in the following pages derives from my belief that some of the most insightful and theologically rich studies of American religious history in

the past few decades have utilized social scientific approaches to uncover the patterns of religious meaning in the "nation with the soul
of a church." Having in mind the provocative and groundbreaking
studies of American religion produced by scholars like Catherine
Albanese, Robert Orsi, and Colleen McDannell, I decided to "experiment" self-consciously with social scientific approaches to studying
the mid-century saga of American Catholicism. What I discovered as
a result of this experiment using different lenses to examine the immediate religious past was a more nuanced, less optative history of
American Catholicism at mid-century: during the very period when
the immigrant Roman faith putatively "came into its own" in the
land of the Pilgrims — decades in the middle of the twentieth century that have been labeled "The Era of Catholic Triumphalism" in
religious histories — major players in the Catholic story were glee-
fully (if unconsciously) laying dynamite to the foundations of an older
(and, arguably, *the* older) American Catholic identity. Thus, from the
viewpoint of the history recounted here, the traumas that a significant section of the Catholic community would undergo during the
final third of the twentieth century did not represent lightning in a
cloudless sky, set off precipitously by the changes mandated by the
Second Vatican Council and the social revolution sponsored by "The
Sixties." Rather, a significant part of the end-of-the-century trauma
had been "set up" in the "Golden Years," when Catholics (like the majority of fellow Americans) "liked Ike," and watched "Uncle Miltie"
on TV.[18]

On the other hand, with this methodological pluralism I have also
endeavored to provide a unified interpretive "voice" by utilizing the
Niebuhrian theological category of "irony" in telling my tale. As
scholars of American history and religion have long recognized, Reinhold Niebuhr's classic work *The Irony of American History* manages
to do justice to both the complexities of America's past and to the rigorous demands of historical theology. In Niebuhr's protean recounting
of American history, "irony" provides the best lens for understanding
the overtly *religious* "meaning of America."

Eschewing both tragedy and sarcasm as overriding interpretive
categories, Niebuhr's use of irony highlights the conundrums and
serendipitous nature of sinful human activity undertaken "for God."
As Niebuhr explained in his preface to his now-classic examination of
American history, irony might be defined as the "apparently fortuitous
incongruities in life which are discovered, upon closer examination, to
be not merely fortuitous." Thus, as Niebuhr utilizes it, "irony" stands

halfway between tragedy and comedy, and usually "elicits laughter" as much as tears:

> This element of comedy is never completely eliminated from irony. But irony is something more than comedy. A comic situation is proved to be an ironic one if a hidden relation is discovered in the incongruity. If virtue becomes vice through some hidden defect in the virtue; if strength becomes weakness because of the vanity in which strength may prompt the mighty; if security is transmuted into insecurity because too much reliance is placed upon it — in all such cases the situation is ironic. *The ironic situation is distinguished from a pathetic one by the fact that the person involved in it bears some responsibility for it. It is differentiated from tragedy by the fact that the responsibility is related to an unconscious weakness rather than to a conscious resolution.*[19]

The following account thus attempts to steer clear of both pathos and tragedy in rendering an account of mid-century Catholicism that is less than triumphant and celebratory. Likewise, it attempts to avoid both sarcasm and fatalism: irony — as Niebuhr applies it — stands apart from sarcasm, which laughs at historical protagonists as though from a higher, "privileged" position, and from fatalism, which views the human condition as inescapably tragic and damned. Niebuhr managed to steer his magisterial interpretation of the religious meaning of America between these shoals because of his profoundly *Christian* sense of history. A Christian reading of America's past is best told from the standpoint of irony, according to Niebuhr, both because *we* as examiners of that past share in it, and because of the human inability finally to control the outcome of history. Irony fits the picture so well, in other words, precisely because the (presumably graced) ending of the story stands so far removed from the intentions and plans of the (presumably graced) actors in the story. Indeed, part of the elegance of Niebuhr's interpretive category of "irony" is that it allows the fractious, untamed, and humorously serendipitous nature of the past to remain intact while also allowing us to see in the surprises of history God's grace, working in fallible human agents.

For Niebuhr, the ironic cast of history is not some alien category imposed from outside the Christian understanding of time and human activity: indeed, the Christian faith "tends to make the ironic view of human history the normative one." Christianity's conception of redemption carries it well beyond the limits of irony, but Christianity's interpretation of the nature of human activity in history is consistently ironic. This is because Christians view the whole drama of human history as taking place "under the scrutiny of a divine judge who laughs at human pretensions without being hostile to human aspirations. The laughter at the pretensions *is* the divine judgment." In Niebuhr's hands, irony as a category of theological interpretation allows the student of the religious past a *critical* but *sympathetic* stance to appreciate both the genuine successes as well as the failures of religious efforts in history. Such a stance studies the past without "laying blame" or searching for conspirators to explain the less-than-perfect outcome of the best laid plans. Niebuhr's great insight was that the biblical interpretation of history is ironic, rather than tragic, comedic, or pathetic, because

> of its unique formulation of the problem of human freedom. According to this faith man's freedom does not require his heroic and tragic defiance of the forces of nature. He is not necessarily involved in tragedy in his effort to be truly human. His situation is, therefore, not comprehended as a pathetic imprisonment in the confusion of nature. The evil in human history is regarded as the consequence of man's wrong use of his unique capacities. The wrong use is always due to some failure to recognize the limits of his capacities of power, wisdom, and virtue. Man is an ironic creature because he forgets that he is not simply a creator but also a creature.[20]

Niebuhr offered his brilliant theological interpretation of American history — published in the early 1950s during the early traumas of the Cold War — with the religious experience of the Protestant "Establishment" in mind as the chief protagonist in his story. To that extent, Niebuhr's hermeneutic of "irony" might appear to represent an arbitrary and "foreign" interpretive voice for considering the experience of "mainstream Catholicism" in the same era. After all, Protestant *biblical* concerns structured the work rather than Catholic *natural law* principles.

But on closer consideration the "foreignness" of Niebuhr's hermeneutic disappears, and its propriety for providing the "narrative voice" for the following story of American Catholics becomes clearer. For Niebuhr's interpretive tool of theological irony was crafted to recount the anomalous historical experience of cultural "insiders" — religious groups that laid claim *to* (and were claimed *by*) the "normative culture" of American public life. Irony — in Niebuhr's estimation — best serves the theological function of revealing the fallible human endeavor of living "for God in the world" *precisely* to those who sought to lay claim to cultural responsibility but who fail "to recognize the limits of their power, wisdom, and virtue."[21]

Even as Niebuhr was penning his magisterial interpretation of the Protestant experience in America, moreover, what Sidney Ahlstrom has termed the "Post-Protestant" era of American history was abirthing — or, perhaps more truly — was being recognized as having already been born. It was in this brave new world of religious pluralism and newly recognized Protestant humility in speaking for the culture that many American Catholics began asking themselves (and others) if the "Catholic moment" had in fact arrived: in what appeared to Catholic eyes as Protestant disarray and "loss of nerve" at mid-century, the graced moment for laying claim to cultural authority appeared at hand. It was, then, precisely at the outset of this exciting era of "cultural arrival" that this history opens, and it is this heady sense of having finally achieved "insiderhood" that defines so much of the Catholic story at mid-century. "Catholic innocence," in Halsey's sense, was gradually overshadowed during these years by Catholic hegemonic aspirations, with ironic results that form the "story line" in the pages that follow.[22]

In an ironic sense perhaps even richer than Niebuhr intended at the time, the eclipse of Protestant claims on the culture at the height of the Cold War abetted the "arrival" of Catholics in the *polis* who felt no such need for cultural humility: the awareness of *hubris* and the profound Augustinian sense of sin that informed Niebuhr's work and that had haunted Catholic ultramontanist fears of American "accommodationists" largely disappeared for many Catholics in the heady decades described here. Exceptions to the cultural triumphalism of the Eisenhower era certainly existed — the highly visible public careers of Thomas Merton and Fulton Sheen come readily to mind — but the very celebrity that these two icons of American Catholicism achieved in preaching an accessibly transcendent gospel came to be used for accommodationist purposes that they themselves disdained and distrusted, and — in Merton's case — came to regret. Indeed, the chief irony in the story that follows may very well turn out to be that the rag-tag group of Catholic personalists and self-styled "Christian socialists" who helped Dorothy Day run the Catholic Worker "houses of hospitality" across the country for the marginalized emerge as the most "American" group of Catholics at mid-century — but more of that in time. The irony in the following story of Catholics at mid-century, thus, runs broad and deep.

Some "Soundings" at Mid-Century

The following nine "episodes" in the history of American Catholicism spanning the twenty-five years in the middle of the twentieth century represent "soundings" of the mainstream of a historically marginal-ized religious community making its way into the verdant pastures of affluence and cultural acceptance; they are offered not as a synthetic narrative of Roman Catholics in America at mid-century, but rather as "interpretive takes" on a religious tradition in transition. This is not, by any means, the *only* story of American Catholics at mid-century, nor even the only important story of American Catholics of the time. It is, however, a story of mid-century American Catholicism that exam-ines the roots of the present "Christ and Culture" debates that exercise that community; it seeks to outline the ironic roots of those debates with (hopefully) equal measures of sympathy and criticism. Such is the nature of Niebuhr's "theological irony" that this study claims as its major narrative voice.[23]

The nine historical essays that follow each seeks to examine and interpret the theological meaning of important Catholic "icons" at mid-century in light of the present historical circumstance. The first chapter considers the odd tale of the "Boston Heresy Case," centered on the Jesuit Leonard Feeney and a group of Catholic hard-liners in the decade following World War II, who taught that non-Catholics were (according to an ancient and very orthodox teaching of Holy Mother Church) well on their way to perdition. Feeney and his "Slaves of the Immaculate Heart of Mary" limned a new fault line between the ancient faith and American culture that perhaps can only be clearly recognized in retrospect. In condemning Feeney's hard-line interpre-tation of the eternal fate of "outsiders" (as it undoubtedly had to do), the "inside" of the Catholic community ineluctably launched it-self into an accommodationist stance vis-à-vis American culture that it probably did not intend, and that opened it to cultural trauma several decades later that it was not prepared to face.

Chapter 2 examines the singular public career of Trappist monk Brother Louis — Thomas Merton to friends "in the world" — whose best-selling autobiography, *The Seven Storey Mountain,* made the revered tradition of Catholic spirituality known and accessible to mil-lions of Americans, both inside and well beyond the Catholic Church.

Merton's genius and spiritual insight offered both succor to anxious Christians at the beginning of the Atomic Age and intellectual legitimacy to Catholics claiming their place in the postwar "Religious Revival" getting under way in the late 1940s — a "legitimacy" that raises a number of questions about the spiritual life of the "revival" sweeping the nation.

Chapter 3 looks at the infamous political career of Senator Joseph McCarthy of Wisconsin, whose "anti-communist crusade" named the first half of 1950s: the "McCarthy era" reveals the profound fears of "internal subversion" that haunted Americans in the early years of the Cold War, as well as revealing Catholic claims to *true* insiderhood in protecting the nation from its foes. The very task of determining the degree to which McCarthy's tortured public career was "Catholic" — no easy task, given the acrimonious debates over this issue both at the time and since — uncovers the profoundly ambivalent nature of American Catholicism's sense of arrival in a culture in which it had long been considered marginal and suspect.

The fourth chapter considers Fulton J. Sheen's television program *Life Is Worth Living* — the first televised religious broadcast to achieve national popularity at the beginning of television's history as the *real* cultural pastime. Sheen's weekly broadcasts in the mid-1950s gave even Milton Berle ("Uncle Miltie") a run for his money in the living rooms across the land on Tuesday evenings and represented the first sustained exposure to Catholic beliefs and practices for millions of Americans. Sheen's very success, however, in a new cultural category — as a "media personality" — made the Catholicism of which he was so devoted an advocate a therapeutic tool for mass culture in ways he could not understand and of which he would not have approved. It further assured American Catholics that their faith was "safe" for America — an assurance that became something of a two-edged sword in the decades that followed.

Chapter 5 examines Dorothy Day's socially radical and philosophically "personalist" experiment in Christian living — the Catholic Worker movement — an approach to being both American and Catholic that she termed the "downward path, that leads to salvation." As recounted in perhaps the most ironic chapter of this study, Day and Peter Maurin crafted a Christian socialist stance that cared for the marginalized through the "corporal works of mercy" and "voluntary, decent poverty" in what might turn out to be the most "American" of Catholic movements of mid-century. Numerically insignificant, the Catholic Worker movement nonetheless offers a prophetic gauge for considering Catholicism's uneasy arrival in America at mid-century through its biting and perceptive critique of fellow religionists being perhaps too much "at ease in Zion."[24]

The sixth chapter considers the famous "Houston Speech" of Catholic presidential candidate John F. Kennedy, a landmark church-state declaration delivered during the 1960 presidential race before a largely hostile audience of evangelical Protestant ministers in Houston, Texas. With a breathtaking reversal of the traditional understanding of Christian responsibilities in the public sphere, Kennedy "secularized" the high priesthood of American culture by announcing that *nothing* — not even religious principles — should take precedence over a president's oath to uphold the laws of the land. Political pundits at the time (and since), as well as religious scholars, have noted the problematic theological implications of such a statement. Political and cultural considerations of the time certainly make Kennedy's statement understandable and perhaps even compelling. But given current Catholic concern over the "naked public square" that relegates religious considerations to the nonpublic sectors of our culture, the ironic possibilities that it was the first Catholic president himself who "secularized" the White House here are rich and sobering.

Chapter 7 examines a landmark date in American Catholic identity — the First Sunday of Advent 1964. Besides opening a new church year as the Advent season always did, that Sunday also opened a new era for American Catholics, as it represented the mandated moment for "turning the altars around" and celebrating the Eucharist in the vernacular (English) for the first time. Centuries-old styles of worship and piety were changed on that Sunday morning for excellent theological reasons, changes that almost all American Catholics now agree were beneficial to the liturgical life of the community. But that Sunday also unleashed deeply divisive "battles for the Mass," setting traditionalists who longed for Gregorian chant and incense over against liturgical experimenters who demanded "guitar masses" and "relevant" songs. Next to sexuality, the battles over liturgical style and substance that began on that Sunday morning divided American Catholics into categories largely unknown up to that date: "conservative" and "liberal" now became designations that Catholics used of each other, posing new and unprecedented questions for an identity that had hitherto been largely undivided and shared.

The eighth chapter considers the intriguing and tragic story of the Los Angeles Sisters of the Immaculate Heart of Mary and their battle with Francis Cardinal McIntyre over apostolic commitments and (perhaps more tellingly) over their "habits." Perhaps even as much as what the good sisters were to do, what the good sisters wore exercised church authorities in ways that reveal an ironic "twist" to the "hopes for renewal" pinned on the results of the Second Vatican Council. The *aggiornamento* mandated by that council led in directions that the good fathers doing the mandating had legitimated but had never envisioned: such is that intrinsic danger of "charismatic" reality.

The ninth chapter, "Thomism and the T-Formation in 1966," seeks to offer a theological reading, à la Niebuhr, of what these mid-century episodes might mean through the lens of Fr. Theodore Hesburg's career at the University of Notre Dame.

Most of the cultural, political, and theological choices between World War II and Vietnam made by the Catholics whose tales are told here were made with the best of intentions and with high confidence in the future of the community in America. Viewed from the end of the century, however, "irony" provides the best theological stance for viewing their import and meaning during a more sober, chastened era of religious history. Finding itself to be neither "outside" the cultural mainstream nor really at home as an "insider" ideology, American Catholicism finds itself discerning anew its "ecological" position (to use Robert Wuthnow's apt phrase) at the end of the century, justifiably proud of its past but also wondering how it arrived at its present pass. As a work of historical theology, these pages hope to contribute to that discernment process by considering the theological implications of selected moments of Catholic history at mid-century.

As James Joyce once remarked, Catholicism means "here comes everybody." American Catholicism certainly shared in the richly textured reality of Catholic Christianity recognized by Joyce, so that no one history (in the singular) can do justice to its varied and complex stories (in the plural) in what used to be called the "New World." The very pluralism of that now-shared insight contributes to the realization that the once monolithic understanding of Catholic Christianity is now over, and "manyness" is as least as important as "oneness" in considering the American Catholic story. That "manyness" emerged in full force — for good *and* for ill — in the decades after World War II, to the joy of many and to the consternation of not a few. The following study is thus offered not as a new synthesis, but as a contribution in uncovering those varied stories. It is thus not about *all* American Catholics at mid-century, and makes no (or, perhaps, few) claims to what postmodernists term "master narrative" — explaining what *all* Catholics thought or did. Such a narrative is now (again, for good and ill) a thing of the historians' past. It *is* about what has won the field as the "mainstream" or "broad middle" that defines the style of increasing numbers of the Catholic tribe at century's end.

The ecclesial and hierarchical implications inherent in the dawning mid-century recognition of pluralism recounted here — especially in a religious tradition dedicated to singularly monolithic "official" understanding of "one Lord, one faith" at least in the past four centuries — have largely defined the American Catholic experience in the last third of the twentieth century. One of the welcome fruits of the excitement and traumas which that recognition has unleashed has been the Catholic community's reappreciation of the living freshness of Scripture, especially of the Psalms, whose ironic musings on history seem especially appropriate as American Catholicism prepares to celebrate the third millennium of Christianity but in a land of profound contradictions and mind-boggling pluralism: "Why do the nations rage, and the people plot a vain thing? The One who sits in the heavens shall laugh. Now, therefore, be wise and be instructed: Blessed are all who put their trust in God."

Chapter 1

Boundary Maintenance

Leonard Feeney, the Boston Heresy Case, and the Postwar Culture

"The first sign of your approaching damnation is that Notre Dame has Protestants on its football team."
— A Feeneyite at a Notre Dame Football game, 1953[1]

St. Cyprian and Emil Durkheim in Boston

On the afternoon of September 6, 1952, the readers of the *Boston Pilot* — the voice of the Roman Catholic archdiocese — found on the front page of their usually staid weekly the text of a trenchant letter from the Holy Office in Rome. The text, dated August 8, addressed a group of Boston Catholics who had kicked up quite a fuss over the ancient theological dictum *extra ecclesiam nulla salus* ("outside the church there is no salvation") — a phrase going back to St. Cyprian in the third century and one of the pillars of orthodoxy for Christian believers.[2]

The letter itself was actually an ambivalent affair: it declared unequivocally that all Christians were "bound in faith" to the truth of that dictum ("No one will be saved who, knowing the church to be divinely established, withholds obedience from the Roman Pontiff, the Vicar of Christ on earth"). At the same time, however, it allowed that a person might be "in the church" by no more than "implicit desire" — an interpretation that had achieved almost normative status among Catholic theologians by the mid-twentieth century, although it had never been officially interpreted as such by Rome.[3]

The doctrinal interpretation thus offered, however, was almost lost in the letter's denunciation of the disobedience of a group of Catholic "hard-liners" in the Boston archdiocese, a group that had taught that all who stood outside communion with the bishop of Rome lived

21

in peril of their souls. But the letter (whatever its subtext) was supposed to end, four years after the uproar, one of the most ironic
and revealing episodes in twentieth-century Catholicism, the "Boston Heresy Case." The heresiarch to whom the published letter was
addressed — Jesuit writer and self-proclaimed theologian Leonard
Feeney — had been dismissed from the Jesuit order for disobedience,
and his followers at the St. Benedict Center in Cambridge, Massachusetts, had organized themselves as the "Slaves of the Immaculate Heart
of Mary," thus constituting the "true remnant" of a church that had
itself fallen into dreadful heresy.[4]

The Boston Heresy Case still excites debate among historians and
theologians of the post–World War II Catholic experience as to what
Feeney and his followers meant for an immigrant church adapting to
a newly affluent, pluralistic culture. The lure of the case is understandable, given the drama of the Feeney episode as one of only two official
heresies ever condemned by Rome in the North American church.[5]
Likewise, the case seems to offer the scholar a classic sociological
example of the insider/outsider paradigm of cultural tension: an immigrant (Irish) reaction to and rejection of the dominant host (Yankee)
culture, a culture represented par excellence in the Boston Irish mind
by Harvard College — the special object of Feeney's wrath as increasing numbers of Catholics attended that "godless" place on the GI Bill.
Further, the Feeney episode appears to fit the classic Troeltschian mold
of a sectarian response to the perils of pluralistic, secular modernity by
positing over against the "fallen" world of postwar America a closed
social group, pure of the contaminations of pluralism and relativism —
a small ark of believers on an especially rough sea.[6]

These historical, theological, and sociological interpretations of the
Feeney affair clearly shed much-needed light on a complex cultural
moment in North American and Catholic history. What they have in
common is a tendency to consider the entire affair from the outside
in, that is, from the standpoint of the exigencies and development of
a normative American culture to which cultural institutions like the
church must conform or risk death by irrelevance.

Moreover, these interpretations of the Boston Heresy Case often
evince not-so-hidden "accommodationist" cultural presuppositions.
These presuppositions are often betrayed by the phrase "The Coming of Age" as the title for chapters dealing with the ways in which
immigrant or nonmainstream institutions and groups in post–World
War II America adapted to the reigning "melting pot" ethos, moving
culturally into middle-class affluence and acceptance.[7]

What has tended to be overlooked in these interpretations of the Feeney episode, however, is the irony of the "boundary redefinition" between Catholicism and American culture that the Feeney case marked with such dramatic clarity: far from representing an authoritarian threat to the democratic institutions of American society, American Catholicism seemed to fall over itself in the years after World War II to become part of what sociologist Will Herberg termed the "Triple Melting Pot," indistinguishable from Protestantism and Judaism in terms of its political, social, and moral positions. It was precisely *this* seemingly uncritical embrace of all things American that first alarmed Feeney and his followers, and their adamant refusal to acquiesce in this cultural embrace ultimately led — quite ironically — to their being "outside the church" themselves. Whatever else one might say regarding the Boston Heresy Case that spanned the late 1940s to the early 1950s, one can safely say that — culturally — the "deviance" that Feeney marked by being thrown out of both the Jesuit order and eventually the Church of Rome as well thus marks an important redrawing of the boundary between American and Catholic culture in the early years of postwar American history, a boundary redefinition that should have warmed Paul Blanshard's heart. A brief examination of what social scientists have long termed "cultural deviance" might help us understand the Feeney affair more clearly.

A basic component of the social-scientific study of deviance is the systematic exploration of the Durkheimian thesis that social deviance (intellectual, political, religious, or whatever) actually performs an essential service to any society by establishing the boundaries that define the group's life. Like waging war, social deviance performs the absolutely critical function of boundary maintenance; that is, "deviance" supplies a focus for group identity by drawing attention to those values and beliefs that constitute the collective conscience of the community. From this Durkheimian point of view, then, all societies might be said to "invent" deviance, for deviance is not a property inherent in any particular kind of behavior, but rather a property conferred on certain behavior by the collective to demonstrate where the line is drawn between behavior that belongs to the universe of the group and behavior that defines the "enemy." Durkheim posited that such boundaries are never fixed in any group but always shift as the group itself discovers new outer limits to its universe. Whenever a community confronts a significant relocation of its social boundaries, either through a realignment of power or the appearance of a new enemy, the emergence of a new deviant cause célèbre is almost essential.[8]

Scholars like Kai Erikson, in his study of Puritan miscreants and antinomians in colonial Massachusetts, and Paul Boyer and Stephen Nissenbaum, in their magisterial study of the Salem witchcraft episode, have offered brilliant applications of the Durkheimian thesis regarding the uses that historical groups have made of firmly drawn lines between "outsiders" and "insiders" for the purposes of social cohesion and cultural identity.[9] But the most provocative recent applications of this revered Durkheimian thesis to the study of historical groups have been undertaken by cultural anthropologists such as the British scholar Mary Douglas. Douglas has argued that there is a strong tendency in some cultures to replicate social divisions in symbolic form by drawing on bodily symbols in every possible dimension of historical experience. Thus, in studies of groups as diverse as African tribesmen and London's "Bog Irish," Douglas has drawn attention to the fact that social deviance in certain cultures manifests itself in a "witch-hunting cosmology" that draws heavily on body symbolism — "orifices" to be guarded, improper "mixtures" to be avoided, fleshly "corruptions" to be amputated, etc. Such a cosmology offers both meaning and direction to groups the social boundaries of which, while normally well defined and clearly marked, are perceived to be under attack either by cultural change or social relocation.[10]

For cultures in which this type of cosmology emerges, Douglas predicts that we should expect the use of bodily images to express both the exclusive nature of the allegiance due to the group perceived to be threatened and the confused social experience of this group vis-à-vis a larger collective. In such cases, the most fundamental assumptions about the cosmos and the human place in it are presented in "socially appropriate images of the human body." Douglas argues that most of the great historical heresies, from Manichaeism to McCarthyism, have operated according to this pattern.[11]

Douglas has attempted to illustrate how groups as different as Darbyite dispensationalists and Ituri forest pygmies have used doctrine as an idiom of control. Such teaching defines and reinforces the purity and goodness of those inside and the (cosmic) evil of those outside the community. Doctrine serves as an easily encapsulated boundary marker defining the body's orifices, as well as a means of guarding against the dangers of poisoning. Doctrine in such groups likewise serves as a guide to action, requiring traitors within to be unmasked and enemies without to be disabled. It provides cohesion and continuity for groups whose boundaries are under attack, from either real or perceived enemies.[12]

Douglas's theories are clearly pertinent for studying a group of post–World War II Catholics who defined salvation solely by incorporation into the Body of Christ (or, perhaps even more tellingly, by being "inside Holy Mother Church"), while declaring all of those *extra ecclesiam* or "outside the church" (that is, most Americans) as going directly to hell. What is less obvious, and thus more interesting, is how her insights may help to uncover the uses to which the Feeney episode was put by the larger Catholic community as its boundaries vis-à-vis the mainstream culture were undergoing dramatic redefinition in the years after World War II.

If, as social scientists posit, all cultures invent deviance when social boundaries are redefined, a good argument can be made that if Leonard Feeney and his Slaves of the Immaculate Heart had not arrived on the scene after World War II, the North American Catholic community might have had to invent him.

Feeney and the St. Benedict Center

Thursday evenings were kept free by Catholic students at Harvard in the late 1940s in order to attend the standing-room-only lectures at the St. Benedict Center.[13] There Leonard Feeney held hundreds spellbound for two to three hours telling anecdotes, reciting poems, and performing his famous impressions. He imitated FDR as he lamented the sorry state of sacramental religion in America ("And in certain underprivileged parts of our country, we have only two paltry sacraments — and not a single bingo game!") or Fulton Sheen testifying to the merits of Coca-Cola in the mode of Isaiah the prophet ("Ho, everyone that thirsteth for the pause that refreshed").[14] The anecdotes and imitations, however, served as a warm-up for the main event of the evening: Feeney's carefully planned lecture on some element of the Catholic faith. Theologian Avery Dulles, then living in Cambridge and a regular at the center, would recall years later that

> not only was the doctrine solid; the oratory was superb. Never have I known a speaker with such a sense of collective psychology. Father Feeney would not move to his main point until he had satisfied himself that every member of the audience was disposed to understand and accept his message.... He would launch into the main body of his talk, leading them from insight to insight, from emotion to emotion, until all were carried away, as if by an invisible force permeating the atmosphere.[15]

The St. Benedict Center had been founded in 1940 by a pious laywoman named Catherine Clarke, who sought to provide an intellectual and social meeting place in Cambridge, with distinct religious affiliations, after it had been decided that Catholic lambs could indeed "eat ivy."[16] The center quickly fulfilled Clarke's vision of a popular meeting place for Catholic students, offering courses in philosophy and church Latin and sponsoring some of the brightest lights in the Catholic intellectual firmament (for example, Dorothy Day and Clare Boothe Luce) as speakers. Among the most popular of these visiting speakers was Leonard Feeney, professor of homiletics at the Jesuit seminary in nearby Weston, but also a well-known literary figure in Catholic circles.[17] His *In Towns and Little Towns* had gone through eleven printings between 1927 and 1930, and *Fish on Friday*, Feeney's collection of Catholic anecdotes and stories, was a staple in parochial schools from coast to coast and a national best-seller in 1934. This recognition had led to his position as literary editor of *America* magazine in the late 1930s, as well as to his being elected president of the Catholic Poetry Society in 1940. By then he had become a regular fixture on both the college lecture circuit and the radio program *The Catholic Hour.*[18]

Feeney's appearances at the center became so popular that in 1943 Catherine Clarke successfully requested the archdiocesan chancery to appoint Feeney as full-time chaplain to the center. The success of this request was due in part to the support of Monsignor (later Cardinal) John Wright, then a rising star in the Boston archdiocese and a regular visitor at the center. Within a year of Feeney's transfer, his Thursday night lectures became events not to be missed in Harvard Square, and the rising tide of Catholic GIs returning from the war who swelled Harvard's student population liked what they heard. With his uproarious and irreverent imitations and funny anecdotes, Feeney offered a coherent universe of meaning over against the social chaos and intellectual confusion that defined postwar America. His genius lay in part in his ability to keep a large audience enthralled by balancing the light and the heavy, the humorous and the serious, particularly amid the grave issues of the newly dawned nuclear age.[19]

As Mark Silk has observed, Feeney, like Billy Graham, drew on national anxieties for what emerged as his crusade at St. Benedict's. "We were never the same...after the dropping of the bomb," Catherine Clarke later wrote of Feeney and the center, and Feeney's message clearly drew on the horrific possibilities that haunted the modern consciousness after Hiroshima.[20] In a cultural environment where schoolchildren practiced bomb drills that consisted of stooping under desks to escape nuclear blasts, Feeney loved to point out what he thought to be the theological moral of the story. Here, he would observe, was the end result of that Protestant tradition that had over-thrown the yoke of Mother Church for "individual autonomy" and "freedom"; here was the abyss to which a culture untutored by the Catholic tradition had led Western civilization.[21]

If nuclear destruction and the amoral license of a modern culture that allowed such destruction formed an important part of Feeney's altar call to his receptive congregation, his preaching arsenal included other related jeremiads. The secular education of Harvard's recently implemented general curriculum for undergraduates — a curriculum in which the Bible could not be studied even as great literature in a uni-versity founded to train ministers — appeared to augur the dead end of a Western intellectual tradition in which spiritual values had formed the heart and purpose of learning. Indeed, James Bryant Conant, Har-vard's president, who had overseen the implementation of the new curriculum, quickly developed into Feeney's theological and cultural bête noire. As one of the most famous scientists involved in the "Man-hattan Project" leading to the first "workable" (*sic*) atomic bomb, Conant handily filled the bill as the perfect example of those "skepti-cal chemists" who were leading civilization to the brink. Feeney loved to tell the story — undocumented and unconfirmed — that Conant had told a dinner party of Cambridge academics that to make a more in-teresting experiment, the U.S. should have dropped ten atomic bombs on Japan. Here, Feeney came to believe, was a skeptical scientist that Catholics would love to hate.[22]

Feeney's message — that the Catholic tradition stood over and against a bankrupt post-Protestant culture teetering on the brink of intellectual anarchy and physical annihilation — reached ready ears. By the late 1940s the center boasted two hundred converts, one hun-dred students sent to the seminary or convent, and an ever-increasing number of students enrolled in center courses in Greek, church history, philosophy, and literature. Likewise, it had founded a publication, en-titled *From the Housetops,* that included articles written by Boston's Archbishop Richard Cushing. The "Catholic moment" appeared to have arrived with a vengeance.[23]

Everything about the center and Feeney's ever-widening ministry seemed to presage success for the future, save for a new and trou-bling beleaguered tone to Feeney's teaching that revealed itself with increasing clarity toward the end of the decade. The new tone emerged gradually and is difficult to document cleanly, as Feeney and the center had always intimated the fortress-like nature of Catholicism in a hostile culture. Indeed, in the first issue of *From the Housetops,* Avery Dulles, one-time Harvard undergraduate and a soon-to-be Jesuit, had set forth the center's cultural presuppositions: "Every culture which is not Catholic is in some degree anti-Catholic.... The belief that one can with impunity consort constantly with heretics and atheists, and casually exchange ideas with them, is a dangerous product of modern liberalism."[24]

Such fear of the Protestant liberalism inherent in American culture, of course, was endemic to "official" Catholic statements until the 1960s and hardly represented anything singular about Feeney or his teaching. On the contrary, it undoubtedly offered a welcome witness to church officials that the center's orthodoxy had not in any way been compromised by its proximity to godless Harvard.

But the strict constructionist reading of the ancient phrase *extra ecclesiam nulla salus* that emerged with increasing frequency in Feeney's teaching by the end of 1947 worried even friends of the center. With unsettling regularity, Feeney began focusing his Thursday night lectures on what he called "the teaching of twenty-nine Doctors of the Church": that it was "wholly necessary for the salvation of every human creature to be subject to the Roman Pontiff."[25] The joy and good humor of the Thursday evening lectures began to disappear as Feeney increasingly focused his talks on those "without" (like Conant), as well as increasingly even on those "within" the fold who were deliberately making light of church doctrine. Indeed, those Catholic leaders who appeared to be deemphasizing doctrine in the postwar religious revival — Boston's Archbishop Cushing, Auxiliary Bishop John Wright, even fellow Jesuit William Keleher (the president of Boston College) — emerged as the special objects of his wrath.

Applying Cyprian's doctrine of salvation with a ferocity and literalness that appeared to beg for confrontation, Feeney (and many of the center students who soon became known as "Feeneyites") broadcast teaching that rejected the ecumenism and movement into the mainstream that defined the postwar religious revival: Harvard was a "pesthole of atheism and Marxism"; its president, James Conant, was a "thirty-third degree Masonic brute"; Boston College, run by Feeney's own Jesuit province, had lapsed into heresy for teaching that non-Roman Catholics might actually be saved.[26]

Catholic "liberals" (such as they were in the 1940s) likewise increasingly became the targets of his contempt. Feeney enjoyed explaining (with both irony and contempt in his voice) that Catholic liberals didn't like talk about the doctrine of salvation because it was not "nice": niceness had replaced orthodoxy as the test of a doctrine's viability. Catherine Clarke would later capture this same contempt in explaining Feeney's position during the gathering storm:

> [The] Catholic liberal is one who, having taken all his cultural standards from a non-Catholic society, tries to make his Catholic dogmas square with those standards.... The situation [has] induced Catholics to attempt to reconcile beliefs they had brought over from Europe with the humanitarian, utilitarian, pragmatic, and political ideals of the new world. It ended up by leaving Catholics with a set of relative standards as regards religion.... A liberal Catholic always knows how God *should* behave, for God's behavior is invariably made to conform with the liberal's own fine feelings.[27]

The previous archbishop of Boston, William O'Connell, would have easily resonated with these words. As something of a prototypical American ultramontanist, O'Connell had forbidden absolution to Catholic mothers who placed the education of their children in the hands of "infidels, heretics, and atheists"; he had frowned on Catholic students attending secular schools like Harvard and loved to show up at civic occasions in full regalia, demanding his due as a prince of the church from discomfited Yankees. His successor, however, was different. Richard Cushing had little time for abetting the outsider image of the church, possessing the shrewdness as well as the warmth of a politician from South Boston, where he was born and raised. Furthermore, he seems to have been deeply influenced by his sister's happy marriage to a Jewish man. The loudly proclaimed "Romanism" of his predecessor was not for him.[28]

By February 1948, Cushing decided to cut short what he perceived to be an emerging cause célèbre and called for an end to religious feuding in a much-publicized speech. Americans, he announced, could no longer afford the luxury of "fighting one another over doctrines concerning the next world, though we must not compromise these."[29] Rather, he called for all Americans of good will to "unite their forces to save what is worth saving in this world." The St. Benedict Center was appalled and chagrined at what they perceived to be the moral compromise of their own spiritual leader, a chagrin that was to grow into alarm the next month when Cushing's Auxiliary bishop, John Wright, gave an even more publicized speech before Harvard's progressive (and in Catholic conservatives' eyes, infamous) Liberal Union to state the Catholic case against universal military training. Feeney's and the center's perceptions of an attack mounted on their little outpost of orthodoxy by church leaders was not just paranoia: the noose was tightening.

On August 25, 1948, Feeney's Jesuit superior, tired of the diatribes against both Harvard University and the Jesuit-run Boston College, ordered Feeney to report to the Jesuits' Holy Cross College in Worcester, Massachusetts, by September 6 to begin teaching there. The picture painted by Catherine Clarke of the resulting crisis (however incongruous) is reminiscent of Luther at Worms. With car waiting and bags packed on the fateful day, Feeney conferred one last time with his disciples, deciding that he could not obey his superior's orders. His conscience was seemingly held captive by a truth larger than mere church authority. For Feeney to leave would mean that true doctrine "would be completely discredited, and Liberal Catholicism more deeply entrenched than ever."[30]

In one sense, while events would become far more dramatic in the spring, the die had been cast on September 6. Feeney had decided that doctrine was far more important than obedience or the bond of unity — an ironically "Protestant" stance for one claiming such distaste and horror of the Protestant tradition. Throughout the fall Feeney's superiors made repeated efforts to change his mind, but to no avail, and just after Christmas Feeney was informed that his "faculties" — the official permission given to priests by church superiors to celebrate Mass and hear confessions — would not be renewed. The irony here was almost too much: the savior of the Catholic tradition was now denied the right to celebrate the sacraments or to preach in any Catholic church. But Feeney would meet the irony with one possibly more complete. In January 1949 he organized his followers into a new religious order without the permission or advice of either his ecclesiastical or Jesuit superiors. Feeney's new "order," the Slaves of the Immaculate Heart of Mary, were pledged to unquestioning (and loudly proclaimed) obedience to the pope and to the fearless (if often literalistic) proclamation of Catholic truth.[31]

The year that began with the creation of the "Slaves" would become considerably more interesting. By early spring of 1949, three of Feeney's disciples teaching at Boston College were gaining considerable renown, or at least publicity, for focusing on the Feeney interpretation of the doctrine of salvation in their classes. Fakhri Maluf, an assistant professor in the Philosophy Department, gained a dubious reputation for failing students who disagreed with Feeney's reading of the purpose of philosophy taught in Catholic institutions, which was, of course, to propagate Catholic doctrine. But all of Feeney's disciples, both in and outside the institution, announced far and wide (including to reporters from the Boston dailies) that New England's premier Catholic university was itself in heresy! The "Feeneyites" on Boston College's faculty — in a move that appeared to the Feeneyites that their deepest fears were well-founded — were subsequently fired.[32]

The Boston Heresy Case erupted into public view during Holy Week 1949. The firings of Feeney's disciples from Boston College made front-page news all over the Northeast: the *New York Times* began a series on Feeney and his group, and *Newsweek, Life,* and *Time* magazines all featured stories on the Boston "troubles." On perhaps the most solemn holy day of the Catholic calendar, Good Friday, Feeneyites stood outside Boston parishes carrying placards warning of the impending subversion of true doctrine by church leaders themselves and selling the latest issue of *From the Housetops.* As one student of the event has observed, the question of salvation replaced the Red Sox as the topic of conversation in Boston bars, and anyone spied in a Roman collar became a potential "lead" in the story. The only analogue church historians could think of was Constantinople in the fourth century, where rioting crowds had battled in the streets over the definition of the divinity of Jesus, and Greek theological phrases became the mottos of chariot teams.[33]

On Easter Monday of 1949, Archbishop Cushing declared that "weighty points of dogma are not debated in headlines or made the occasion of recrimination and inordinate attack on constituted authority."[34] Feeney, Cushing announced, had been officially silenced by church authorities in Rome, and all Catholics were warned that anyone attending or assisting the St. Benedict Center would be denied access to the sacraments. For devout Boston Catholics — however sympathetic to Feeney's anti-accommodationist message — the case was over. *Roma locuta, causa finita:* "Rome has spoken, the case is finished."[35]

Thereafter events took on a life of their own, so that both Feeney and the archdiocese grew implacable in their respective positions. By October 28, 1949, when Feeney received word from Rome announcing that he had been dismissed from the Society of Jesus for contumacious disobedience, he and his followers had already taken to appearing on Boston Common on Sunday afternoons. There they would boom their doctrine at "Brimstone Corner" at the Park Street "T" station, warning (through bullhorns) of the nuclear wrath to come and denouncing the enemies of Holy Mother Church — Masons, the Boston hierarchy itself, but especially the Jews. The official Roman condemnation of their heresy, printed on the front page of the *Pilot* four years later, almost seemed like an afterthought.[36]

By 1957, when Feeney and his "Slaves" moved from Cambridge thirty miles west to Harvard, Massachusetts, they had become synonymous with social pathology: interrupting Notre Dame football games, demonstrating against interfaith chapels like the one at Brandeis University ("We are asked to turn our Lord over to that people which for two thousand years has reviled Him"), and denouncing the prince of Satan's legions, Archbishop Cushing himself. Always a passionate advocate of being inside Holy Church as the only ark of salvation, Feeney and his disciples now found themselves (both ecclesiastically and psychologically) cast into the rough seas of non-Catholic reality.[37]

A "Comic Opera Heresy"?

What can one make of this "comic opera heresy," as Cushing's biographer would later term it? What is the student of mid-century Catholicism to do with this tempest in a Boston teacup? Feeney himself clearly nourished elements of the Boston Irish hatred toward Brahmin Yankee culture — an ancient antipathy that focused on WASP institutions like Harvard for the purposes of identifying the despised descendants of Cromwell in the New World. "Atomic anxiety" also played its part in the Boston Heresy Case, just as it did in the popular Billy Graham crusades then sweeping the country, sponsoring eschatological fears of the abyss toward which Western culture seemed to be rushing in the wake of Hiroshima. Likewise, the new cultural pluralism that emerged with dramatic clarity in postwar America, a pluralism in which Norman Vincent Peale, Fulton J. Sheen, and Joshua Liebman constituted the interdenominational chaplaincy to a genuinely post-Protestant America, aroused fears about the blurring of theological lines to which the St. Benedict Center responded. But, even allowing for the personal and social pathologies that informed the Boston Heresy Case — and such pathologies clearly did play a role — one can safely state that the uproar was about theology, just as Feeney and his followers claimed.[38]

On strictly theological grounds, Feeney's teaching was not as outrageous or pathological as might appear from the vantage of post–Vatican II Catholic reality. Catholic propagandists in Counter-Reformation Europe had certainly believed their Protestant opponents, no less than Moslem infidels, to be beyond the reach of grace, and a rigorist interpretation of Cyprian's phrase clearly uncovers the motives undergirding much of the missionary activity between the sixteenth and twentieth centuries. The urgency of "snatching souls" from the jaws of hell inspired Jesuit Francis Xavier in India as well as Puritan John Eliot in Natick, Massachusetts, to go out and preach the good news to the "people that walked in darkness" (Isa. 9:2).

Pius XII's encyclical *Mystici Corporis,* promulgated in 1943, unequivocally identified the Roman communion with the mystical body of Christ, allowing for the salvation of pagans and non-Catholic Christians by positing their "implicit desire" for institutional church affiliation (that is, by making the righteous outside the communion into "closet Catholics," either because of their ignorance of the church's claims or because of serious inability to affiliate themselves with it). Thus, in pressing for a rigorist interpretation of *extra ecclesiam nulla salus* in 1945, Feeney was indeed "simply sailing before prevailing Roman winds."[39]

Twenty years later, of course, the Second Vatican Council sponsored an initially quiet (and then exceedingly loud) ecclesiological revolution by positing in its most important document that the true church "subsists" in the Holy Roman Church. This seemingly simple rephrasing of the relationship between the mystical body of true believers and the Roman Church (the former "subsisting in" rather than "existing in" the latter) actually elucidated a new Catholic worldview for viewing non-Roman Christians by allowing that elements of the True Faith could be found outside institutional Catholicism.[40]

Long before 1965, however — certainly by the end of the decade following the Second World War — most North American Catholics had ceased to believe that their good Protestant and Jewish neighbors were going to eternal ruin at death, invincibly ignorant or not. Leonard Feeney had recognized as early as 1945 this quiet but quite important revolution in Catholic thinking about boundaries between Catholics and North American culture. Indeed, Feeney's insight saves the Boston Heresy Case from comic opera and makes it an important episode in the North American Catholic experience. Here Mary Douglas helps scholars to discern the meaning of Feeney and his disciples.

Despite the fact that they found themselves living in a culture that had been shaped in important ways by Protestant values, Catholics in

North America had always found the communal boundaries between the safe "inside" and the hostile "outside" rather fluid — a fluidity that manifested itself in vociferous (indeed, perhaps too vociferous) pledges of loyalty to the American way. At the same time, however, North American Catholics had always maintained a staunchly ultramontanist loyalty to Rome, making American Catholicism, on the whole, a model church in terms of obedience, doctrinal orthodoxy, and financial support. The strains between this orthodoxy and American cultural support and identification had certainly been tested at certain moments in American history. Perhaps the most dramatic test had occurred at the end of the nineteenth century when, during the heyday of American cultural imperialism, Rome had felt it necessary to denounce certain culturally affirmative impulses within Catholicism that it labeled "Americanism."[41]

Whatever the truth of that charge in 1899, the boundary markers between the Catholic community and American culture had shifted even more dramatically by 1945, when Catholics were laying claim to being a legitimate part of the cultural mainstream. By the late 1950s, Catholic intellectuals like John Courtney Murray could proclaim not only the congruency of Catholic and American democratic principles, but the mutual dependence of those principles if American democratic culture were to survive. Catholics entering the mainstream of the upper reaches of American government (including the presidency within fifteen years of the war) spelled a new relationship to the outside culture, a relationship that Feeney perhaps intuited more than understood.[42]

Feeney's rigorist interpretation of *extra ecclesiam nulla salus* arguably stood much closer to its meaning held by Pope Innocent III in the thirteenth and St. Francis Xavier in the sixteenth centuries than did that of his "liberal" Catholic opponents who found his teaching abhorrent.[43] Indeed, in the era between the Reformation and Vatican II, "the church" in official dogmatic statements had meant precisely what Feeney said it did: those in union with the bishop of Rome. The salvation of those outside of that union was somewhat problematic, although scholastic categories like "implicit desire" and "invincible ignorance" had allowed an eschatological loophole for virtuous pagans (like those found to inhabit Dante's *Paradiso* and righteous Protestants).[44]

The most interesting piece of evidence in the entire Feeney episode that witnesses to the lingering perception of that older understanding is Feeney's official church censure itself. The letter from Rome in

1952 deplored Feeney's deviance because of discipline, not because of heresy. While placing less emphasis on Feeney's teaching regarding Cyprian's revered phrase, it highlighted the Jesuit's disobedience to duly constituted church authority as the reason for censuring him. Indeed, the letter from the Holy Office printed on the front page of the *Pilot* evinces something like ambivalence, as though the church found itself caught in a no-win situation, trying to hold on to its claims to unequivocal truth even while censuring one who had proclaimed that truth a little too literally.[45]

The point of the story is that Feeney, for all of the private demons that undoubtedly drove him, had changed the interpretation of St. Cyprian's dictum far less than had the experience of postwar American Catholicism itself. The boundary line marking those saved from those condemned had moved (or perhaps, been moved) to include others (that is, most Americans) who had no desire, implicit or otherwise, to join the Roman communion.

As Mary Douglas might read it, Feeney and the entire Boston Heresy Case served an absolutely essential function for North American Catholicism at a crucial moment in its history: Feeney and his disciples provided the occasion for "boundary redefinition" in a new cultural context. Doctrinal positions that had been considered rigorous but nonetheless orthodox at an earlier moment in North American Catholic history were now perceived to be beyond the pale — beliefs that the collective now declared to be deviant and even dangerous to the life of the community. The collective conscience had changed, the boundary between what constituted "inside" and "outside" had moved or been scaled down, and the official interpretation of what it meant to be "outside the church" had changed with it.

From this vantage, Feeney's case provides a critical marker in charting the relationship of Catholicism to postwar American culture. Indeed, it might be argued along Durkheimian lines that the Catholic community in 1949 *used* Feeney and his followers to redefine itself vis-à-vis American culture, embracing the American cultural values of respect for pluralism, egalitarianism, and democracy with an alacrity and enthusiasm that today appears perhaps too effusive. An older, hardline interpretation of the church's relationship to those "outside" of its body — an interpretation almost sectarian in its rigorous denunciation of the belief that one might "with impunity consort constantly with heretics and atheists" — was now declared to be deviant, damnably so. The sociological, political, and economic reasons for this redefinition were and are reasonably clear; the theological justifica-

tion for this redefinition, however, remained obscure — at least until
the Second Vatican Council. Indeed, the later, *ex post facto* theological justification for this boundary redefinition, offered at Vatican II,
raises quite legitimate questions about the role of cultural (as opposed to theological) impulses redefining the relationship of "Christ"
to "culture."

At least part of the *poignancy* of the story of the Boston Heresy Case
is that, in hindsight, both the "conservative" Feeneyites and their "accommodationist" ecclesiastical opponents — Roman-trained bishops
so feared by American cultural progressives like Paul Blanshard — were
engaged in an extremely delicate theological debate about the proper
relationship of the gospel to human culture (in this specific case, American culture) without a lucid or clearly thought-out understanding of
the likely long-term effects of "boundary moving": redefining one's
relationship to the "outside" ineluctably changes the "inside" as well.
Thus, from the vantage of the late twentieth century, we can say that
Leonard Feeney and his epigoni can certainly be accused of utilizing
a naively literal, pathological, and precritical appropriation of church
doctrine in a post-Enlightenment, pluralist world no less than fighting
ethnic, class, and psychological assurance battles in the language of
theology. At the same time, however, Feeney's opponents blithely abandoned the fortress of the immigrant Catholic subculture for the fair
and broad plains of mainstream American culture with an optimism
and enthusiasm that, in retrospect, appears at best equally uncritical.
Catholics, no less than mainstream Protestants, stood in danger of
embracing a "culture religion" that Gibson Winter at the time termed
"the suburban captivity of the churches."

If America was, indeed, "the land too easily loved," then many
postwar Catholics appeared to stand among the front ranks of its
admirers. At least part of the *irony* of the story, therefore, is that
the "accommodationist," winning side of the Boston Heresy Case announced and celebrated the removal of the old boundary between
Holy Mother Church and the Redeemer Nation without adumbrating a new one that elucidated a clearly defined boundary between the
claims of the church and the claims of the culture. The social, economic, and political rewards of "letting down the drawbridge" from
the Catholic fortress were so great that few "mainstream Catholics" —
a new term that would emerge in the next few decades — saw much
danger at the time. American Catholicism, quite suddenly, was no
longer exactly a "church" in the older, dogmatic sense of Cyprian's
phrase — the sole locus of truth and fidelity on the darkening plains

of history. But it was not exactly a "denomination" in the American Protestant sense either, as it continued to make claims to unqualified authority vis-à-vis other Christian believers.[46]

The Boston Heresy Case foreshadowed a Catholic future that would take the route charted by those whom Feeney termed "accommodationist liberals." This may seem like a penetrating glimpse of the obvious today, now safely on the other side of Vatican II, but it was not always so obvious. There was a time, before Knute Rockne's day, when one expected everyone on Notre Dame's football team to be a good Catholic.

Chapter 2

Young Man Merton

Thomas Merton and the Postwar "Religious Revival"

"[Gethsemani Monastery] is the real capital of the country in which we are living. *This* is the center of all the vitality that is in America. This is the cause and reason why the nation is holding together."
— THOMAS MERTON[1]

The Seven Storey Mountain

While Leonard Feeney was spellbinding (and then haranguing) students at St. Benedict's Center in Harvard Square, another Catholic — far away from the madding crowd and, quite literally, speaking to almost no one — was about to change the ground rules of postwar spirituality in America. For on the morning of October 21, 1946, Father Louis of Gethsemani Monastery in Kentucky — Thomas Merton to his friends "in the world" — sent off to his literary agent, Naomi Burton, a manuscript that would help to change the face of postwar religion in America. The manuscript, an autobiographical work quite consciously modeled on St. Augustine's *Confessions* and named after Dante's seven mountains of Purgatory, was published by Harcourt, Brace & Company on October 4, 1948, as *The Seven Storey Mountain*. Both the publication itself and its popular reception portended several things about post–World War II religious culture, not least being the arrival of what "may turn out to be the most significant Christian figure in 20th century America."[2]

Within days of its appearance, the publishers decided to increase the copies of the original printing, first to seventy-five hundred copies, and then to twenty thousand. Much later, the book's editor at Harcourt, Brace, Robert Giroux, called it "the biggest seller of my career." Between October and December 1948, the book sold more quickly than anything else on the market, and finished 1948 (just three months after publication) as the number three best-seller of the year. Between January 1 and Labor Day 1949, the book sold two thousand copies every working day, with a record ten thousand copies ordered in a single day. In all, six hundred thousand copies of the original cloth edition were sold before it went into a number of paperbound editions.[3]

Even before publication, Giroux had sent galley proofs to three icons of the English-speaking Catholic world — Evelyn Waugh, Graham Greene, and Clare Boothe Luce — and had received advance warning of the book's importance. Waugh, never one to overpraise a fellow Catholic writer (or anyone else, for that matter), wrote back to Giroux observing that this was a book "which may well prove to be of permanent interest in the history of religious experience." Graham Greene, in a similar vein, called it an "autobiography with a pattern and meaning valid for all of us," while Clare Boothe Luce (before Merton, perhaps the most famous American Catholic convert of the century), observed that "it is to a book like this that men will turn a hundred years from now to find out what went on in the heart of man in this cruel century."[4]

There are, of course, easily discernible social, intellectual, and religious impulses in Merton's book that help to account for the tremendous popular acclaim that it generated. Like the post–World War II "religious revival" itself, just then emerging as a discernible phenomenon, Merton offered seemingly secure, *interior* truths in a suddenly very unsafe, post-Hiroshima world. Over against the new threat of nuclear destruction and the spread of atheistic communism in eastern Europe and southeast Asia, Merton offered his American readers the promise of a rich interior life in perfectionist language redolent of both the Puritans and the Transcendentalists.[5]

Moreover, Merton's book announced the emergence of something like a Catholic analogue to Protestant neo-orthodoxy; that is, it announced the arrival of a mature and "chastened" American Catholicism just when third-generation immigrant Catholics were leaving their cultural ghetto. Much of American Catholic life in both the nineteenth and twentieth centuries had been consumed with "fitting in" and striving after bourgeoisie "normalcy." In answer to the charge of being outsiders in an overwhelmingly Protestant culture, Catholic intellectual and ecclesial leaders had sought to prove how thoroughly *American* their religious tradition was. Thus, the heroes of American Catholic culture had been, generally speaking, "Americanist" accommodationist leaders who sought a church adapted to a democratic, pluralist culture.[6]

Merton's autobiography offered a dramatically different Catholic claim on American "insiderhood": Merton offered stinging critiques of both the shallow, therapeutic spirituality that would help engender the religious revival then emerging, and of the secular worldview of intellectuals like Mencken and Dewey that had defined much of the life of the mind in the twentieth century. Over against both, Merton (like the American giants of Protestant neo-orthodoxy, Reinhold and H. Richard Niebuhr) offered his readers an existentially satisfying, "transcendent" piety that was both rooted in an ancient prophetic tradition and profoundly critical of "culture religion" masquerading as biblical faith.[7]

For American Catholics, Merton offered a sophisticated and aesthetically mature "take" on an ancient faith to a religious group just then riding the sociological escalator out of immigrant status into middle-class affluence. Merton's Catholicism seemed refreshingly free of the immediate working-class Catholic past, with its badly imitated Gothic churches and its memorized catechism lessons. Merton's style of Catholicism, on the contrary, seemed to be a faith "come of age" — at home in America and comfortable enough with the culture to critique it without bitterness or carping. Here was a style of Catholicism conversant with both the latest European trends of neo-Thomism as well as with the newest currents of American intellectual culture. For third-generation children of immigrants seeking to reappropriate their faith for a newfound middle-class niche, Merton was a godsend.[8]

Somewhat later, however, Merton — despite his recorded enthusiasm over having discovered the "real capital of the country" at Gethsemani — viewed his autobiography as something of a spiritual albatross. Indeed, Merton's later ambivalence about the astounding success of his first book is attributable to a number of rather sound reasons: the autobiography evinced a "contempt for the world" that Merton would later regret and attribute to his own spiritual immaturity; the autobiography drew increasing numbers of very loud visitors to his "silent" monastery to meet him and seek his spiritual counsel (including, incongruously enough, carloads of Southern Baptist seminarians from nearby Louisville), visits that disrupted the life of his brother monks and caused Merton much spiritual (and physical) disquiet; the autobiography's popular success did its own part in contributing to the problematic overcrowding of Gethsemani Monastery by attracting young men (especially returning GIs) distinguished more by their earnestness than by any discernible call to the monastic life, so that the monastic buildings designed to hold 70 monks eventually came to house close to 270 men.

Whatever one makes of Merton's later ambivalence about the astounding success of his autobiography, the remarkable reception of *The Seven Storey Mountain* presents the historian of religion with a number of anomalies as well. Merton's autobiography does not fit easily into the "peace of mind" genre of religious best-sellers just then flooding the bookstores at the beginning of America's postwar religious revival. Unlike Rabbi Joshua Liebman's *Peace of Mind* (published in 1946 and "naming" the popular theology that surged in the postwar revival), Monsignor Fulton J. Sheen's *Peace of Soul* (1949), or the 1952 classic of the genre, Norman Vincent Peale's *Power of Positive Thinking,* Merton offered no easy-to-master psycho-theology to his readers; nor did he promise a gospel that would let folks "feel better about themselves." Liebman, Sheen, and Peale (the interreligious "trinity" of the postwar revival) provided the "bibles of American auto-hypnotism" — what one of the most perceptive scholars of the movement has termed "therapeutic pop psychology masquerading as religion" — to a culture in need of precisely what the movement itself promised: peace of mind. Merton's book, in contrast, offered a far different message: a perceptive and self-critical "confessional" account of one soul's journey to a monastery of Trappist monks (Cistercians of the "strict observance") in the middle of the Kentucky countryside. It likewise celebrated what (on the face of it) appear to be rather un-American virtues: recollection, passivity, and — perhaps most un-American of all — contemplation![9]

Further, the book's very similarities to Protestant neo-orthodoxy in its cultural critique present the historian of religion with difficulties when it comes to explaining Merton's popularity and cult-like success. While neo-orthodox thinkers like the Niebuhr brothers became voices to be reckoned with in Protestant divinity schools and denominational bureaucracies across the land in the years before and after World War II, they had a minimal effect (at best) on the "folks in the pews": no lines formed in front of Scribner's bookstore to buy their newest titles, and neither generated anything remotely like a popular following outside of American seminaries.

Why then did a book written by a monk, chastising the "busyness" and venality of American culture, in a way analogous to the somewhat *unpopular* Protestant neo-orthodox theology of the Niebuhr brothers, sell so well? Why did carloads of earnest Catholics (and Southern Baptists) suddenly begin appearing on the steps of an obscure monastery, seeking the ghostly counsel of a monk who had ostensibly turned his back on "the world"? Why may Father Louis of Gethsemani Monastery "turn out to be the most significant Christian figure in 20th century America"? Why, indeed, may Merton and his poetic autobiography turn out to be "the man that Christianity needed in a time of transition that began not with Vatican II but the Second World War"?[10]

A number of insightful studies, produced by both historians of religion and by students of spirituality, have offered cogent "clues" as to why Merton emerged with such dramatic suddenness on the American religious landscape in the years immediately after World War II: this chapter seeks to build on their insights.[11] But this chapter seeks to offer as well a complementary interpretation, utilizing the insights of that perceptive scholar of social psychology, the late Erik Erikson, for help in adumbrating Merton's complex (and conflicted) relationship with what most scholars of American religion have termed the "postwar religious revival." More specifically, this chapter seeks to utilize Erikson's famous theory of the "great man" (hereafter "great individual"), elucidated in classic form in his famous psychobiography *Young Man Luther,* to examine Merton's relationship with postwar American Catholic culture.[12]

Erikson offered, in his now-famous study of the psychological factors informing the childhood and adolescence of Martin Luther, a controversial but provocatively rich analysis of the historical reasons for Luther's "greatness" in Western culture: social changes in western Europe in the early sixteenth century had produced new psychological needs which could not be satisfied by the traditional ideological answers — theological, philosophical, or cultural — provided by society. This resulted in a "socially generalized identity crisis," a crisis in which

> large numbers of people fail[ed] to make an effective transition to adulthood. One way in which the difficulty could be resolved was for a "great young man" such as Luther to articulate the crisis and its solution for himself in such a way that others could recognize *their* problem and the possibility of solutions for themselves in *his* solution. In other words, the new identity and ideology he forge[d] for himself [was] *culturally paradigmatic.*[13]

Erikson has thus posited that the identity crises and resultant "conversions" of "great individuals" throughout history were not unusual primarily in terms of depth or intensity; rather, what made them "great" was both that their crises were structurally similar to what millions of other people were experiencing at the same time, and that their crises and conversions were highly personal *and* "ideological" in a public and generalizable way. Luther's achievement, in Erikson's view, was thus that he recognized his personal crisis of scruples for what it was: a vast ideological/theological problem that plagued his age, and not just a private difficulty. Luther was forced, then, to shape both his personal difficulties and his resolution of those difficulties into a "culturally paradigmatic" identity crisis in which many others in his culture saw themselves reflected. In "solving" his own personal problems, then, Luther developed a "solution" of sorts for one of the major problems of his age.[14]

If Erikson was correct in his theory of how one individual can work through and embody the tensions of his or her age, offering in turn a "culturally paradigmatic" answer for others to follow — and this chapter will argue that Erikson offers an important insight to American religious historians for understanding Thomas Merton's dramatic appearance on the Catholic religious landscape on precisely this point — then Merton's publishing success and later cult-like status in the two decades after World War II is not inexplicable or ambivalent at all: indeed, Merton's emergence as the spiritual guide for a generation of postimmigrant American Catholics might even have been predicted.

However, given Erikson's insight, there is irony and even pathos in the story as well, for despite Merton's well-known disdain for "peace of mind" peddlers masquerading as spiritual guides, *The Seven Storey Mountain* and Merton's later career as apologist for the Catholic contemplative tradition would itself become one more "commodity" in the postwar revival, itself hawking "fix it" solutions to the anomie and anxiety of a newly fluid and uncertain nuclear age. In ways he could not have foreseen or approved of, Brother Louis of Gethsemani helped to "legitimate" and mainstream Catholic spirituality for postwar America.

A Pilgrim's Progress

Thomas Merton's personal pilgrimage to the Monastery of Our Lady of Gethsemani near Louisville, Kentucky, was but the last stage of his own peripatetic family history. Born in 1915 to an American mother and an artist father from New Zealand who had met at an art school in Paris, Merton's early family life and schooling were either cosmopolitan or rootless, depending on one's viewpoint. Educated in a series of French grammar schools and at an undistinguished but respectable British public school (Oakham), Merton began his university studies at Clare College, Cambridge with the hope of a career in the

British diplomatic service. But after a dashing good time in the public houses and on the rugby fields of Cambridge, and a less than stellar showing on his examinations, Merton decided to take up residence with his grandparents in Flushing, Queens, enrolling in Columbia University in January of 1935. It was at Columbia that Merton first met a group of professors and students who would remain important to him for the rest of his life: they were the individuals who helped Merton ("providentially" he believed to the end of his life) discern what he came to see as his extraordinary vocation.[15]

Upon his arrival at Morningside Heights, Merton had believed that he should pursue a career in literature, both as an author and as a professor. Thus, on completing his undergraduate studies in literature, Merton began work in Columbia's graduate program (under the direction of the English Department's legendary Mark Van Doren) on the British "mystical" poet William Blake. To his considerable surprise, Merton discovered (as many had before him) that Blake had a quite unexpected effect on his intellectual life:

> As Blake worked himself into my system, I became more and more conscious of the necessity of a vital faith, and the total unreality and unsubstantiality of the dead, selfish rationalism which had been freezing my mind and will for the last seven years.... By the time I began the actual writing of my thesis, the groundwork for my conversion was more or less complete.[16]

The "completion" of that process — of the type that scholars of religious experience usually refer to as "intellectual conversion" — came in stages that Merton could date and pin down with alarming specificity: in February 1937, Merton happened to be passing Scribner's Bookstore in Manhattan and saw a copy of Etienne Gilson's *Spirit of Medieval Philosophy* in the window. Gilson's work simultaneously repelled and fascinated him, but it offered Merton an entrée into a whole new universe of discourse — the heady world of the continental neo-Thomist revival just then bursting into full flower. The profoundly intellectual nature of Merton's conversion strikes the reader of Merton's spiritual saga repeatedly. Thus, in describing the effect of Gilson's book on his personal pilgrimage, Merton observes,

> The one big concept which I got out of its pages was something that was to revolutionize my whole life.... The word *aseitas*. In its English translation "aseity" simply means the power to exist absolutely in virtue of itself.... This notion made such a pro-

found impression on me that I made a pencil note at the top of the page: "Aseity of God — God is being per se."[17]

Later, Merton would observe that Gilson's work had led him from being "an atheist to one who accepted the full range of religious experience." Indeed, by the beginning of June 1937, Merton had devoured Gilson and had moved on to Jacques Maritain, whose *Art and Scholasticism* convinced him that he should approach Blake's poetry through the thought of Maritain and St. Thomas Aquinas. This grazing in the verdant pastures of French neo-Thomism led to long discussions and close friendships with several fellow Columbia students who were themselves toying with the idea of conversion to the Roman Church. By the beginning of November 1938, Merton's intellectual conversion was complete, and Merton himself later recorded the "voice" that impelled him, as he was reading about Gerard Manley Hopkins's conversion to Catholicism, into the waiting arms of Holy Mother Church:

> Suddenly, I could bear it no longer. I put down my book, put on my raincoat, and went out into the street. And then everything inside me began to sing, to sing with peace. I turned the corner of 121st Street [to Corpus Christi Church]...and saw Fr. Ford coming around the corner. I went up to him and said, "Father, I want to become a Catholic."[18]

Merton was conditionally baptized on November 16, 1938, and immediately found himself torn by practical questions as to *how* to live out his newly found and hard-won Catholic identity. During one of his regular "bull sessions" nearly a year later, on November 30, 1939, close friend Bob Lax asked Merton what he wanted to be, to which Merton responded, "A good Catholic." Lax rejoined that such an answer was not good enough by half, that "what you should say is that you want to be a saint!" His friend's rejoinder struck Merton as ridiculous; but there was also an ineluctable attraction to the idea, especially given the direction of conversations with friends at the time. America was certainly in need of Catholics with such a call, Merton realized, as it was

> a country full of people who want to be kind, pleasant, happy, and love God, but do not know how. And they do not know where to turn to find out....[The vision] is to find somebody capable of telling them of the love of God in language that

no longer sounds hackneyed or crazy, but with authority and conviction: the conviction born of sanctity.[19]

It dawned on Merton gradually that perhaps he, of all people, might be one of those called to speak of the love of God "with a conviction born of sanctity" and began the spiritual pilgrimage that ended during Holy Week 1941 in a retreat at Gethsemani Monastery outside Louisville. Merton's account of that first visit is charged with a religious emotion and celebratory intensity that has helped to make the simple buildings of Gethsemani among the most visited shrines in Catholic America. His autobiography recounts his stepping "out of the world" into a cloister with the words "God Alone" written above the door, into a world where "solitude is an impregnable fortress"; the now-famous but terrifying question of the porter, "Have you come to stay?" — a question that Merton felt "sounded much like the voice of my own conscience"; the realization during the Maundy Thursday liturgy that this was a place defined by "hundreds of pounds of spiritual pressure compressed and concentrated, weighing down on the heads of the monks."[20]

Merton was, quite simply, bowled over by the spiritual power of the place; and his later recollections of that retreat in *The Seven Storey Mountain,* however "improved" by journalistic hindsight, still strike the reader with affective and poetic power. The idea of a life organized around the solemn chanting of the church's Divine Office and hard physical labor hit him like a personal invitation from God, so that his account of it approaches the rhapsodic:

> [The Abbey church] rings with a chant that glows with living flame, with clean, profound desire. It is an austere warmth, the warmth of Gregorian chant. It is deep beyond ordinary emotion, and is one reason why you never get tired of it. It never wears you out by making a lot of cheap demands on your sensibilities.... When we began to chant the Magnificat I almost wept, but that was because I was new in the monastery. And it was precisely because of that that I had reason to weep with thanksgiving and happiness, as I croaked the words in gratitude.[21]

The new convert's first visit to that place that would shortly become known as "Merton's monastery" dissolved the remaining doubts as to his "call." Just as his good friend Bob Lax had argued years before, Merton felt himself called to live out his newfound Catholic identity as, of all un-American things, a saint! And Merton would seek that sainthood "in struggle, not in acceptance, in becoming, not in being." Even so, many of Merton's friends drolly wagered that he would last somewhere between a week and a year in the deserted Kentucky countryside, as he who loved the companionship of people (especially women), parties, and long conversations into the night was entering the most austere order in the Catholic Church. Thus, three days after the bombing of Pearl Harbor — on December 10, 1941 — Thomas Merton entered the Monastery of Our Lady of Gethsemani, a few hundred acres that would be his world for the next twenty-seven years.[22]

As Michael Mott has noted, from the moment Merton entered his "house of silence" one searches his writings in vain for any evidence that he ever found his monastic life anything but a liberation. Thus, in the celebratory conclusion of *The Seven Storey Mountain,* published seven years later, Merton had only one complaint: that even with the famous penances and fasts that defined a good part of the Trappist year, his life was not austere enough.[23]

Merton's ferocious creative energies found an outlet in the strictly regimented life of the cloister in a daily journal, a journal started ostensibly in obedience to his abbot, who was also his spiritual director. In retrospect, this journal might also be seen (consciously or not on the abbot's part) as a "safety valve" for Merton's life-long need to understand his world by writing about it. By March 1, 1946, this journal had evolved into a "new project" — something Merton described in a letter at the time as "creative, more or less poetic prose, autobiographical in its essence, but not pure autobiography. Something like a cross between Dante's *Purgatory,* Kafka, and a medieval mystery play.... It has been brewing for a long time."[24]

One might more properly say that Merton's account of his spiritual pilgrimage had been brewing his entire life; even so, when Merton sent off the manuscript to his literary agent, he reported that the monastery's censors — those charged with screening works to be published by the monks — had already raised questions about granting a *Nihil obstat,* the church's "stamp of approval" on works of theology, to the "new project." There were far too many references, they felt, to the sex and drinking of Merton's preregenerate days (especially at Cambridge), and one even suggested that a correspondence course in writing might help Merton grapple with his problematic lapsing into "slang" in the manuscript.[25]

Merton's "slang," however problematic to the monastery's censors, nonetheless helped to make the work both accessible and a lively read to hundreds of thousands of readers. While the publication set off little immediate critical notice (the *New York Times* never got around to reviewing it), three Catholic book clubs immediately put the work on their lists within weeks of its appearance, and by Labor Day 1949 — ten months after its appearance — *The Seven Storey Mountain* had sold three hundred thousand copies.[26]

Merton's best-seller, as Evelyn Waugh noted not altogether favorably at the time, was a curious blend of accessible popular culture and the "high tradition" of Western mysticism and spirituality. And as Merton's most exhaustive biographer has observed, there was a helterskelter element to the book's index, "where one name jostled another with no regard to chronology or decorum," that tickled Merton's sense of literary irony: "Ameche, Don; Anselm, St.; Aquinas, St. Thomas; Armstrong, Louis; *Art and Scholasticism* (Maritain)." For Merton had quite consciously borrowed literary conventions from a wide variety of sources — St. Augustine's *Confessions,* Dante's *Purgatorio,* Maritain's works on Thomistic philosophy, St. Therese's *Story of a Soul,* even Marcel Proust's *Remembrance of Things Past* — to craft the account of one soul's spiritual pilgrimage in order to proclaim a perfectionist "moral of the story" in the book's epilogue:

> In practice, there is only one vocation, whether you teach or live in the cloister or nurse the sick, whether you are in religion or out of it, married or single, no matter who you are or what you are. You are called to the summit of perfection: you are called to a deep interior life, even to mystical prayer, and to pass the fruits of contemplation on to others.[27]

Merton's own description of his work as "poetic prose" comes closest to the mark in describing the book's literary style, as it was — by turns — ironic, poignant, funny, and prophetic. In its profoundly critical (and even mocking) description of the spiritual dead-end at which American liberal culture found itself, it resembled the early works of Reinhold Niebuhr. For like that earlier cultural prophet, Merton seemed to be at pains to remind his readers that the old Christian doctrine of original sin went a long way toward diagnosing the deplorable state of the "atomic age." One thinks of Niebuhr's prophetic denunciation of the "easy liberalism" of his time in *Moral Man and Immoral Society,* as well as of Dante's cry of existential despair on the opening page of the *Divine Comedy,* in reading Merton's description of his preregenerate days. Early in the book, he recounted the death of his father, an event which left him with the quite mistaken impression that he was free; but

> it would take me five or six years to discover what a frightful captivity I was in.... And so I became the complete 20th century man. I now belonged to the world in which I lived. I became a true citizen of my own disgusting century: the century of poison gas and atomic bombs. A man living on the doorsill of the Apocalypse.[28]

But for all of its critical edge, the book flattered its readers as well, offering casual and quite off-hand references to the "great minds" of the twentieth century — T. S. Eliot, James Joyce, Carl Jung, Aldous Huxley — implying, of course, that his readers were as conversant with the transatlantic life of the mind in the postwar world as he. Cheek-in-jowl with his sophisticated discussion of Eliot's poetry and Jung's psychological insights, however, was the constant theme of the work: the primacy of the spiritual in an unspiritual age. It was a heady blend of profound spiritual insights and chatty gossip about the New York intellectual world: Catholic readers had seen nothing like it, and they ate it up like hotcakes on Spy Wednesday.

Erikson and the Postwar Revival

For the past several decades scholars studying postwar American Catholicism have reached something like a consensus on Merton's seminal presence on the religious landscape: Henri Nouwen has listed him as one of the "most important spiritual writers in our century," while Lawrence Cunningham has gone even further, calling Merton the most significant spiritual writer of his generation. Jean Leclercq, perhaps the most widely respected historian of monasticism in our time, has ranked Merton's influence in the history of monasticism with that of the fathers of the early church and of the giants of the High Middle Ages, while Walter Capps has called him "the West's most influential fashioner of contemporary spirituality."[29]

What has been clearly documented by a wide variety of scholars, then, is the way in which Merton handed on — in the best sense of "tradition" — to a wide American audience the riches of the Western spiritual past, in the process fashioning the first modern synthesis of contributions made by the Greek philosophers, the fathers of the Western church, the Thomists of the High Middle Ages, and the Carmelite school of spirituality. And in fashioning this synthesis, Merton *re-vealed* American Catholicism to itself, articulating "what we may sense but cannot say," leading the Catholic community to a future with new possibilities. In this sense, Merton himself might be (and has been) described as a "symbol" of modern American Catholicism — a symbol in the Catholic sacramental sense of revealing and enfleshing the true nature of a reality hidden by appearances. As Jean Leclercq has observed in describing Merton's complex relationship to his historical predecessors and to the *risorgiamento* of the post–Vatican II church,

> When he went back to the sources, Merton shook off the hampering shackles of the very recent past which grew out of the 19th century, and he did much in the way of liberating his immediate background from such confines. He preferred theology and spirituality to usages which had come down as formalism.[30]

A variety of scholars have thus agreed on Merton's central role in elucidating a new, postimmigrant American Catholicism in the years after World War II; the explanation of the why of Merton's critical role, however, has been less cogent and unanimous, "the right person at the right time" coming closest to describing the received wisdom. It is precisely here that Erik Erikson's theory of the "great individual" can help exegete Merton's role in defining what became, in effect, a new style of American Catholicism.

Basic to Erikson's theory of the great individual is the concept of the "identity crisis," a term which Erikson coined but which has now become part of the argot of our time. For Erikson, every individual undergoes some form of this crisis at some point in his or her psychological development, usually in late adolescence or early adulthood. For at issue in the identity crisis is the development of an effective adult identity, an identity that always involves the acquisition of an "ideology" — that is, a "relatively comprehensive and unified understanding of the nature and meaning of oneself, and of one's role in the world."[31]

In some, or probably most, young people, in most periods of history, this crisis is minimal; in some individuals, and in certain periods of history, however, this period will be clearly marked off as a critical period — a period when an entirely new ideology is needed to reorient the individual in changed (or revolutionary) cultural surroundings. Indeed, Erikson argues that "in some periods of history, people need a new ideological orientation as sorely as they need air and food." When such individuals uncover such an ideology, they experience a kind of "second birth" that can easily be described in religious language: in resolving the conflicts of this crisis, they experience a sense that they have been "born again."[32]

Erikson posits that for these great individuals, the very "danger" of their psychological situation forces them to mobilize capacities to "see and say, to dream and plan, in new ways," in the process contributing important original insights to an emerging style of life that speaks to many other "adolescents" undergoing similar crises. Thus, Erikson's notion of the culturally paradigmatic identity crisis can help to explain how the "intensely *private* struggles of great ideologists are of such immense public significance": the *personal* solutions of such great individuals enable others to recognize the possibility of solution for themselves in them.[33]

In such a reading of the crisis of the late medieval church, young man Luther's identity crisis was simultaneously highly personal *and* also

> intellectual and ideological in a publicly definable and generalizable way. Thus in forging a new kind of Christian identity for himself, Luther also forged a new theology; and in solving his own personal problems, he developed a solution of sorts for a major problem of his age.[34]

From an Eriksonian perspective, postwar American Catholics generally and Thomas Merton specifically faced a crisis analogous to that of young man Luther. The bombs of Hiroshima had effected more than the destruction of a Japanese city: the clearly defined walls of the Catholic ghetto likewise appeared atomized in a cultural context in which "being Catholic" now became an acceptable and comfortable way of "being American." In the post-Protestant milieu of mid-century, American Catholics found themselves securely riding the sociological escalator out of the working class into suburban, middle-class affluence. The tight "in-group/out-group" boundaries that had defined their ethnic identity throughout the nineteenth and the first half of the twentieth centuries no longer provided an easy demarcation of social location and tribal bonding. The secure but somewhat narrow world of parochial school networks, Catholic labor unions, and Communion breakfasts now appeared cramped and unsatisfying in light of the invitation to join the larger cultural feast. "Poetry" no longer meant just Joyce Kilmer; reaching Fordham was no longer to reach the top of the university ladder. But with this entry into a broader world also came a crisis of identity: if "being Catholic" no longer provided a ready-made secure but ghetto-ized identity, as it had for most American Catholics for over a century, then what *did* it mean? Much like good burghers of Luther's time, new social and psychological needs could no longer be satisfied by the traditional "ideological" answers. A new ideological identity in the Eriksonian sense — a new way of being an American Catholic — now became imperative.[35]

Merton's personal "identity crisis" — an essentially *intellectual* crisis of confidence in the power of modern culture to "save" him — found resolution in the powerful spirituality embodied, among other places, at Gethsemani Monastery. A convert to the church from the "wider" established world of Anglo-American culture — the world of Cambridge and Columbia and the New York literary scene — Merton was perhaps the first American Catholic to recognize the richness *and* the possibilities of the ancient Western tradition of spirituality, and make that tradition accessible to Americans precisely at the cultural moment when millions were searching for "peace of mind." But the "peace of mind" he rhapsodized about in the account of his spiritual pilgrimage both shared in *and* critiqued the popular movement of that name just then emerging on the American religious landscape. Unlike Norman Vincent Peale's *Power of Positive Thinking,* Merton promised no easy spiritual uplift in an optative mood of "five easy pieces." The path to such peace was arduous and long — thus the titular reference to the mountains of Purgatory — and the attainment of such peace involved a sophisticated critique of the busyness and venality of the affluent and materialistic culture of America. Merton hardly fitted in to the "piety on the Potomac" genre of popular piety that would soon be made famous by the "sermons" of Dwight David Eisenhower. In accord with the nature of his own conversion that began with reading Etienne Gilson, Merton proposed a new intellectual model for American Catholicism, a model in which ideas and serious reflection would have to take the place of memorized "answers" and "relying on Father."[36]

Thus, to call Merton a "popularizer" is hardly to do justice to the crucial role he played for postwar American Catholic culture. And yet he was *precisely* that — in the best sense of the term — for millions of readers. From the moment he first visited Gethsemani Monastery, he recognized with an insight granted to cultural prophets that a vibrant life of the spirit, to be cultivated by businessmen and shopkeepers no less than monks, was *(mirabile dictu)* exactly what both he and his culture needed. *This*, he proclaimed after his first visit to Gethsemani in a tone of belated discovery, is the "real capital of the country. *This* is the center of all the vitality that is in America!"

Merton thus made accessible and attractive to millions of mid-century readers a spiritual tradition that had been present but largely unknown in American culture. The "truth" of his experience was also, it would seem, the truth of many others engaged in a similar search for identity and meaning in the brave new world after 1945. Merton offered to fellow Catholics a "high" tradition of spirituality at exactly the cultural moment when the older traditions of the immigrant ghetto, with fish on Friday and Catholic book clubs, were crumbling.

Far from being outsiders to the life of the mind and the peaks of spiritual sophistication, Merton seemed to say, Catholics were the *real* insiders! Dante predated Emerson by centuries; St. Bonaventure addressed the anomie of human existence at least as well as Freud. Merton forged for himself a sophisticated and rich spiritual identity that spoke meaningfully to many others engaged in precisely the same task of welding together an identity made up of three seemingly disjunctive terms: "modern," "American," and "Catholic." And it was the first of these terms that made his resolution of the other two so timely: the answer to the identity crisis for American Catholicism was *not* to be a retreat into obscurantism, "mind cure," or even a monastic flight from the world. The answer, rather, would be a creative reappropriation of ancient ideas *in a new way,* a way open to everyone, and not just to a religious elite. There was, after all, "only one vocation...no matter who you are or what you are." All were called, he argued, "to the summit of perfection."

Twenty years before the Second Vatican Council, Merton announced a perfectionist, "populist" vision of Catholicism in decidedly American tones redolent of the Transcendentalists and Charles Grandison Finney. In a real sense, the psychological "homework" necessary for the revolution that took place at Vatican II had begun long before anyone ever considered calling that council; from an Eriksonian perspective, Brother Louis of Gethsemani Monastery had issued something like a clarion call to such a Catholicism in 1948.

As was the case for fellow cultural critics on the Protestant side of the fence, Merton's shadow fell well beyond the enclave of fellow religionists, indeed, in due time well beyond the confines of Christianity itself. Like the famous Niebuhr brothers, Merton resurrected a revered intellectual alternative to the busyness and materialism of twentieth-

century American culture as an answer to the anomie and sense of
"lostness" in which many suburban Americans found themselves. Unlike the Niebuhrs, however, Merton's alternative was presented in the
form of a "personal journey" that eschewed "theology" as the form
for presenting his chastened cultural critique, offering instead spiritual
autobiography as the locus for his lessons in a return to older "orthodoxies." Merton's brand of spiritual autobiography, in fact, harkened
back to a genre at least as old as *Walden*, if not older, casting his story
in a reassuringly "American" light, despite the European nature and
history of monasticism. At the same time, however, Merton blazed a
new path in this genre — a path that welded modern therapeutic concerns with serious (or at least ancient and revered) theological insights
to create a new kind of "popular" spiritual literature, a literature with
an intellectual legitimacy and seriousness lacking in the best-sellers of
Liebman, Sheen, and Peale.

For hundreds of thousands of Catholic Americans, Merton emerged
as a Catholic spiritual writer whom even non-Catholics had to recognize as significant. Millions of other Americans in 1948 and after were
clearly "ready" for Merton's heady blend of cultural critique, spiritual journeying, and prophetic call to stand apart and (of all things)
contemplate.

According to an Eriksonian reading of the situation, of course, Merton's personal example does not *explain* the postwar Catholic revival
in any von Rankian sense of "proof." Americans read Merton — or
would have read someone *like* him, in such a reading — because they
were ready for his message, not because he personally "empowered"
them to undertake a journey for which they were otherwise not ready.
Merton's success and influence thus derives from the "emotional congruities" of his personal dilemma and that of millions of other people.
Further, an Eriksonian reading does not discount the weight of myriad
other cultural, political, and sociological factors in the situation; but it
does argue that the relationship of great individuals to their cultural
milieu is an exchange that goes "both ways." The great individual
brings to his or her age creative insights and new "pathways" that
are congruent with the needs and crises of the moment.

The remarkable success of *The Seven Storey Mountain* and Merton's subsequent popularity until his death in 1968 rather points to
the applicability of Merton's personal synthesis of "American" and
"Catholic" to the lives of many others. As Richard Bushman has
argued in a similar application of Erikson's theories to the role of
Jonathan Edwards in the events of the First Great Awakening,

Something common to all, some prevailing strain on their institutions, some pressure in the culture, prepared people for the new life he urged upon them. They listened because the truth of his experience was also the truth of theirs.... Insofar as this analysis is convincing, it confirms Erikson's conception of leadership as the application of the leader's personal identity solution to the needs of his age.[37]

Merton's populist, perfectionist vision of American Catholicism, reflecting the gains of his own intellectual conversion, thus offered a model of postimmigrant, post-working-class spirituality to newly arrived middle class Catholics looking for role models in the strange landscape of the suburbs. It is just one of the delicious ironies of the story, of course, that they found such a role model in the person of a Trappist monk, who had "abandoned" the world for life in a silent monastery. Indeed, perhaps the ironies here might serve as a metaphor for so many other ironies in the postwar Catholic story: how ironic that immigrant Catholicism, having eschewed intellectual issues for over a century, discovered the resolution to its identity crisis in the intellectual conversion of a graduate-student-turned-monk. The irony is further compounded by the fact that a significant popular "resolution" to Catholicism's postwar identity crisis would not be found in sacramental or hierarchical models of Christianity, but rather in the essentially democratic and perfectionist preserve of "spirituality." Further, there is rich irony in the fact that Brother Louis of Gethsemani Monastery in Kentucky might very well turn out to be "the most significant Christian figure in 20th century America."[38]

But perhaps the chief irony of *The Seven Storey Mountain* is that Merton's own deep disdain for the thin therapeutic spirituality being marketed by the likes of Norman Vincent Peale did not protect his autobiography itself from becoming the chief postwar Catholic "spiritual classic" of just such a "therapeutic" spirituality. While many devout Catholics and other Americans undoubtedly found in Merton a profound source of spiritual insight as well as a timely introduction to ancient spiritual resources largely unknown in America, still others — and arguably most of his readers — approached Merton's autobiography as simply one more "commodity" being sold in the spiritual bookstore, along with Liebman, Peale, and Sheen. While several hundred young ex-GIs were inspired to follow Merton into the silent corridors of Gethsemani, the great majority of Merton's readers — close to a million if the book sales data is reliable — did not seek out the monastic life, or indeed organize contemplative groups in their parishes. In this final ironic sense, Merton "legitimized" the possibility of a sophisticated, accessible Catholic spirituality for a middle-class, suburban constituency without really "converting" them to the radical implications of Cistercian or Benedictine spirituality. The "busyness" and activism of Catholic parish life, the measurement of success by numbers and building programs — what has been termed "brick-and-mortar Catholicism" — these continued unabated, and even became more noticeable during the 1950s and early 1960s. One wonders what Brother Louis thought of all those parish reading groups plowing their way through his book before tackling *Peace of Mind*.

Chapter 3

Catholicism as a Cultural System

*Joe McCarthy, Clifford Geertz,
and the "Conspiracy So Immense"*

> "While I cannot take the time to name all the men in the State
> Department who have been named as active members of the Com-
> munist Party and members of a spy ring, I have in my hand a list of
> 205 names...." — SENATOR JOSEPH McCARTHY[1]

Senator McCarthy and 205 Communists

While Leonard Feeney was limning a new fault line between American culture and Catholicism in Boston, yet another player in this
Catholic "ecological" story emerged quite suddenly in (of all unlikely
places) Wheeling, West Virginia. None of the 275 people present in
the Colonnade Room of Wheeling's McClure Hotel on the evening
of February 9, 1950, had a clue that a new era in American history
was about to dawn in their presence — not the Ohio County Republican Women's Club, who had invited the speaker that evening; not
WWVA, the local fifty-thousand-watt radio station that would broadcast the speaker's words throughout the Ohio Valley; not even the
speaker himself, Senator Joseph McCarthy of Wisconsin.[2]

Wheeling was to be the first of five Lincoln Day appearances on the
rubber chicken circuit for Senator McCarthy, the only exciting part of
which was supposed to have been stopovers in Reno and Las Vegas —
where the senator could indulge his interest in gambling for a few
hours — on the way to his final appearance in Huron, South Dakota.
Indeed, according to later retellings of that evening, McCarthy hadn't
given a great amount of thought to what he was going to say that
night, as the expected news coverage was likely to be local at best.
From a prepared "textual" point of view, then, much of McCarthy's
speech in Wheeling promised nothing that the national news media

would have geared up for in any event. Significant portions of the address that his Washington office staff had prepared for him — full of standard right-wing accusations about betrayal in high places and the threat of world communism — was substantially the same one he had already delivered in Madison, Wisconsin; the data it cited about the alleged growth of communism since the end of World War II had already been used two weeks earlier by Richard Nixon, then a rising Congressional star from California.[3]

The question of how faithfully the senator followed the "prepared text" that evening in Wheeling — and thus the question of whether McCarthy "ad-libbed" his way into national fame or clawed his way there by cold calculation — would itself become the topic of fierce debate, not least among members of the Senate's Tydings Committee, which would be formed in the maelstrom set off by that evening's address. But whether by plan or by chance, Senator Joseph McCarthy held up a piece of paper in his hand well into his address before his sympathetic but unsuspecting audience and announced:

> Ladies and gentlemen, while I cannot take the time to name all the men in the State Department who have been named as active members of the Communist Party and members of a spy ring, I have here in my hand a list of 205 — a list of names that were made known to the Secretary of State as being members of the Communist Party and who nevertheless are still working and shaping policy in the State Department.[4]

Charles R. Lewis, night editor of the Associated Press bureau in Charleston, West Virginia, was astonished by the claim of 205 communists in the State Department that he found in the wire story sent in later that same evening by a part-time correspondent present in Wheeling and asked him to verify it. Shortly before 2:00 a.m. on February 10, Lewis sent off a 110-word story to newspapers nationwide. What would later be termed the "McCarthy era," however, began in an eerily quiet manner: one study of 129 national newspapers revealed that only 18 carried the Associated Press story on Friday, February 10, and only 3 of them featured it on their front pages. All of that, however, would quickly change.[5]

The paranoia, political witch-hunts, and fierce concern about world communism that would mark American culture between 1950 and 1954 — that is, during the "McCarthy era" — spawned a cottage industry among cultural and political pundits, both at the time and since, offering readings as to what the senator from Wisconsin "meant" for America's newfound but uncomfortable role as "Leader of the Free World." Indeed, while the McCarthy crusade was still in progress, intellectuals from both sides of the political divide began to publish interpretations of its import. A small but consistently interesting group in this endeavor were intellectuals concerned to deconstruct McCarthy's exact relationship to, and degree of symbolic expression of, American Catholicism. For, not least among the observable forces shaping Joseph Raymond McCarthy's life was the fact that he was a theologically untutored but nonetheless doggedly pious second-generation Irish-American Catholic.[6]

The question of whether and the degree to which "McCarthyism" represented a "Catholic crusade" in the postwar years has exercised both Catholic and non-Catholic intellectuals since the fateful February evening in Wheeling. And the problem is that convincing evidence has been brought forward by both "sides" to this debate to establish their claims.

Intellectuals spanning the religious spectrum from the professional anti-Catholic Paul Blanshard to the ecumenical and urbane editors of the Protestant *Christian Century* to the liberal Catholic editors of *Commonweal* have outlined a quite believable and easily documented scenario in which American Catholics (and especially Irish-American Catholics) constituted the hard-core support group for McCarthy's anti-communist crusade. This position would appear to have at least some statistical support: an early Gallup poll taken in March 1950 — that is, a month after the Wheeling speech and well before any "hard" evidence could be presented verifying such an accusation — showed that 49 percent of Catholics polled (a significantly larger percentage than respondents who identified themselves as Protestant or Jewish) believed McCarthy when he said that he had proof that that a number of communists worked in the State Department. The Gallup poll's statistical measure of Catholic support for Senator McCarthy would fluctuate over the next four years; what would remain stable was that Catholic support for the senator was significantly higher than that by Protestants and "others."[7]

Likewise, Catholic periodicals like the *Brooklyn Tablet,* Catholic voluntary groups like the Catholic War Veterans of New York and that city's Policemen's Benevolent Association, and Catholic prelates like Francis Cardinal Spellman (the "point man" of the American hierarchy) offered McCarthy early, vociferous, and unmistakably *Catholic* support from the time of Wheeling until well after his death. As this group correctly points out, the most consistently loyal groups of

McCarthy supporters were Catholic voters from Massachusetts and Catholic police and firemen in New York City, overwhelmingly Irish in both locations. Indeed, according to a still-disputed rumor publicized at the time by columnist Drew Pearson, McCarthy's entire anti-communist crusade was allegedly born over dinner at Washington's Colony restaurant at the instigation of a Roman Catholic cleric, Father Edmund Walsh, S.J., founder and dean of Georgetown University's powerful and prestigious School of Foreign Service (see further below, p. 67).[8]

Further, there is a pleasing historical "cleanness of line" to this side of the argument: McCarthy fit neatly and handily into a larger Catholic crusade against communism that began with the papal encyclical *Quanta Cura* in 1864, and that had reached fever pitch in the decade after World War II. With the fall of "Catholic nations" in eastern Europe like Poland and Hungary within five years of the end of the war, prelates like Joseph Cardinal Mindszenty and Archbishop Aloysius Stepinac emerged as icons for the suffering and persecution that ensued when "godless communism" triumphed in a culture. More than any other religious group in America, Catholics saw anti-communism as somehow uniquely *their* issue because of the suffering of their co-religionists behind the "Iron Curtain." In the eyes of those American Catholics who formed themselves into "Mindszenty Circles" after the cardinal's trumped-up arrest and imprisonment in 1948, the fight against communism was the Catholic cause par excellence. Fitting McCarthy into this historical stream, it might even be argued that if the senator from Wisconsin had not emerged when he did, then certain American Catholic groups would have had to invent him.[9]

Scholars on the other side of this debate, however, have convincingly argued that from McCarthy's first appearance in the national consciousness, Catholic support for the senator and his cause was divided at best and cannot ever be termed monolithic or in any way "official." This group in the debate points out correctly that widely respected Catholic leaders like Monsignor George Higgins of the National Catholic Welfare Conference's Social Action Department and Chicago's legendary auxiliary bishop, Bernard Sheil, were outspoken and quite consciously *Catholic* critics of McCarthy's crusade, calling the Wisconsin senator to task for sponsoring a campaign made up of "lies, calumny, and absence of charity." Likewise, the two most respected Catholic journals of opinion — *Commonweal* and *America* magazines — took critical stands on "Tail Gunner Joe's" tactics and public calumnies. It was, moreover, a Catholic senator,

Dennis Chavez from New Mexico, who rose in the congressional chamber to denounce McCarthy's chief congressional witness, Louis Budenz, for "cashing in" on the Catholic ticket. "I speak as a Roman Catholic," Chavez announced to a hushed chamber, proceeding to denounce Budenz for "using the Church I revere as a shield and a cloak."[10]

The "evidence" itself, therefore, at least as it has traditionally been framed by the two sides to this debate, would seem to allow the historian to take a Solomonic if finally unsatisfying middle position: both positions — and therefore neither — are probably correct. Quite clearly, McCarthy courted and received loyal (and sometimes even fanatical) support from widely read Catholic journals like *Our Sunday Visitor,* which both perceived and publicly touted the senator's concerns as distinctly "Catholic." But self-consciously Catholic opposition to McCarthy was likewise fierce and public, championed by Catholic intellectuals like John Cort and Robert Hartnett, S.J., the editor of *America* magazine.

Indeed, it is precisely *how* this debate is usually framed that has contributed to the resulting hermeneutical confusion. McCarthy's anti-communist "mission" clearly resonated with the spiritual ideals, fears, and political perceptions of great numbers of American Catholics, resulting in a fairly widespread perception — among both Protestants and Catholics — that indeed it *was,* somehow, related on *some* level to "being Catholic" in America. But granting this to be the case, it would be a gross simplification (as well as historically untrue) to portray "McCarthyism" as *Catholic* in any strictly institutional or ecclesiological sense: some bishops supported him, others did not; some Catholic periodicals valorized him, others roundly condemned him. As Bishop Sheil of Chicago correctly noted in the very speech in which he denounced McCarthy in 1954, "the Catholic Church does not take positions on matters of public controversy."[11]

But whatever side of the controversy one takes, what *is* clear is that American Catholics in the early 1950s felt compelled to "pronounce" on Joe McCarthy's crusade precisely *as* Catholics: Senator Dennis Chavez, no less than the *Brooklyn Tablet*'s Patrick Scanlon, offered rather self-consciously *Catholic* positions on McCarthy's anti-communist program. *Commonweal,* no less than *Our Sunday Visitor,* felt it imperative to make its position on McCarthyism clear "for the record." How, then, to understand the somewhat intangible but nonetheless discernible relationship of the senator from Wisconsin to American Catholic concerns from 1950 to 1954?

Religion as a Cultural System

The model of "religion as a cultural system" advanced by anthropologist Clifford Geertz offers the student of the McCarthy era a fruitful and creative lens for understanding the powerful ways in which Joseph McCarthy's language and message profoundly resonated with the perceptions and fears of many Catholic Americans — precisely on the level of religious symbol — while also recognizing the mood shaping the somewhat different Catholic "cultural system" of Catholic anti-McCarthyites. Using Geertz's model, it is less true to say that McCarthy "manipulated" his Catholic followers than that he recognized the congruence between his political concerns and the symbol system that many American Catholics already shared.[12]

Geertz argues that, on some level, all religions operate as a "system of symbols" to establish

> powerful, pervasive, and long-lasting moods and motivations in men by formulating conceptions of a general order of existence, and clothing these conceptions with such an aura of factuality that the moods and motivations seem uniquely realistic.[13]

Geertz's examination of the cultural resonances of religious symbols, of the "moods and motivations" inspired by religious systems, would seem to respect both the congruities and the disharmonies between McCarthy's crusade and American Catholicism, while highlighting the complex ways in which American anti-communism of the McCarthy type elicited strong Catholic support precisely as "religious." For, from Geertz's anthropological perspective, the symbols of any religious tradition

> function to synthesize a people's ethos — the tone, character, and quality of their life, its moral and aesthetic style and mood — their worldview, the picture they have of the way things in sheer actuality are. In religious belief and practice, a group's ethos is rendered intellectually reasonable by being shown to represent a way of life adapted to the actual state of affairs.[14]

Geertz thus argues that successful religious symbols offer epistemological *congruence* with the cultural experience of believers; that is, symbols — and the "priests" who interpret them — offer a self-evidently "true" bridge of meaning that connects the language and concerns of religion with political and social reality. For Geertz, any effective *cultural* expression of religious symbols elicits a *mood* and a *worldview* that offers a convincing "picture...of the way things in sheer actuality are." This congruence between transcendent religious truth and political/social reality, embodied in the cultural expression of religious symbols, helps human beings to address the uncomfortable suspicion, raised by certain empirical events, that "perhaps the world and the human place in it has no genuine order at all — no moral coherence." It is precisely against this deep-seated human fear of moral incoherence in the "real world" that religious systems operate as *cultural* systems. Religious systems formulate, by means of symbols,

> an image of such genuine order of the world which will account for, and even celebrate, the perceived ambiguities, puzzles, and paradoxes of human existence. The effort is *not* to deny the undeniable, but to deny that there are inexplicable events.[15]

For Geertz, then, to say that people are "religious" is to say that they are motivated *toward the world* by a set of transcendent symbols, and that these motivations offer a specific "directional cast" to their social, political, and personal lives — directional casts obviously open to formulation, persuasion, and manipulation. By Geertz's definition of religion, then, people using the very same religious symbols but "persuaded" or "shaped" in different ways are liable (and even likely) to respond to similar cultural and political contexts differently, *not* because the codes and formal creeds of their communities "officially" enjoin them to so respond, but because the symbols of their belief system have induced "moods" that direct them differently. One's "take" on religious symbols, then,

> alters, often radically, the whole landscape presented to common sense, alters it in such a way that the moods and motivations induced by religious practice seem themselves supremely practical, the only sensible ones to adopt given the way things "really are."[16]

Using Geertz's anthropological understanding of religious symbols, it might very well be both possible and fruitful to trace the ways in which Joseph McCarthy's profound fears of a communist "conspiracy so immense" appealed to, and elicited support from, a significant segment of the American Catholic community precisely because of certain "moods and motivations" induced by a specific type of (ethnic) American Catholicism. At the same time, Geertz's approach uncovers the deep *Catholic* motivation for opposing the senator's crusade precisely on religious grounds.

In Geertzian terms, Joseph McCarthy "synthesized the ethos" of many American Catholics in ways both he and they recognized: he made sense of their "worldview, the picture they have of the way things in sheer actuality are." McCarthy offered for millions of ethnic (and not so ethnic) Catholics an explanation of the postwar political and international circumstance that was "rendered intellectually reasonable by being shown to represent a way of life adapted to the actual state of affairs." The "sell-out" at Yalta, the Iron Curtain (with the concomitant betrayal of millions of Eastern European Catholics), the seeming loss of nerve at home — all of this in the face of the church's consistent and well-reasoned anti-communist stance suddenly fell into place. The "Prayers for the Conversion of Russia," said immediately after Sunday Mass in hundreds of Catholic parishes across the land, now made as much political and diplomatic as soteriological sense: the stakes were high, both here and abroad; "our enemy the Devil" lurked on Capitol Hill no less than in the Kremlin. Holy Mother Church, as they always had been taught, was the last refuge of human dignity and freedom on the darkling plains of history.

Thus, to argue for a Catholic "cast" to McCarthy's crusade has very little (or nothing) to do with formal Catholic theology, official teaching by theologians and bishops, or public ecclesiastical pronouncements on social and political questions. It rather has to do with considering the different kinds of dispositions, motivations, and self-perceptions that informed the cultural reception and expression of Catholicism among many Catholics.

Considered from Geertz's vantage, it is not surprising at all that Senator McCarthy's anti-communist crusade received the amount of support it did among Catholic Americans, nor that it elicited such strong denunciation from certain Catholic leaders. For cultural "outsiders" just beginning to ride the middle-class escalator into affluence and cultural acceptance — precisely the social location of many of his co-religionists in 1950 — McCarthy's fears of subversion and internal betrayal struck a deep cord of anxiety, one might even say a "religious" cord. For other co-religionists, McCarthy represented precisely the kind of celebrationist, accommodationist "culture religion" that many American Catholics had always found suspect and thin — precisely because of a specific Catholic "take" on the official symbol system that eschewed linking politics and theology, history and eschatology. Thus, much like Leonard Feeney five years previously, Joseph Raymond McCarthy defined a fault line within American Catholicism that makes his anti-communist crusade, ironically enough, precisely a "Catholic issue" in a distinctive way. For, far from uncovering a monolithic "Catholic" position on American cultural issues, McCarthy's anti-communist crusade revealed at least *two* American "cultural systems" emergent from, and pledging allegiance to, Roman Catholic symbols. *Both* systems evinced profound "moods and motivations" shaped by those symbols, although in contradictory ways.

"Tail Gunner Joe"

From the moment that McCarthy entered the political arena in 1938, the whirlwind from Wisconsin seemed to have a knack for "stirring things up," and then professing astonishment (and perhaps actually feeling astonishment) at the resulting furor his campaign antics unleashed. Born in Grand Chute, Wisconsin, in 1908, Joe was raised in a resolutely religious household in which Catholicism was regular, strict, and unquestioning, "scrupulously if unthinkingly observed." Graduating from the local grade school at fourteen, young Joe interrupted his formal schooling to work on the family farm until he was twenty years old, when he returned to school and finished four years of high school in a year. In the fall of 1930, he entered Marquette University, listing "boxing" — prophetically enough — as his chief extracurricular interest and commitment. Indeed, the first media press record we have of him is found in the Marquette student newspaper, the *Tribune,* which noted that "McCarthy is a husky, hard-hitting middleweight who promises an evening's work for any foe." After just two years in the undergraduate college — in which he was also president of his class — McCarthy transferred to the university's law school, from which he graduated in 1935.[17]

After a brief, restless career as a small-town lawyer, McCarthy launched his first campaign for public office in 1939 for a Wisconsin state judgeship. The young lawyer ran against a stuffy and pedantic incumbent who in 1916 had lied about his age in his initial judicial race, claiming 1866 rather than 1872 as the year of his birth in order to emphasize his maturity. In a public letter during the campaign, McCarthy — who knew of the earlier untruth — emphasized the problematic nature of the judge's age, and then intimated questions of the judge's probity when the judge let the real story surface. The tactics of McCarthy's first campaign were thus *formally* legal — if *materially* problematic — and eerily presaged a "style" of politics that would come into its own in 1950. The upshot of these tactics, however, was that on April 5, 1939, McCarthy was elected to the state judiciary in what was claimed as the most astonishing upset in the history of Wisconsin's tenth district, taking office — at thirty years of age — as the youngest man ever elected a circuit judge in Wisconsin history. Richard Rovere, hardly a sympathetic chronicler of McCarthy's career, noted later that "Judge McCarthy" came to be known throughout the state for his "five-minute divorce judgments."[18]

When World War II broke out, McCarthy left the bench to join the Marines, in whose service McCarthy claimed to have suffered a "war injury," the problematic nature of which provided several hostile scholars grist for their anti-McCarthy mill. Whatever the nature (or reality) of that injury, McCarthy fruitfully mined his association with the Marines in the 1946 Wisconsin Republican primary against Senator Robert LaFollette, Jr., as a "marine war hero" with the moniker of "Tail Gunner Joe." Claiming that he carried "ten pounds of shrapnel" in his leg as a result of a war wound, he testified under oath that he had flown thirty-one "combat missions" in his country's service. Few reporters at the time inquired into McCarthy's war record, less out of respect for McCarthy's word than because so few newspapers took McCarthy's campaign against the son of one of Washington's "progressive saints" seriously. Astonishing everyone, especially those newspapers who had dismissed his candidacy, McCarthy won the 1946 primary over LaFollette, leading the *Milwaukee Journal* to label the outcome "one of the most startling victories in the political history of Wisconsin, an upset that not only stunned the state but bewildered political observers all over the nation."[19]

Years before the purported "Colony Restaurant Meeting" — in the course of which McCarthy was supposed to have been given the idea of anti-communism as a successful campaign issue — "red-baiting" rhetoric made its appearance in McCarthy's 1946 campaign strategy against his Democratic opponent. McCarthy's rhetoric and tactics made both Democratic *and* Republican leaders nervous about his candidacy. Thus the *Madison Capitol Times* sensed "deep religious divisions" during a campaign debate between McCarthy and his Baptist Democratic opponent, Professor Howard McMurray of the University of Wisconsin. These two prophetic intimations of McCarthy's later crusade incarnated themselves in the homily of the Catholic pastor of Appleton, Wisconsin, the week before the 1946 state election, who urged his listeners to vote against the "Communist candidate."[20]

McCarthy won an overwhelming victory over McMurray and moved to Washington and the Senate, in which he earned a reputation early as a relentless (and somewhat unreflective) conservative, opposing Fair Deal legislation and public housing while lobbying for sugar interests. James O'Neill, who published a study of the voting records of the six Catholic senators in the 80th Congress in 1954, reported that young Senator McCarthy had the most conservative record by far.[21]

The question of when and how communism emerged as a senatorial reelection issue for McCarthy has decimated several forests: certainly McCarthy had utilized the fear of communist domestic infiltration in his 1946 senate race in Wisconsin; likewise, the fear of domestic subversion was in the Washington air. In March of 1947, F.B.I. Director J. Edgar Hoover branded the American Communist Party a "Fifth Column," and during that same year the House (of Representatives) Un-American Activities Committee (HUAC) made headlines regularly in its charges of "domestic subversion." Roy Cohn, soon to become McCarthy's legal counsel and the bête noire of almost all liberals, later reported that McCarthy had announced to him that prior to the fall of 1949 that he had neither much interest in world or domestic communism nor much knowledge of it. According to Cohn's version of the tale, McCarthy confided that shortly before Thanksgiving 1949, the senator was approached by three men bearing an F.B.I. report and "literally overnight" was persuaded to take up anti-communism as a "cause."[22]

The better-known version of McCarthy's "conversion" to anti-communism was first reported by columnist Drew Pearson in March 1950. In it, McCarthy purportedly had dinner on January 7, 1950, at Washington's Colony Restaurant with the Jesuit founder and dean of Georgetown's School of Foreign Service, Fr. Edmund Walsh, Professor Charles Kraus of that same school's Political Science Department, and William Roberts, a prominent Catholic attorney in Washington. After dinner, McCarthy allegedly announced that he was in desperate need of a 1952 reelection issue. Roberts proposed the St. Lawrence Seaway project as a possible issue, to which McCarthy retorted, "That hasn't enough sex." McCarthy himself then floated the idea of sponsoring a pension plan for the elderly in which everyone over sixty-five would automatically get $100 a month: all three others present opined that this would be economically unsound. Finally, Fr. Walsh is supposed to have queried, "What about Communism as an issue?" McCarthy allegedly liked the idea immediately, announcing "the government is full of Communists. The thing to do is hammer at them."[23]

The debate over the question of whether the "Colony dinner" actually ever occurred — or over whether it occurred as Drew Pearson reported it — has spawned an interesting literature in its own right. Whatever the source for McCarthy's newfound interest in and knowledge about domestic communism, however, his announcement at the Republican Women's Club dinner in Wheeling, West Virginia, thirty-three days later quickly made the morphology of McCarthy's crusade secondary.

Two weeks prior to McCarthy's address in Wheeling, Richard Nixon — also seemingly obsessed with the problem of world communism — had announced that there were 540 million people on the "side" of freedom, 600 million "neutrals," and 800 million on the "Russian side." McCarthy's famous Lincoln Day speech changed those figures somewhat dramatically, numbers coming easily if not very reliably to the senator before the Republican Women of West Virginia: he declared 80 *billion* people "under the absolute domination of Soviet Russia," while "on our side the figure has shrunk to 500,000." Three paragraphs of the Wheeling address on "leaks" in the State Department came directly from an article published the previous week in the *Chicago Tribune;* the speech's condemnation of Alger Hiss — a WASP "insider" in the eastern Establishment — was almost identical to that used by Nixon in a speech before the House of Representatives on January 26. The address's accusation that an FBI investigator had revealed to McCarthy that the State Department had buried the exposure of spies in its midst was taken directly from hearings before the Senate Judiciary Committee in 1949.[24]

McCarthy singled out a number of high government officials by name in his address, all of whom were familiar in right-wing circles. None of this was new or especially shocking to his hearers. What was shocking and explosive was McCarthy's claim to have a list of 205 "known traitors" in the State Department, the source of which appears to have been a letter written by Secretary of State James Byrnes to Democratic Congressman Adolph Sabath of Illinois, a letter that had been inserted into the *Congressional Record.* As would soon be discovered, Byrnes's letter — a reply to an inquiry about the screening of four thousand federal employees transferred to the State Department from wartime agencies — contained no references whatever to Communist Party membership or proven disloyalties by anyone; it was also three and a half years old in 1950.[25]

It was not until the next morning, when McCarthy was shown the front page of the *Wheeling Intelligencer* while being driven to the airport, that the first inklings of the wide press coverage his speech would draw dawned on the senator; it was also on that "morning after" that

McCarthy first realized that someone soon would demand to see his list of 205 communists. He did not realize how soon that would be: during his plane's thirty-minute stopover in Denver the next day, reporters waiting for his plane asked McCarthy to comment on the State Department's immediate denial of his charges. As had been the case in the past and would be the case in the future, McCarthy bluffed his way through the interview: unfortunately he had left the list of "207 bad risks" in a suit on the plane. "Left Commie List in Other Bag" was the line that the *Denver Post* ran under a photograph showing Joe searching through his briefcase. At this point — as at other points in the four years that would follow — McCarthy either did not understand the import of his words or did not care: he switched the number of traitors from 205 to 207 at Denver, as he would in the next few days switch it again to 57 without batting an eye himself while giving headaches to reporters attempting to report figures accurately.[26]

The common wisdom — suspected by some at the time and held by most scholars since — was that McCarthy had no list, either of 205 or 207 or any other number of "traitors" in the State Department. The Sabath letter contained no names, and McCarthy himself never produced such a list. But events quickly sped out of Tail Gunner Joe's control: on February 22, 1950, the Senate passed Resolution Number 231, which authorized and directed a "full and complete study and investigation as to whether persons who are disloyal to the United States are or have been employed by the Department of State." The Resolution also named Maryland Democrat Millard Tydings chair of the investigating subcommittee: the "McCarthy era" had been begun in earnest.[27]

The "Tydings Committee" opened its hearings on March 8, 1950, in a Senate caucus room filled to overflowing with newspaper and television reporters; by March 21, Tydings told a news conference that, to date, McCarthy had not provided his committee with the name of a single person accused of being a communist by the State Department, and McCarthy himself had refused to lodge definite charges against any of the hundred names he had submitted to the committee. On March 29, 1950, the *Washington Post* carried a cartoon drawn by Herblock that christened both the era and the ideology that defined it: the cartoon showed a large GOP elephant being dragged by "right-wingers" toward a barrel dripping with tar and labeled "McCarthyism," while the elephant asks, "You mean I'm supposed to stand on *that?*" Herblock's new term caught on immediately.[28]

On July 17, 1950, the Tydings Committee released a 313-page

document after its five-month investigation, denouncing McCarthy in "scorching language that ignored traditional Senate courtesy." It stated that both McCarthy's charges and his methods were "a fraud and a hoax perpetrated on the Senate of the United States and on the American people. They represent perhaps the most nefarious campaign of half-truths and untruths in the history of the Republic."[29]

The Tydings Committee Report notwithstanding, however, at some indefinable point in his post-Wheeling crusade, McCarthy himself seems to have become persuaded of the truth of the communist conspiracy charges that would dominate the rest of his political career. Thomas Reeves thus convincingly highlighted one of the chief ironies of the "McCarthy era": while his critics railed at him for his cynicism and immorality, those who knew McCarthy well believed the Wisconsin senator to be quite sincere in his accusations of internal subversion and external attack. "His basic innocence of history made him natural prey for the hard-line right wingers who flocked around him. Reporters usually confused McCarthy's eagerness for publicity with political cynicism."[30]

By the fall of 1950, McCarthy's fame was such that his Washington office received up to twenty-five thousand letters a day, a fact that McCarthy read as popular confirmation of his new crusade. Indeed, if anything, his fame grew in the following year: on June 14, 1951, the Wisconsin senator made headlines across the country by delivering a two-hour, forty-five-minute attack on Secretary of Defense George Marshall in the Senate chamber, the written text of which — submitted to the *Congressional Record* — constituted sixty thousand words on 169 pages. McCarthy accused the former hero-general of being a "mysterious, powerful figure" who, along with Dean Acheson, was part of

> a conspiracy so immense as to dwarf any previous such venture in the history of man. A conspiracy of infamy so black that, when it is finally exposed, the principles shall be forever deserving of the maledictions of all liberal men.[31]

Joseph Raymond McCarthy appears to have struck a responsive cord in the hearts of at least *some* American Catholics immediately upon his emergence as an anti-communist prophet: just three weeks after his Wheeling speech, Patrick Scanlon, editor of the Catholic *Brooklyn Tablet* and the figure who would emerge as McCarthy's loudest and most loyal champion, announced that "every American is burdened with the obligation of saving the country before it is too late.

Write your support of Senator McCarthy NOW!" Likewise, when Senator Dennis Chavez of New Mexico rose on the Senate chamber on May 12 to denounce one of McCarthy's chief witnesses before the Tydings Committee, the Reverend Lawrence McGinley, Jesuit president of New York's Fordham University, denounced Chavez as a "modern Pharisee...the kind who is always ready to point a self-righteous finger at their fellow man." Moreover, the *Los Angeles Tidings* (that city's Catholic paper) said of Chavez's attack that "for a Catholic to do this to one of our Prodigal Sons — amid the joyous howls of all the atheist conspirators against God and mankind — is in my view unspeakably low."[32]

The response of several Catholic leaders to the Catholic senator from New Mexico itself serves to highlight an important Catholic "presence" in McCarthy's Tydings Committee battle: Louis Budenz, McCarthy's "star witness" in the hearings, made much of the *Catholic* roots of his anti-communist ideology. Himself a former editor of the American Communist Party's *Daily Worker,* Budenz had been one of Fulton J. Sheen's "star converts" in the 1940s. Catholicism became an issue in Budenz's testimony before the committee "largely because he made it so." As the University of Notre Dame's popular publication *Ave Maria* put it in arguing for the former communist editor's reliability in giving evidence, "he was himself tangled in the meshes of communism for a while, but the heartcalls of Faith and the motherland won him back."[33]

But Dennis Chavez hardly stood alone in the early days of the McCarthy era as a Catholic concerned about the "religious" nature of the Wisconsin senator's crusade. Monsignor George Higgins, the head of the Social Action Department of the National Catholic Welfare Conference, recognized in Budenz a potentially serious threat to the reputation of the Catholic Church in America. Higgins argued that Budenz should make it clear that the church's stand against communism "goes hand in hand with a radical program of social justice," a stand that many of McCarthy's Catholic supporters failed to include in their denunciations of communist subversion. Likewise, Fr. John Cronin, a colleague of Higgins at the NCWC, similarly concerned about the reputation of the church in light of the "Catholic" ethos of both McCarthy's witnesses and support, attempted to steer the Wisconsin senator into a more cautious path throughout the Tydings investigation, largely to no avail.[34]

It was McCarthy's attack on George Marshall, however, that galvanized Catholics fearful of the senator's effect on both Catholics and on the perceptions of those outside the church: "the conspiracy so immense" denounced by McCarthy in June 1951 provoked a number of critical responses from Catholics growing ever more uncomfortable with the kind of Catholic support generated by Tail Gunner Joe's rhetoric. *America* magazine editorialized that McCarthy's speech was both "unfair and unjust" in smearing a man with a brilliant record of loyalty to his country; *Commonweal,* a Catholic periodical run by laymen and therefore freer to offer opinions than the Jesuit-run *America,* went considerably further by accusing the senator of "sheer intellectual dishonesty and recklessness." But perhaps most telling in offering an index of the feelings of the "official" Catholic leadership made nervous by cheers offered by Catholic patrolmen's organizations to McCarthy's accusations was the report issued by the American bishops at the end of 1951. When the U.S. Catholic bishops gathered for their annual meeting in November 1951, one of the chief issues on their agenda was "public and private morality." In a statement released to the press at the end of their gathering, they condemned the idea among "some" Catholic politicians that "anything goes" in the rough-and-tumble world of politics, and announced that "dishonesty, slander, detraction, and defamation of character are as truly transgressions of God's commandments when resorted to by men in political life as they are for all other men."[35]

In August 1951, William Benton of Connecticut rose in the Senate chamber to introduce a resolution demanding McCarthy's expulsion from the Senate, not only because of the slanderous cast of much of his rhetoric, but also because of the problematic financial management of campaign funds: the body organized a special commission under the chairmanship of Senator Guy Gillette to examine Benton's accusations, a commission that released its report over a year later — in early January 1953. McCarthy's long struggle with the Gillette Commission was to prove decisive in moving the moderately critical *America* magazine toward an openly anti-McCarthy stance. Equally important in mobilizing Robert Hartnett, S.J., the editor of the magazine, was McCarthy's attack on the Democratic presidential candidate, Adlai Stevenson, at the infamous "McCarthy Broadcast Dinner" on October 27, 1952, at Chicago's Palmer House. In that speech broadcast nationally to an audience estimated in the millions, McCarthy announced his intention to give the "history of the Democratic candidate for the Presidency who endorsed and would continue the suicidal Kremlin-directed policies of the nation." The line that drew the fifteen hundred listeners cheering to their feet in the Grand Ballroom of the

Palmer House was McCarthy's calculated "slip of the tongue": "Alger, I mean Adlai," repeated several times throughout the address.[36]

In the November 22, 1952, issue of *America*, Hartnett — long a supporter of both Stevenson and the Democratic Party's social reform programs — blasted the Wisconsin senator's "cheap stunt" in Chicago as a typical example of "what are euphemistically called 'McCarthy's methods.' " McCarthy immediately replied to Hartnett's attack in a long "letter to the editor" published three weeks later in the magazine. In typical fashion, the brunt of McCarthy's letter was directed not to defending the facts of his Chicago speech but how he felt about the Jesuits at *America*. McCarthy told the good father that

> while you owe no duty to me to correct the vicious smear job which you attempted to do on me, you do owe a heavy duty to the vast number of good Catholic people who assume that at least in a Jesuit operated magazine they can read the truth. Being an ardent Catholic myself, brought up with a great respect for the Priesthood, which I still hold, it is inconceivable to me that a Catholic Priest could indulge in such vicious falsehoods in order to discredit my fight to expose the greatest enemy of not only the Catholic Church, but our entire civilization.[37]

Far from convincing Hartnett of the "heavy debt" owed McCarthy as a "Catholic Priest," however, the senator galvanized the Jesuit editor's emergence as a stubborn and resourceful leader of McCarthy's Catholic foes, both political and journalistic. McCarthy's new Jesuit opponent, moreover, found his "critical voice" just in time to help defuse widespread Protestant perceptions of McCarthy's crusade as "Catholic" in a deeply troubling way. Starting in 1951 — with the publication of Paul Blanshard's *Communism, Democracy, and Catholic Power* — a number of Protestant leaders had begun to publicly question the paucity of Catholic criticism of the senator's methods and rhetoric. Indeed, as Donald Crosby has observed in his study of McCarthy and the Catholic Church:

> Many Protestants [saw] in Joe McCarthy the lurid image of everything they had come to fear in American Catholicism: like many Catholics he showed a certain disinterest in civil liberties, he demanded conformity to his own set of opinions, he was intolerant of all opposition, he dogmatized endlessly, and he made a shambles of the democratic process by abusing the witnesses who came before his congressional committee.[38]

Organized Protestant criticism of McCarthy's crusade precisely as "Catholic" deepened noticeably after 1953, with the Wisconsin senator's reelection for a second term. Protestant outrage, however, was provoked by several published "red flags" in Catholic periodicals. The popular columnist for the deeply conservative *Our Sunday Visitor,* Richard Ginder, opined in the July 26, 1953, issue of that Catholic weekly that "the Senator would not have so many enemies if he were a high-ranking Protestant and a Mason." And even liberal Catholic columnist Francis Lally, calling for more nuance in denunciations of Protestant "loss of nerve" in the *Boston Pilot,* nonetheless agreed that a number of Americans perceived American Protestantism to have taken on a "pink hue," believing that "if the Reds are not in the pews they are at least in the pulpit." But it was after the head of McCarthy's "investigating committee" — Joseph B. Matthews, a former Stalinist turned Methodist minister — announced in the July 1953 issue of the *American Mercury* that the "largest single group supporting the Communist apparatus in the United States today is composed of Protestant clergymen" that something resembling an undeclared "war of religion" broke out.[39]

Matthews's public accusation was reported in Catholic publications like the *Los Angeles Tidings,* which sympathetically noted that McCarthy's congressional aide had attacked the Protestant clergy precisely because a "disconcerting number" of them "have brought dishonor on the regiment," opining that honor would "return only with the purge or the penance." Matthews's accusation and the published Catholic applause that it generated angered most Protestants and added nothing to their deep (if often unspoken) fears of Catholic support for the senator's crusade. Likewise, Protestant anger was further exacerbated in August 1953, when Francis Cardinal Spellman — long a bitter opponent of ecumenical endeavors and of prominent Protestants in New York City — announced to a group of newspaper reporters that Protestant anger after the Matthews affair seemed disingenuous, as McCarthy simply "is against communism and is doing something about it." In response, Dr. Reuben Nelson, general secretary of the American Baptist Convention, announced at an ecumenical convention that he was "deeply concerned" that the leader of America's largest Catholic diocese could publicly "advocate McCarthyism." By early 1954, three of the most visible Protestant leaders in America — Dean James Pike of New York's Episcopal Cathedral, Washington Cathedral's Dean Francis Sayre, and the Reverend Robert McCracken of New York's Riverside Church — joined publicly in accusing the "official" American Catholic Church of not only failing to repudiate McCarthy's methods but of offering him widespread support as well. On March 21, 1954, Pike and Sayre exchanged their cathedral pulpits in New York and Washington to question — in the context of the chief morning worship service at both cathedrals — why the Catholic Church had not formally condemned McCarthy's wild accusations and slanderous methods. And their accusations of widespread Catholic support would appear to have had statistical backing: a Gallup poll taken in January 1954 showed 58 percent of American Catholics approving of both McCarthy's methods and charges of internal subversion, while only 23 percent disapproved.[40]

Conservative Catholic publications like the *Brooklyn Tablet* were, predictably enough, outraged by the gauntlet thrown down by the Protestant leaders in early 1954. Other Catholics not as taken with McCarthy's cause, however, tended to blame Catholics themselves: liberal Catholic columnist Donald McDonald told the Newman Club at the University of Iowa that Protestant accusations of widespread Catholic support for the senator were generated by the large number of American Catholics who had either remained silent or who had "already canonized the man."[41]

The stage was thus set for Robert Hartnett's "full court press" against McCarthy in the pages of *America,* published during the first great national event televised nationally — McCarthy's now-famous "Army Hearings" in the spring of 1954. From the beginning of its editorial critiques of McCarthy's crusade in 1952, *America* magazine had found itself under growing pressure from both readers and from fellow Jesuits to "soften" its anti-McCarthy stance. By mid-April 1954, the magazine was deluged with letters from Catholics questioning both its loyalty and its orthodoxy. So many criticisms came into the rectory of St. Patrick's Cathedral on Fifth Avenue that it reportedly cancelled its subscription; in the midst of the uproar, someone shot a bullet through the front door of the most prominent Jesuit church in New York City, St. Ignatius Loyola on Park Avenue. The mailed criticisms and the bullet notwithstanding, however, the Jesuit editor of the magazine published a vigorous attack on both McCarthy's campaign and his methods in the May 22, 1954, issue of *America.* " 'Peaceful Overthrow' of the U.S. Presidency" — the title of Hartnett's editorial — was ostensibly in response to McCarthy's acceptance and subsequent use of classified documents from a "young Army Intelligence officer," justified by the Wisconsin senator on the grounds of a "national emergency." Hartnett's editorial attracted more attention than any other

Catholic piece (pro or con) ever published on McCarthy, and was immediately picked up by the Associated Press Wire Service on May 18 (the day on which the May 22 issue of *America* was published): significant sections of the *America* piece appeared in the May 18 editions of the *Boston Daily Globe,* the *Baltimore Sun,* and the *Washington Post.*[42]

Hartnett observed in the two-page editorial that came to be considered the "classic" anti-McCarthy Catholic response:

> In *The Idea of a University* Cardinal Newman warned against "a man of one idea ... of the view, partly true but subordinate, partly false, which is all that can proceed out of anything so partial." Mr. McCarthy seems to think that all the operations of government boil down to one: eliminating people *he* judges subversive. The President, the Army, the State and Justice Departments all have a lot of other things to do. The folly of the McCarthy formula is shown in Indo-China, where the fate of the free world is slowly, relentlessly being shaped, with conspicuously no help from Mr. McCarthy. If he insists on his piecemeal and "peaceful" overthrow of the Presidency, he may do great harm to U.S. policy by his so far very successful diversionary tactics.[43]

As early as the November 1952 exchange between McCarthy and Hartnett, the religious superior of the New York Jesuits, Father John McMahon, came under increasing pressure from both within and outside the order to "do something" about *America* and its editor on the "McCarthy issue." McMahon had initially refused to commit himself to such a course; but on May 29, 1954, McMahon announced to the editors that the topic of McCarthy was now off-limits, not out of sympathy with McCarthy supporters but out of concern that the magazine's position was dividing Jesuits and that it appeared to be breaking a long-standing command not to engage in "disputes among Catholics."[44]

McMahon's concern about *America*'s stance abetting "disputes among Catholics," however, soon became moot, as the nation (Catholics included) watched in mesmerized fascination as the senator from Wisconsin came apart on the first great "TV event" in postwar America: the Army-McCarthy Hearings were only seventeen minutes old when McCarthy interrupted testimony with "point of order, Mr. Chairman" — the first of hundreds of such random interruptions in the proceedings. By early June, the nation had seen enough of Mc-

Carthy's menacing monotone, his self-conscious bullying of witnesses, and his perpetual five o'clock shadow. By then, McCarthy had been reduced to a figure of farce, and comedians and mimics across the country would provoke roars of laughter by droning "point of order, Mr. Chairman" every few minutes in their stand-up routines. As late as September 1954, however, a Gallup poll showed that 40 percent of Catholics surveyed still approved of the senator and his methods, as opposed to 23 percent of Protestants surveyed.[45]

Long before the emotional climax of the hearings on June 9 — when Joseph Welch, the Army's counsel, attacked McCarthy for implicating one of the Army's young lawyers for belonging to a liberal legal association by shouting "Have you no sense of decency, sir, at long last? Have you left no sense of decency?" — McCarthy's national political career as high-priest of anti-communism was over. But even during his "political twilight" that began at the end of the summer of 1954, the senator's Catholic supporters still rallied to his side: in response to the forced resignation of McCarthy's most visible legal aide, Roy Cohn, McCarthyites threw a "testimonial" dinner at New York's Astor Hotel, an event subsequently described as a "conspicuously Catholic demonstration." The principal addresses of the evening were offered by William F. Buckley, Jr., Dean Clarence Manion of the University of Notre Dame's Law School, Father James Gillis, and Professor Godfrey Schmidt of Fordham University. The reporter from *Commonweal* — noting that the Catholic War Veterans of Queens County, the Holy Name Society, and the Ancient Order of Hibernians had organized the evening — likened the event to "graduation exercises of an Irish Christian Brother high school. I felt, with a chill, very much at home."[46]

On August 2, 1954, the Senate announced the formation of a "select committee" to investigate the by then voluminous charges against McCarthy's conduct, a committee which two weeks later issued a unanimous report recommending censure of the Wisconsin senator. On December 2, the United States Senate voted overwhelmingly (67 to 22, with John F. Kennedy being one of the three unrecorded votes) to "condemn" Joseph Raymond McCarthy — a vote that came as a shattering blow to the senator's Catholic supporters. The *Wanderer,* a conservative Catholic journal that had been a consistent McCarthy supporter, reported that the censure vote manifested "a world in revolt against God and his Law, a world not only locked in mortal combat between East and West, but savagely at war with itself and with all that remains of what was once Christendom." While *America* re-

mained neutral in reporting the censure, *Commonweal* noted darkly
that the "religious issue had entered the dispute with all its wide-
ranging political implications," but that "social responsibility asserted
itself to rebuke the destructive Adventurer." By the time of the "destructive Adventurer's" death less than three years later — on May 2,
1957 (reportedly of alcohol-related ailments) — it appeared that Eisenhower America had moved on to other concerns, leaving behind the
memory of the "McCarthy era" like a particularly vivid but chimerical
bad dream.[47]

"I Felt, with a Chill, Very Much at Home"

As *Commonweal* so cannily noted in reporting the senator's humiliat-
ing censure at the hands of his congressional colleagues, the "religion
issue" had indeed entered the dispute over McCarthy and his methods
("with all its wide-ranging political implications"). But the "religion
issue" did not just separate Catholics from Protestants. McCarthy did
indeed provide a particularly effective "lightning rod" for attracting
deep but vibrant American Protestant fears about Catholic "outsiders"
trampling on American democratic values and civil liberties. "Tail
Gunner Joe" had had a remarkably successful career in selling his
methods and rhetoric to millions of fellow Catholics in America in far
higher numbers than to Protestants, a fact that successive Gallup polls
statistically documented, to the alarm of many non-Catholic Americans and to the discomfiture of Catholic liberals at the time and since.
It was surely no accident that the major players in the "conspiracy
so immense" adumbrated by McCarthy were all "WASPs with three
goddamn last names" (as Roy Cohn so colorfully put it). Arrayed
against the "forces of darkness" incarnated in the likes of Whittaker
Chambers, Alger Hiss, and George Marshall — Protestant "insiders"
who had purportedly betrayed the nation at the very highest levels — McCarthy enlisted the aid of the American descendants of Oliver
Cromwell's Irish Catholic "victims." And at least on the level of "intu-
ition," many Americans — both Protestant and Catholic — understood
this unpleasant "religious underside" of the McCarthy crusade and felt
compelled to address the religion issue directly. Therefore, on at least
one level of symbolic discourse, it would appear problematic to imply
that McCarthy's was *not* a "Catholic crusade."

Using Geertz's model of religion as a cultural system to interpret
the Catholic support for the senator, one might argue that it was neither a statistical accident nor cold-blooded political calculation that

consistently produced dramatically more Catholic supporters for Mc-
Carthy's crusade than Protestants: McCarthy's political language and
views of the way "reality in sheer actuality *is*" in fact operated in explicitly *religious* ways for millions of American Catholics who stood
by the senator long after his congressional colleagues formally condemned him. To use Geertz's language, McCarthy's anti-communist
crusade drew on religious symbols that functioned to "synthesize a
people's ethos — the tone, character, and quality of their life," their
"moral style and mood: their worldview." McCarthy's four-year career
of anti-communism drew on Catholic "motives" in a Geertzian sense:
that is, McCarthy elucidated for millions of American Catholics "a
certain overall course, gravitating toward certain [usually temporary]
consummations." McCarthy offered the directional cast and interpretative framework for religious symbols that were already very much
in place. And that directional cast saw the "forces of light" being very
much under attack in the postwar world, an attack aided and abetted by those ancestral Protestant opponents who had persecuted their
Catholic forebears. After the closing off of millions of fellow believers
behind the Iron Curtain of eastern Europe, the quite conscious attacks
on the institutional church and its leaders in places like Hungary and
the frightening silence of America's (Protestant) political leadership in
the face of such genuine persecution, McCarthy's concerns and accusations appeared perspicaciously true. Even to intimate otherwise
appeared disingenuous, or possibly something more sinister.[48]

For McCarthy's Catholic supporters, the senator drew on a familiar
world of religious symbols that provided a "cosmic guarantee not only
for their ability to comprehend the world" — as complex and byzan-
tine as that postwar political world was — "but also, comprehending
it, to give a *precision* to their feelings, a definition to their emotions,
to enable them to endure it." Their response to subversion and god-
lessness both within *and* without, in both the State Department and
behind the Iron Curtain, was thus both religious and cultural — or,
perhaps better, was a religious response with a "directional," cultural
cast to it. For Catholics who read the *Brooklyn Tablet* as the voice
of reason itself in political and cultural affairs McCarthy offered a
clear-cut model to comprehend the evil in their world as well as the
solution to that evil.

"Oh, you're from Brooklyn," went the backyard conversations in
this world. "What parish?" McCarthy, whether consciously or not,
quite effectively drew on the religious symbols of this "parochial"
symbol system — parochial in both a literal and a metaphorical

sense — in constructing his political crusade, in a sense offering hermeneutical, interpretive explanations for the daily use of those symbols
in politics and world events.[49]

The more surprising — and more ironic — part of the story, however, lies in the fact that McCarthy's methods and rhetoric also
prefigured a deep fissure within the American Catholic community
itself, a fissure that would deepen and grow wider in the decades
after McCarthy's death. McCarthy's anti-communist campaign revealed that the parochial world of the *Brooklyn Tablet* now defined
a progressively smaller part of the American Catholic world. Much
like the career of Leonard Feeney a decade earlier, McCarthy unwittingly revealed and helped shape a very different "style" of American
Catholicism from that of the *Brooklyn Tablet* — what Clifford Geertz
might term a different "cultural system" of Catholicism. *America* magazine lived — quite literally, in Geertz's sense — in another cultural
system from that of the *Tablet*.

The deep resonances that McCarthy's rhetoric and actions evoked
among many Catholics rang hollow here. For Catholics of the cultural system that *America* magazine addressed — one in which parish
identification no longer offered an entire *gestalt* — Joseph McCarthy
appeared more like a bully or a buffoon than a prophet. The Jesuit magazine under Robert Hartnett's editorial hand addressed a very
different Catholic audience in terms of both tribal and ideological loyalties — less "parochial" in both a literal and a metaphorical sense,
better educated, far less concerned with "proving" Catholic loyalty in
the face of implicit Protestant nativism.

For American Catholics living in *this* cultural system, McCarthy's
brand of "tribal religion" with its well-defined immigrant-ethnic political loyalties offered symbolic discourse with no personal resonance at
all. Picking up a cultural stance inherited from the Maryland Anglo-
American Catholic families in the face of both Irish immigrants and
Protestant nativists, this "cultural system" of Catholicism found both
McCarthy's rhetoric and his methods distasteful and embarrassing.
And recognizing the implicit Catholic "altar call" that McCarthy
issued to fellow American believers, these Catholics sought to eluci-
date a quite different cultural stance toward the domestic communist
threat. Having nothing to "prove" about their Americanness and little
or no sense of Catholicism as a "tribal" affair, these Catholics sought
to distance both their church and themselves from the senator's cause.
The "tone, character, and quality" of their "take" on the Catholic
symbol system predisposed them to a very different set of motives vis-

à-vis American culture. The "manner and directional cast" in which their Catholicism "comprehended the real world" left them deaf to McCarthy's religious rhetoric. The "perceived ambiguities, puzzles, and paradoxes in human experience" that their Catholicism addressed did not need the "conspiracy so immense" offered by Senator Joe to make sense of the American circumstance. In an explicitly religious sense, these Catholics were committed to a very different "cultural system" of Catholicism, one in which religious symbols no longer functioned in primarily tribal or class terms. Indeed, in an ironic twist that McCarthy and his followers could never understand, the very "tribal" nature of his crusade made it distasteful to Hartnett, Chavez, Sheil, and their partisans. The "mystic chords of memory" rang hollow for them in Senator McCarthy's speeches: *their* cultural "take" on the Catholic symbol system left them unmoved by McCarthy's warnings of a "conspiracy so immense."

Education, class, and political loyalties certainly played important roles in the Catholic opposition to McCarthy's blandishments; but finally such opposition — like the support of McCarthy's followers — *was* "religious," just as many anti-McCarthy Catholics at the time claimed. Indeed, the "cultural system" of Catholicism espoused by McCarthy's opponents would soon come to define a "Catholic mainstream" that would view both McCarthy and the *Brooklyn Tablet* as remnants of a simpler, more tribal style of Catholicism no longer useful in "synthesizing a people's ethos — the tone, character, and quality of their life." But this was not always the case; there was indeed a time when the graduation exercises of a Catholic high school came close to defining the American style of Catholicism.

Chapter 4

"Life Is Worth Living"

Fulton J. Sheen and the Paradoxes of Catholic "Arrival"

"There can be no world peace unless there is soul peace. World wars are only projections of the conflicts waged inside the souls of human beings."   — FULTON J. SHEEN[1]

Tuesday Evenings with "Uncle Fultie"

On the evening of February 12, 1952 — in the "obituary slot" of eight o'clock on Tuesday evenings, opposite Milton Berle and Frank Sinatra — the Dumont Television Network premiered a new show that would make television and televangelism history. For the premier of the show in a medium still new enough to cause general cultural excitement, the Adelphi Theater on Fifty-fourth Street just off Broadway in New York City had been besieged with many times the number of requests for tickets than could be granted for its eleven hundred seats. The stage of the theater had been built to resemble a study, filled with books, and the only "props" that were provided were a statue of the Virgin Mary (soon to be christened "Our Lady of Television") and a blackboard that would serve as the site of the longest-running gag on television during the 1950s. An attentive member of the audience might have noticed that there were no "cue cards" or teleprompters anywhere in sight, as the star of the show had decided to speak for the twenty-eight minutes of the program without a written script or notes of any kind. At exactly 7:59, a slim but surprisingly short man in flowing red robes strode to the center of the stage and, facing the cameras with deep-set eyes that many had described as "hypnotic," announced, "Good evening. My name is Fulton Sheen. Welcome to 'Life Is Worth Living.'"[2]

The man with the hypnotic eyes who would serve as the host of the longest-running religious show on prime-time television was no stranger to publicity or to the media: Sheen was already a celebrity "convert maker" in 1952, having brought into the fold of Holy Mother Church the likes of Congresswoman and author-playwright Clare Boothe Luce (wife of *Time/Life* mogul Henry Luce), Louis Budenz, the communist managing editor of the *Daily Worker,* and motor scion Henry Ford II. Further, Sheen's radio broadcasts for over two decades on *The Catholic Hour* at six o'clock on Sunday evenings had already made him "perhaps the most famous preacher in the U.S., certainly the best-known Roman Catholic priest." Indeed, Billy Graham himself — no slouch on these matters — had already dubbed him "one of the greatest preachers of our century."[3]

While Sheen was already an exceptionally successful National Director of the Propagation of the Faith (Catholicism's international "missionary society"), famous for sending millions of dollars to Rome for the missions since his appointment in 1950, and while his 1949 *Peace of Soul* had climbed to the best-seller charts of the *New York Times,* he hardly fit the profile of either a television celebrity or a "peace of mind" peddler. Having earned doctorates at the Catholic University of America and at Belgium's University of Louvain (along with the prestigious *agrégé* and the Mercier Prize from the latter institution), Sheen had taught at Washington's Catholic University as a quite popular professor for twenty years before his television career. His first book — *God and Intelligence* — had been an extended Catholic answer to the pragmatic philosophy of John Dewey. Further, much of his writing and speaking up to (and after) 1952 had been aimed precisely at the therapeutic pretensions of Freudians and "soft religion" of the type that would become popularized by Norman Vincent Peale.[4]

The television series that Sheen launched that February evening in 1952, however, would extend his fame far beyond the boundaries of his students at Catholic University, beyond his largely Catholic Sunday-evening listening audience, and even beyond the avid audience of *Peace of Soul.* His famous sign-off at the end of every telecast — "God love you" — would be heard for five seasons at the very beginning of television's national presence and make his program the "most widely viewed religious series in TV history." According to the American Research Bureau, the "audience rating" for his program in 1952 was 23.7 — the highest ever recorded for anyone on TV in those pioneering years — leading the bureau to estimate that Sheen's program was watched in 2.3 million homes by 5.7 million people. Thus, by his second season, the Admiral Radio Corporation was sponsoring his weekly program "to the tune of $1 million flat."[5]

Sheen offered twenty-eight-minute presentations in front of rapt audiences with titles like "Science, Relativity, and the Atomic Bomb" and "The Philosophy of Communism" — presentations that were essentially ecumenical and nondogmatic but unmistakably theological in character. While the titles and subject matter of these "lectures" might appear too intellectual to appeal to a wide prime-time audience, Sheen played his presentations broadly: he mixed serious scholastic philosophy with old-shoe jokes and sight-gags on his blackboard, and punctuated his discussions with references to his "little angel."[6]

Perhaps his most famous single telecast — certainly the one that drew the most press attention — was aired on February 24, 1953, and was entitled "The Death of Stalin." Sheen delivered a hair-raising reading of the burial scene from Shakespeare's *Julius Caesar,* with the names of Caesar, Cassius, Marc Antony, and Brutus replaced by Stalin, Beria, Malenkov, and Vishinsky. "Stalin must one day come to judgment," Sheen intoned to a mesmerized audience at the height of Senator McCarthy's anti-communism crusade, "and Stalin's spirit, ranging for revenge...shall come hot from hell, and shall cry 'Havoc.'" Several days later the dictator suffered a sudden stroke and died a little over a week later, on March 5, 1953. Sheen's performance made front-page news across the nation in the reporting of the Russian's death.[7]

The audience that chose to watch these presentations of "Uncle Fultie" — as opposed to the deeper belly-laughs offered at the same time by "Uncle Miltie" — contained Protestants and Jews as well as Catholics. Stories abounded in the popular press of Jewish cabbies jumping out of taxis with still-running meters to find a bar with a TV tuned in on Tuesdays at 8:00 p.m. and of Protestant "PKs" (preacher's kids) lined up in front of the tube before bed. Les Brown could thus dub Sheen "probably the most popular religious personality to have worked on TV." Long before the days of the "700 Club" or the Crystal Cathedral, a quite large and surprisingly diverse media audience planned their Tuesday evenings around a Catholic cleric standing in front of a blackboard, spouting homespun scholastic advice as to why, indeed, life might be worth living.[8]

Even more dramatically than Fr. Feeney and his Slaves of the Immaculate Heart and more popularly than Thomas Merton's widely read but essentially "high brow" spiritual autobiography, Fulton J. Sheen announced the somewhat ironic "arrival" of Catholics into the American cultural mainstream in the decade after World War II. The irony of this arrival — more evident in hindsight than at the time — was certainly related to the singularly popular (and interdenominational) reception accorded to Sheen's packaging of Catholic scholastic philosophy on prime-time TV. The student of postwar religion and culture, however, is left with the question of how it was that Sheen, a Thomistic philosopher to the core and a cleric of the Roman Church, could play so well in a decade that produced Paul Blanshard and "Protestants and Others United for the Separation of Church and State." How to explain the singularly popular reception accorded an *agrégé* from Louvain who read Shakespeare in front of TV cameras? The paradoxes of this "celebrity," in fact, are reflected in the somewhat contradictory presentations of Sheen himself in scholarly evaluations of the postwar era. For scholars of the mid-twentieth-century American religious experience, while all agreeing on Sheen's singular importance, nonetheless have had a difficult time "pegging" the import of that popularity.

Will Herberg, in his insightful and trenchant sociological commentary on the "religious revival" of the 1950s, portrayed Sheen as the Catholic member of the interdenominational trinity selling the "American Way of Life" as American culture's real if idolatrous religion. According to Herberg, Sheen thus played a singularly important role in mediating the Catholic emergence into the American cultural mainstream:

> It was during these years that the [Catholic] Church finally arrived in America, emerging from its former status as a *foreign church* to join the national consensus as one of the three versions of the "American Way of Life."[9]

In a similar vein, Donald Meyer has argued that Sheen's media career was primarily "calculated to fortify Catholic self-conceptions." William McLoughlin, in examining the same "ecumenical revivalism" of the 1950s analyzed by Herberg and McLoughlin, has commented on the common efforts of Sheen, Norman Vincent Peale, and Billy Graham to "arouse the public to its need to return to the cultural values that preceded the advent of atheistic liberalism," while Martin Marty has portrayed Sheen as the icon marking the end of Protestant-Catholic tensions in America, so that "a congenial public found it could enjoy the soothing ministries of both Catholic Sheen and Protestant Billy Graham as if there had never been a war between the faiths." Focusing on a different (and scarier) part of the 1950s, Donald Crosby has dubbed Sheen "the prophet and philosopher of American Catholic anti-Communism," while the best critical study of Sheen to date has taken Sheen at his own word and has deemphasized the anti-communist part of his career, borrowing Sheen's own self-perception to describe his life in apostolic terms — as a life dedicated to "working out a Christian response to the challenge of the times."[10]

Given the complexities of both the times and the man, there is more than an element of truth in all of these historical evaluations. But Sheen's media career — both for twenty-five years on the radio and, even more clearly, for five years on national television — offers the student of the postwar era as well a privileged glimpse into the paradoxical nature of the Catholic "arrival" in the American cultural mainstream in the early years of the Age of Anxiety. Indeed, Sheen's public career as "perhaps the most famous preacher in the U.S." can perhaps be best understood as adumbrating the ironic nature of American Catholic "insiderhood" itself.

Christ and Culture

H. Richard Niebuhr, in many ways the "founder" of the discipline of the sociological study of religion in America, has expounded a classic set of models that helps in understanding the paradoxical nature of this arrival of Catholics into the cultural mainstream in the 1950s. In his seminal study *Christ and Culture,* Niebuhr offered five models for understanding the range of relationships of Christianity to human culture. These five models have been utilized by several generations of scholars seeking to understand the patterns and meaning of American religion.[11]

It is the contention of this study that Sheen's widespread and surprisingly ecumenical media popularity, evinced in *Life Is Worth Living,* announced an ecological move of Catholics from the margins to the center of American culture, and that his career helped to provide an epistemological "bridge" over which American Catholicism moved from one Niebuhrian model, that of "Christ above Culture," to a more widely accepted model that has largely defined the American cultural mainstream in the twentieth century, that of "Christ of Culture."

Niebuhr argued in his classic study that the ultramontanist "Christ above Culture" model informed immigrant Catholicism for the century before World War II; in this model, Christianity and its institutional expressions acted as preceptor and guardian of human culture, all the while remaining above the battle-scarred plains of history. The church thus oversaw schools, hospitals, orphanages, and universities — both to serve the humanitarian needs of culture and to educate culture in the truths of the gospel. The church's "service" to humanity, however, contained within it (at least potentially) an invitation to human culture not unlike that of the spider to the fly: the church itself became the embodiment of divine grace in history.[12]

American Catholicism, in the decade after World War II, stood prepared for a "model change," away from a secure but somewhat ghetto-ized world of "parochial reality" into the alluring big stage of mainstream culture itself. The model of religion and culture that Niebuhr believed informed that larger world, what he termed "Christ of Culture," offered an essentially accommodationist, therapeutic understanding of Christianity. In this model, religion seeks to meet the needs of a particular culture by "baptizing" the highest aspirations of culture with theological import. In Niebuhr's estimation, mainstream Protestantism in America from the nineteenth century until well into the twentieth defined this "culture religion" model, offering itself as the spiritual glue of American culture:

> This Christ of culture does not call upon men to leave homes and kindred for his sake: he enters into their homes and all their associations as the gracious presence which adds an aura of infinite meaning to all temporal tasks.[13]

Utilizing Niebuhr's models to examine the celebrity career of Fulton Sheen as witnessed in *Life Is Worth Living* allows the paradoxes of that career to remain in place while uncovering their meaning for Catholic participation — and even leadership — in the "American Way of Life" in the decade after World War II. America, for a variety of reasons, was ready and eager to listen to a scholastic philosopher-turned-media-celebrity at the outset of the Cold War, a Catholic bishop whose telecasts were filled with Thomistic distinctions between "formal" and "material," "substance" and "accidents," and whose preparation for his weekly program consisted in fifteen minutes of prayer before a tabernacle. Catholicism, or at least a significant number of American Catholics, was likewise ready and eager to provide answers for a culture under attack from without (the spread of communism in eastern Europe and southeast Asia) and within (the emergence of genuine ethnic, racial, and religious pluralism). The "peace of soul" advertised by this celebrity bishop had little to do with the "gospel of social anesthesia" that would be offered by "Peace of Mind" genius Norman Vincent Peale, although he most certainly sought to proclaim the "peace which the world cannot give."[14]

The irony and confusing popularity of Sheen's success in *Life Is Worth Living* was not lost on canny observers at the time, although that irony was largely ignored in favor of less tension-filled interpretations in evaluations of his importance: Sheen the anti-communist, Sheen the "Peace of Mind" promoter, Sheen the popularizer of theology for the new media of television. While these interpretations get at part of the story, the elusive figure of Sheen himself always transcends reduction into one — or even all — of them. Quite paradoxically, it would seem, a Catholic bishop and scholastic philosopher, standing in front of a blackboard on nationwide television, was just what America needed in 1952. And many American Catholics were likewise eager to interpret Sheen's popular reception as announcing a long-overdue acceptance of their own "religious affiliation" as now, somehow, safely "American." But Sheen's ironic "celebrity" announced a Catholic acceptance and arrival in American culture which developed in ways he could not see, and which would eventuate in cultural positions he would have disdained.

A Catholic Media Star

Peter John Sheen began his American pilgrimage humbly enough: born in El Paso, Illinois, in 1895 to a hardware store owner and his wife. "P.J." took his mother's maiden name (Fulton) as his own early in life, claiming that his maternal grandfather had given it to him when he enrolled in St. Mary's Grammar School in 1900, although scholars have subsequently speculated about this coopting of a more "distinguished" moniker with varying degrees of charity. Educated at St. Viator's College in Bourbonnais, Illinois, and then St. Paul's Seminary in Minnesota, Sheen was ordained in 1919 and immediately sent east to the Catholic University of America to pursue graduate work in philosophy, earning an S.T.D. in 1920. Sheen made his debut as a preacher (to great accolades) while still a graduate student at Catholic University, both in Washington churches and at the Paulists' "mother church" in New York City, St. Paul the Apostle, a church famous for the quality of its pulpit eloquence. Thus, by 1925, when he earned an *agrégé* in philosophy from Belgium's prestigious University of Louvain "with the very highest distinction," Father Fulton Sheen (as he was now known to the world) had developed quite a reputation as a preacher, both in America and in Europe. Sheen's European experience was crucial in shaping his subsequent personal life and public career, both in exposing him to the sophisticated intellectual and cultural world far beyond Midwestern parishes on the prairies, and in making Thomistic philosophy the ground of his thought and piety, a grounding that would inform the five seasons of his "televised chats" on *Life Is Worth Living* no less than his several dozen books.[15]

Sheen was ordered back to the diocese of Peoria for a year of parish work in 1925, an order that must have chaffed his now polished sensibilities after the Louvain faculty conferred a distinguished *agrégé* on the young American cleric and awarded Sheen's dissertation the coveted Mercier Prize — an award announcing its recipients as future Catholic intellectual "stars." The dissertation written for the *agrégé* — an extended Thomistic response to modern philosophical "cultured despisers of religion," chief among whom stood John Dewey — was published in 1926 as *God and Intelligence in Modern Philosophy: A Critical Study in the Light of the Philosophy of St. Thomas Aquinas,* and sealed Sheen's call to the School of Theology at Catholic University that same year. Subsequently transferred to the Philosophy Department in 1931, Sheen would remain as a professor at CU for twenty-five years, publishing a steady stream of books and articles that sought to fortify the Catholic scholastic edifice against the "acids" of modernity.[16]

But Sheen's academic treatises would be gradually displaced by more "popular" works that sought a wider and less academic audience. And along with these more popular works, Sheen began a punishing lecture schedule, so that by the late 1930s and early 1940s he annually filled over 150 speaking dates, including his famous series of Lenten sermons at St. Patrick's Cathedral which he preached annually for thirty years. In terms of national media visibility, however, Sheen's "break" came in 1930, when he was invited by the National Council of Catholic Men to speak on the first Sunday evening radio broadcast of *The Catholic Hour.* The text for his premier appearance on March 9, 1930, entitled "Man's Quest for God," had been criticized before the broadcast as being too scholarly; in fact, it generated hundreds of letters of praise within days of its telecast. By the end of his first series of talks on *The Catholic Hour,* which ran from March 9 to April 30, 1930, the National Council of Catholic Men had received 1026 responses from listeners, of which 994 were positive. The requests for transcripts of his talks bespoke an immense radio audience who listened to him: *The Catholic Hour* received 163,800 requests for copies of "The Divine Romance" delivered during his first season in 1930, 104,000 requests for the transcript for "Manifestations of Christ" in 1931, and 117,000 queries for "The Hymn of the Conquered" in 1933. It was hardly a surprise when *Commonweal* magazine praised *The Catholic Hour* generally, and more specifically Sheen's talks on it, as "the outstanding achievement of Catholic Action in the United States." In 1934, in recognition of his important role in "propagating" the faith, Father Sheen became "Monsignor." Indeed, the situation of American Catholicism vis-à-vis American culture might very well be charted by marking the cultural passing of one radio priest, Father Charles Coughlin of Detroit, and the rising popularity of Sheen.[17]

One of the most surprising aspects of Sheen's popularity on radio was that upward of 30 percent of the mail received regarding his talks came from non-Catholics, and Sheen would later reminisce that perhaps his most satisfying achievement in his radio ministry was both the improved image and reputation of the Catholic Church in the culture generally, and the greater religious understanding between Protestants, Jews, and Catholics that it seemed to engender. Thus, both *Catholic Action* and *Time* magazine celebrated Sheen's tenth anniversary season on *The Catholic Hour* in 1940 with much panoply: *Catholic Action,* recognizing Sheen's singular contribution to the popular image of a more "American" Catholic Church, hailed Sheen's telecasts as "the most popular religious series ever given on radio," while *Time* — highlighting Sheen's ecumenical appeal — noted that Sheen "can make religion sensible and attractive to great masses of people." And the statistics would appear to back up their encomiums: *The Catholic Hour* had spread from twenty-two to ninety-five radio stations in ten years, and 1.75 million copies of Sheen's talks had been mailed out.[18]

But in addition to the essentially personal piety that Sheen dispensed, there was a political and social side to his public gospel as well. A "noticeable thread of patriotism" ran through the fabric of Sheen's oratory, evinced in *Catholic Hour* talks like the 1936 broadcast "The Prodigal World," and, perhaps his best political synthesis, *Communism and the Conscience of the West.* While Donald Crosby has termed Sheen "the prophet and philosopher of American Catholic anti-communism," Sheen seldom involved himself in the purely political aspects of the anti-communist crusade and would have nothing to say on the public record regarding the senatorial antics of Joseph McCarthy, who would emerge in the early 1950s as the head inquisitor of American anti-communism. In an interview granted twenty years after the McCarthy era, Sheen observed that "I have no inter-

est in politics.... There was no reason that I should have discussed
him [McCarthy], and he was not an authority on communism in any
case."[19]

But Sheen's demurring regarding his anti-communist message notwithstanding, the American Legion of New York awarded Sheen its
gold medal for his "exemplary work on behalf of Americanism,"
and the University of Notre Dame bestowed on him its second annual "Patriot Award" as "an outstanding patriot who exemplified the
American ideals of justice, personal integrity, and service to country."
It is now something of a truism, of course, to recognize the Catholic
anti-communism of the 1940s and 1950s as a "vehicle of Americanization" for a religious body still perceived by many in the mainstream
as essentially "foreign." As one Catholic historian has observed,

> In fighting the red peril, the Catholic could dedicate himself to
> action which was both Catholic and American... demonstrating
> the compatibility of faith and patriotism.[20]

Whatever motives beyond the purely theological that may have inspired Sheen in wedding his Catholic message with that of anti-
communism, it is not pure speculation to note that the high-water
mark of American Catholic self-confidence, cultural influence, and
optimism — what David O'Brien has termed "the climax of American Catholic history" — occurred precisely in the decade after World
War II, when Sheen was emerging as a major media presence. In 1949,
the year after receiving the American Legion's Gold Medal, Sheen published what would become one of his most famous books, *Peace of
Soul*, a work that won a rather long berth on the best-seller lists. Sheen
announced on the second page of what would become one of the
best-sellers of the year that "modern man" was characterized by three
"alienations": alienation from self, from humanity, and from God. The
answer to these "modern heresies," Sheen confidently asserted, was
the Christian good news of redemption from guilt, despair, and cynicism through faith. During the first two months of 1950, *Peace of
Soul* ranked at number 6 on the *New York Times* best-seller list, far
ahead of Paul Blanshard's anti-Catholic diatribe, *American Freedom
and Catholic Power*, which stood at number 16. Indeed, Winthrop
Hudson has argued that the publication and widespread accolades accorded Sheen's book announced his arrival along with "Billy Graham
and Norman Vincent Peale as the preeminent spokesmen of religion
during these years."[21]

Contemporary scholarly evaluations of Sheen's "peace of mind" best-seller are divided, some ranking him with Norman Vincent Peale and Rabbi Joshua Liebman as one of the chief popularizers of "mind cure," while others assert that he was about a different business entirely: Sheen had become involved in a nasty public brawl with the psychiatric profession which had made headlines for over six months during 1947–48. Sheen himself stated that his book was an attempt to clarify his views about an issue that had come close to "getting out of hand." As Kathleen Fields has observed, Sheen certainly did walk a fine line "between a sentimentalized 'peace of mind' religion and a more orthodox Catholic theology" in his best-seller; but he also "never compromised his religious beliefs or lost sight of his Catholic soul" in the book. Her evaluation probably comes closest to offering a balanced evaluation of Sheen's most popular publication:

> Rather than following the trend toward turning the "American Way of Life" into some form of civil religion, Sheen crafted an adaptation of Catholicism to the American situation to meet the challenge of the times.[22]

In 1950, the year after publication of *Peace of Soul,* Fulton J. Sheen was made a bishop of the Catholic Church and was appointed national director of the American wing of the Society for the Propagation of the Faith, one of the most important Roman appointments an American could earn. For many American non-Catholics at mid-century who knew little or nothing about the Roman Church, Sheen was the first (or only) association they could make with the church, an association that radiated an intelligent, warm faith that appeared to be very much at home in the American environment.[23]

The Dumont Television Network's invitation to a Roman Catholic bishop to host a weekly program in 1952 was thus not as risky as perhaps it might seem at first sight: here was a proven commodity who reflected American Catholicism's newfound pride and confidence, but also one who provided "reassurance and comfort to the American people in a confusing modern world." Sheen's television program, as envisioned by Dumont TV executives, would be grounded in the same ecumenical "theology" that had produced *Peace of Soul:* the general hope was that Sheen's televised "chats" would be "received and discussed by Americans as *general religious pronouncement*[s], rather than as sectarian address[es]."[24]

"My Little Angel"

The Dumont Network's initial idea in 1952 was to sponsor Sheen's religious broadcasts as a "public service" — part publicity for a still-emerging popular medium, part goodwill gesture to the communications overseers in Washington. *Life Is Worth Living,* moreover, became the first "religious" program on television to be financed by a commercial sponsor: the Admiral Corporation reportedly paid a cool one million dollars to cover the air time, and Sheen himself was paid a (then-impressive) salary of $26,000 a show, all of which he donated to charity.[25]

But whatever the Dumont Network's original intent, after Sheen's premier appearance on February 12, 1952 — shortly after which Dumont was swamped with phone calls and fan letters — quite another game plan emerged. Sheen's almost immediate popularity surpassed almost all reasonable expectations of Dumont executives, and *Life Is Worth Living* would become the Dumont Network's most-watched program for three TV seasons — outdrawing even Dumont's prime entertainment weekly event, *The Jackie Gleason Show.*[26]

From early in his first broadcast season, two of Sheen's on-camera "props" captured the popular imagination and became icons for his show. The blackboard in Sheen's "study" on the stage of the Adelphi Theater became the object of a running gag about his "angel" — an off-camera stagehand who erased the board for Sheen as he moved around the set. At least once during the course of the majority of his weekly appearances, Sheen would make reference to "my little angel" cleaning the board for him — a reference which quickly became the running sight-gag that an entire generation of Catholic school children growing up in the early 1950s remember waiting for during the half-hour broadcasts. Likewise, the statue of "Our Lady of Television" on the set achieved a popularity such that Sheen had it reproduced and sold to viewers as a means of raising money for the Society of the Propagation of the Faith.[27]

By the close of his first season on national television, Sheen's angel and Our Lady of Television had worked their magic: by April 1952, Sheen was receiving between eight thousand and eighty-five hundred letters a week — some seeking advice and solace, almost all singing his praises — while the Dumont Network received five thousand requests a week for tickets to a theater whose seating capacity stood at eleven hundred. Jack Gould, in a review of the show for the *New York Times* shortly after its premier, opined that Sheen offered "a remarkably absorbing half hour of television." The viewer, regardless of individual faith, "finds himself not only paying attention, but doing some serious thinking as well." Sheen won an Emmy in 1952 for his weekly program. By 1955, the show had moved over to the American Broadcasting Company (ABC), and it was during that season that his popularity peaked, with an estimated audience of thirty million viewers.[28]

Sheen himself never wavered in his own perception as to *where,* exactly, his true audience was: indeed, it can be reasonably argued that he was the first religious figure in the history of the new medium of television to shape his message to the "invisible audience" watching him:

> The several thousand persons in the Adelphi Theater are not my audience, not the people with whom I try to set up a *rapport.* For my words are aimed at little family groups seated about their television sets in their own living rooms. Whatever makes me forget *them,* for a minute, is a disturbance.[29]

Sheen's twenty-eight-minute weekly "chats" to millions of Americans mixed scholastic philosophy with quite practical advice about how to live a more focused life — often through the use of old-shoe jokes and home-spun metaphors that seemed to find new life through Sheen's use of them. Sheen thus talked of "flea-less dogs" in making his point about how a lack of *telos* in one's life could lead to frenzied "scratching," and of a two-year-old child's habit of saying "do it again" to get at the eternal freshness of life for those with religious faith. In a broadcast on the problems facing parents in raising children, Sheen observed — in a "swipe" at the psychiatric profession typical of him — that "some probably believe the reason why Cain turned out so badly was because Eve had no books on child psychology," and in a broadcast about "security" in their age of anxiety, Sheen observed that "we are like passengers who, taking a trip at sea, search not for the cabins but for the lifeboat." Sheen appeared to have perfected the "knack" of expressing fairly profound philosophical and theological truths in colloquial and accessible ways that made it appear self-evident to the interested but untutored listener:

> Do we find it difficult to imagine that space and time are relative? You listen to me for about six minutes trying to describe the theory of relativity. It seems like an hour to you. If you were

listening to Milton Berle for an hour, it would seem like a minute. *That* is relativity of time.[30]

Sheen did not go without his critics, however: the *Christian Century,* the unofficial "voice" of mainstream progressive Protestantism at mid-century, was a consistent critic of Sheen throughout the 1950s. In editorials with titles like "Bishop Cloys as Critic," the magazine found the good bishop's theology problematic, if not simplistic. Thus, A. Roy Eckhard responded to Sheen's retelling of the story of the birth of Christ, published in the December 1953 issue of *Collier's* magazine, in an editorial published in the new year in the *Christian Century:*

> Obviously the bishop is a man keenly aware that we have to meet people where they are. But unless our strategy pays serious attention not only to reason and history as such, but to the perplexities reason and history *raise,* it builds on sand.[31]

Eckhard, in fact, was expressing a view that even many of Sheen's fellow Catholics — both academics and educated laity — shared, but were too polite (or nervous) to express in public: perhaps Sheen was *too* "popular" and simplistic at times.[32]

There were, in fact, significant parts of Sheen's printed and televised gospel that sounded indistinguishable from "mind cure" spirituality of the type preached by Norman Vincent Peale: on the opening page of his 1949 best-seller, *Peace of Soul,* Sheen had observed that "there can be no world peace unless there is soul peace. Wars are only projections of the conflicts waged inside the souls of modern men." Similarly, in his book entitled *Guide to Contentment,* Sheen told his readers that the "accumulated wisdom of the human race has always acknowledged that there was *some* kind of relationship between peace of soul and health. Today, medicine and psychiatry are combining to prove that there is some *intrinsic* relationship between holiness and health." To the casual reader, and even to the critical observer, much of Sheen's message and spirituality appeared to fit hand-in-glove with the "religion-as-pop-psychology" strain of popular spirituality.[33]

In October 1952, at the beginning of his second television season, Sheen had been questioned about what many in his national audience considered his corny sense of humor and use of tired jokes to illustrate serious issues; Sheen responded that "I've always been inclined to strike a light note," and moved on. But what both Eckhard and Sheen's Catholic critics missed — or at least down-played — was that while Sheen packaged his talks in "aw shucks" kinds of metaphors and stories, he tackled the most serious issues facing the postwar West head on, going to the heart of difficult philosophical and ideological questions on prime-time TV. Even at his most popular and whimsical, Sheen remained the Thomistic philosopher, approaching reality through the categories of scholastic philosophy and neo-Thomistic anthropology. Thus, on his earliest show dedicated exclusively to communism during his first television season — entitled, tellingly enough, "The Philosophy of Communism" — Sheen argued that the problem at the heart of communism was philosophical, and not geopolitical or military. Economic determinism, and not Soviet armies in Eastern Europe or "reds" in the U.S. government, was the troubling issue:

> Notice that whenever the Communists try to convince us of their superiority, they make moral judgments about us. They say we are "immoral" and "unethical," while they are right and good. These moral judgments do not belong in the economic category. Whence comes their moral worth if reality be not moral? If economics is at the base of reality, how can it be said that *any* system is "right," and another is "wrong"?[34]

While Sheen's programs were clearly designed to be both entertaining and broadly "ecumenical" in tone, there remained, throughout his five television seasons, a core "take" on reality that separated Sheen's presentations from both Billy Graham's style of evangelical Christianity and Norman Vincent Peale's more "generic" type of mind cure spirituality. Gretta Palmer, a Sheen convert and unapologetic admirer, noted in an extremely flattering article printed in *Catholic Digest* that "few speakers would have dared to trust American audiences to find the movement of the reasoning mind exciting enough to compete on TV." That "reasoning mind" so eulogized, in fact, was relentlessly Catholic.[35]

Indeed, one might very easily label Sheen's distinctive style as "public Catholicism" (to use David O'Brien's apt phrase): Sheen quite consciously crafted the neo-scholastic philosophy and natural law theology learned at Catholic University and at Louvain to address broadly cultural questions while retaining the epistemological and anthropological assumptions of Roman Catholicism. Human identity and meaning were to be considered in terms of "ends" (*telos*) and "finalities," not in terms of human needs and drives: "When are we most happy? When we do that for which we are made." Education on every level was about "moral formation" in the *habitus* of virtue, not about imparting information in a neutral manner; the problem with communism was rooted in anthropology, not in economics.[36]

In a broadcast in his second season about positions on the political spectrum, Sheen revealed his "epistemological slip" by offering an encomium on St. Thomas Aquinas, whose philosophy provided the intellectual *Grundwerk* for Sheen's telecasts, as it did for the entire academic mainstream of pre–Vatican II Roman Catholicism:

> His works represent the greatest masterpiece in the realm of philosophy. His gigantic powers of intellect naturally led him to God. His "first principle" was: you cannot begin religion with faith; there must be a *reason* for faith, and a motive for belief.[37]

What many media commentators and most non-Catholic viewers took to be ecumenical and nondenominational "inspirational" chats were actually profoundly Catholic reflections on the cultural state of the American union. Dressed up by Sheen in homely metaphors and accessible stories, natural law Thomism — which had asserted for centuries that the Holy was accessible and to a large extent understandable to the human intellect and that human agents could *participate* with the divine in the work of redemption — sounded amazingly up-beat and fresh; indeed, it sounded not far removed from the up-beat, "can do" spirituality just then claiming the American religious mainstream in books, movies, and state of the union addresses. Thus, many religious and cultural pundits at the time, and since, have categorized Sheen as the Catholic member of the "interdenominational Trinity" hawking peace-of-mind spirituality during the Fifties Revival.[38]

But from the very beginning of his public career as a preacher in 1920 through his last television appearance in 1957, Sheen remained a committed devotee of Thomistic ultramontanism. Sheen never wavered in his firm belief that Catholicism provided the best — and very possibly the *only* — answer to the question of human existence. However "ecumenical" the viewing audience and media critics perceived Sheen's chats to be, the not-so-hidden subtext of Sheen's message was relentlessly Catholic, Thomistic, and neo-scholastic.

It was not, then, just ecclesiastical "hype" when a Vatican official described Sheen to a reporter from *Time* magazine as "our right arm in the U.S." Likewise, James Conniff, in a hagiographic portrait of Sheen masquerading as "press release" journalism, commented tellingly about Sheen's television show that the bishop was *"preaching* to more Protestants than any priest ever has." Consciously or not, Conniff had ironically expressed precisely how church officials viewed Sheen's show, whatever disclaimers Sheen himself voiced about "teaching" and not "preaching" during his twenty-eight minute presentations. A distinctively "Catholic" ethos pervaded the weekly production of *Life Is Worth Living* that Conniff clearly recognized and described: the published scripts of his first television season, appearing as *Life Is Worth Living* in 1953, were "dedicated to our Heavenly Mother, Who stands behind me at every telecast, and before whom I kneel in filial love." In discussing "War as a Judgement of God," Sheen laid the blame for the wars of the twentieth century at the feet of a culture-wide defection from the salutary Catholic commitment to natural law:

> All nations must learn, in sorrow and tears and blood and sweat, that wrong attitudes toward natural law and the moral law are simultaneously and necessarily a wrong attitude toward God, and therefore bring inevitable doom, which is the judgement of God.[39]

Sheen presented the appearance of the Virgin Mary to a group of un-lettered peasant children at Fatima in Portugal as the *key* to world peace in the twentieth century; indeed, Fatima had become a "kind of gathering place for all the people of the world who believed that peace is made somewhere else than at the tables of politicians." A large part of his years-long public battle with the psychoanalytic profession was based on his belief that people mistakenly used psychoanalysis in the place of confession, seeking a "peace" that Freudians most assuredly were incapable of offering: "guilt over un-admitted sins accounts for many of modern man's psychological ills." Further, psychoanalysis it-self was being presented as a kind of "gussied up" confession, deluding many otherwise intelligent people:

> The popularity of psychoanalysis has nearly convinced everyone of the necessity of some kind of confession for peace of mind. This is another instance of how the world, which threw Christian truths into the wastebasket in the 19th century, is pulling them out in isolated, secularized form in the 20th century, meanwhile deluding itself into believing that it has made a great discovery.[40]

Fulton J. Sheen, as preacher, as "radio priest," and as host of televi-sion's most successful religious weekly broadcast, never deviated from a theological model of Christianity's relationship to social reality de-scribed by H. Richard Niebuhr as "Christ above Culture": the role and duty of Christianity (which for Sheen always meant Catholicism) was to lead, shape, and finally convert human culture along the lines laid out by the *institutional* church. The gospel call to conversion and obedience was *both* individual and corporate; the vehicle and object of that proclamation was quite concrete and organized. The Roman Catholic Church was the true (and, in the years before the Second Vatican Council, only) body entrusted to proclaim Jesus' word in history. It was neither accidental nor irrelevant that the good bishop appeared before millions of television viewers every week wearing his episcopal robes and *zucchetto:* the modern world had strayed from the salutary and healthful oversight of Holy Mother Church, and redemption — individual, cultural, historical — could be found only by returning to Her oversight and care.

Thus, while Sheen's message might be "dressed up" in accessible and "folksy" language, the epistemological model of reality that informed that message remained — as it did for virtually the entire hierarchy in the years before Vatican II — faithfully Thomistic, neo-scholastic, and ultramontanist. The Vatican's perception of Sheen as "our right arm in the U.S." was, then, neither overstated nor just rhetorical: Sheen was *both* formally and materially a bishop of the Holy Roman Church, loyal to its mission and vision. As national director of the Society for the Propagation of the Faith (*Propaganda Fide*), Sheen zealously sent millions of dollars annually to Rome for the church's missionary endeavors. To understand Sheen's *self-perception* in any other way is to substantially misunderstand both the man and his career. Sheen's career as "convert-maker to the stars" was thus neither extraneous nor secondary to his media presence: his celebrity conversions witnessed to his true "agenda" as a missionary. However, the "meaning" of Sheen's public career as "media celebrity" — both for Catholics and for religious Americans generally — offers a somewhat ironic and different message than that of ultramontanism and of the "Christ above Culture" model of religion that shaped his message and spirituality.

American Catholics in the decade after the end of World War II were ripe and waiting for a "model change." As the stories of Feeney, Merton, and McCarthy illustrate so well, the old immigrant relationship to the church, organized around the life of the local parish in which (quite literally) "father knows best," no longer fit the social reality made possible by the GI Bill and the promise of suburbia. "Father" was no longer (necessarily) the best educated person in the parish; religious life now extended beyond the borders of the parish lines — even beyond the borders of the church itself, as more and more Catholics read *Guideposts* and watched Billy Graham's revivals on television. That institution which during the "Age of the Immigrant" had promised and provided a haven above the battle-scarred plains of life in a hostile culture could now be utilized as an escalator into the middle class. As Will Herberg had so cannily recognized, Catholics were no longer strangers in a strange land: along with Jewish Americans and Protestants, Catholics now constituted one of the three legitimate and legitimizing ways of being American. "The American Way of Life" — Herberg's famous moniker for the *true* religion of American culture during the Fifties Revival — could be lived in bourgeois Catholic style no less than in WASP culture.

In Niebuhr's terms, this emergence from the "Age of the Immigrant" into the bracing air of middle-class respectability meant that the older paternalistic model of "Christ above Culture" no longer fit the aspirations and needs of the Catholic middle class: the church as the source of *all* wisdom and knowledge was all very fine and good for grandma and grandpa, fresh off the boat. As the best-selling spiritual autobiography of Thomas Merton illustrated, many American Catholics in the years after World War II, college-educated and suburban, sought a very different way of construing their relationship with American culture — one in which they could join the cultural conversation as equal partners, neither dictating terms nor being dictated to. Many, if not most, middle-class Catholics in the mid-1950s thought that they recognized such a model in the relationship that Protestants had had with American culture at least since the Gilded Age, a relationship elucidated in Niebuhr's "Christ *of* Culture" model.

The "Christ of Culture" model offered both social respectability and a soothing "therapeutic," *functional* definition of religion's role: far from celebrating difference and boundary maintenance, this model of religion's relationship with culture sought to help its devotees "fit in" better; it was a perfect fit for the "organizational man." Both culture *and* religion worked together in providing spiritual succor. The highest aspirations of (American) culture touched the goals of the gospel itself. For Catholics living in postwar America, with its stress on internal conformity and external defense, this model was a godsend.

It was, of course, precisely the allure of this model of religion and culture that Leonard Feeney presciently recognized and decried: whatever else *extra ecclesiam nulla salus* meant, Feeney recognized that it would seem to imply *some* tension between the gospel and human culture. Feeney's crusade was, quite ironically in retrospect, crushed from the top of the authority structure of the American Catholic hierarchy.

The paradox here is that Sheen himself — like Feeney a devoted ultra-montanist and loyal advocate of the "Christ above Culture" model — helped to provide a "bridge" over which a significant portion of the Catholic middle class could migrate from this model to another.

The good bishop, with his angel and statue of "Our Lady of Television" presiding over his weekly presentations, believed that he was engaged in the "missionary" task of helping Americans find the answers they sought in the rich tradition of Catholicism. "I went to television to help my sponsor, the good Lord," Sheen told a *New York Times* reporter in 1952, and we have no reason to doubt his word. But the very salience of his presentational style and rhetoric with that of "mind cure" advocates and sponsors of the "generic religiosity" of the Fifties Revival helped to mask essentially missionary, scholastic motives. From the beginning to the end of his media career, the neo-scholastic and resolutely Catholic Thomism that Sheen had imbibed at Louvain informed his preaching, writing, and television "chats." The public *perception* and hermeneutical usage of those "chats" by a Catholic middle class adjusting to the cultural mainstream, however, represented something very different from what either Sheen or his hierarchical supporters would have approved. "The most influential voice in Christendom" was, ironically enough, providing a quite popular and ecclesiastically approved bridge for Catholics wishing to leave behind the "Catholic ghetto" and move into an affluent culture where religious homogeneity, not difference, assured social acceptance. Sheen made Catholicism look both friendly and American — a religion of people worried about their crabgrass, like their Methodist neighbors.[41]

Quite paradoxically, then, Bishop Fulton J. Sheen's *Life Is Worth Living* both abetted and announced the "arrival" of Catholics into the American cultural mainstream, but with a model of "Christ and Culture" he would have disdained and with a resulting relationship with the Catholic tradition that would have worried him. As in the case of Brother Louis of Gethsemani Monastery in Kentucky, one might fruitfully wonder what Sheen would have made of the "uses" his media popularity provided for American Catholics seemingly more worried about the "American" than "Catholic" part of their identities in discerning how and why life was worth living.

Chapter 5

"The Downward Path"

Dorothy Day, Anti-Structure,
and the Catholic Worker Movement

"It is hard for us ourselves to become simple enough to grasp and
live with these ideas. It is hard for us, and hard for our readers
and friends throughout the country. We are still not considered respectable, we are still combatted and condemned as 'radicals....'
And following St. Paul, I am certainly praying that we continue
so, because this is indeed 'the downward path which leads to
salvation.'"   — DOROTHY DAY[1]

"A Spectacle unto the World"

At almost exactly 2:05 on the sunny afternoon of June 15, 1955,
Dorothy Day and six of her disciples from the Catholic Worker house
of hospitality in the Bowery — looking much like the homeless people
they served — were promptly arrested for failing to cooperate during
a civil defense air-raid drill known as "Operation Alert." While the
sirens blared, Day and her fellow miscreants sat blithely the benches of
City Hall Park at the foot of the Brooklyn Bridge. Shortly thereafter,
they shared the police van they were loaded onto with twenty-three
other "culprits," mostly from the War Resisters League and the pacifist Fellowship of Reconciliation. The twenty-fourth suspect arrested
with them was the only real innocent that afternoon — a shoeshine
boy named Rocco Parilli — who had walked into the park simply to
get a drink of water, only to find himself hauled off with the rest of
the protesters. One can only wonder what Parilli made of this "spectacle unto the world" when they were all released on bail after a
considerably more dramatic spectacle later that evening.[2]

On the morning following the arrest, the *New York World Telegram* offered a sarcastic description of a suspicious "riot" that had
broken out at 11:00 p.m. the previous evening, when these protesters

were arraigned before the night court judge. The unamused judge, viewing their civil disobedience as a heinous attack on American freedom and civic preparedness at the height of the Cold War, had asked one of the Catholic Worker protesters, Judith Beck, if she had ever been hospitalized in a mental institution for "stunts" like the one she had undertaken that afternoon, to which she pertly replied, "No, have you?" The furious judge therewith shouted that she be taken to Bellevue Hospital for observation. The *World Telegram* then narrated the outbreak of a "riot staged by [these] so-called pacifists of such dimensions that additional squad cars had to be called out and twenty-nine reserve policemen." When the 29 reserve policemen had managed to restore order among the "dangerous" group, Judge Kaplan described them all as "murderers" for their seditious and cavalier flaunting of practice drills that sought to save the lives of women and children.[3]

Day and her fellow Catholic Workers subsequently issued a formal statement about their "action" in City Hall Park, which declared that they undertook their protest

> not only to voice our opposition to war, not only to refuse to participate in psychological warfare, which this air raid drill is, but also as an act of public penance for having been the first people in the world to drop the atomic bomb and to make the hydrogen bomb.[4]

The protest, arrest, and subsequent comic opera drama on June 15 (minus the participation of Mr. Parilli) was the first of a series of acts of civil disobedience from 1955 until 1960 on the part of the Catholic Worker movement, protesting the air-raid drills in some thirty American cities, called "Operation Alert" by the federal government and mandated to prepare the civil population of the United States for the eventuality of an atomic attack by its new enemy in the Cold War era, Soviet Russia. The 1955 drill sought to "acclimatize" American citizens both to the nuclear threat itself and to the presence of the nearest atomic shelters, while also giving the federal government practice in operating from thirty-one scattered shelters in the vicinity of Washington, D.C. Day and her fellow Workers alternated between seeing the drills as risible and blasphemous and refused any cooperation with what they perceived to be a monstrous perversion of civil power. Thus, in June of 1956, Day and her fellow Workers were again arrested, this time in Washington Square Park, a block away from New York City's Civil Defense Headquarters, after a "civil disobedience" organizing meeting at the Quaker Meeting House on East Twentieth Street.

Yet again, on July 16, 1957, the Workers were arrested, but now given a thirty-day jail sentence by the judge, Walter Bayer, who called them "a bunch of individuals who breathe contempt of the law." He bade them to "read your Bibles and see what our Lord Jesus Christ did for penance. You must be bound by rules and regulations. You use your religion as an excuse to tell others to break the laws."[5]

These yearly "operations" were continued until 1960, when Day and the other Workers decided to give up their "annual little war games" (as Day termed them). In every case, their custom was to inform the police beforehand of their intention to violate the civil defense directive mandating that civilians seek officially designated "shelters" at the wailing of the air-defense sirens, so that there would be no confusion about their presence outside during the drills. At the 1960 incident, when the Mott Street crew were not among those of the thousand or so protesters arrested by the police, one of the Workers, Ammon Hennacy, inquired of the police if they were not shirking their duty. But Dorothy Day consistently reiterated that she wanted no martyr's crown for suffering persecution at the hands of a godless state, as she stated immediately after the 1957 operation: "We love our country and are only saddened to see its great virtues matched by equally great faults. We are a part of it, we are responsible too." Further, she always sought to make it clear that she didn't want to harass hardworking folks like the policemen who arrested them who were only doing their duty: "we bend over backward to show our respect for the desire for the common good, which most laws are for."[6]

The "spectacle" made by Day and her fellow Catholic Workers in these quiet but powerful acts of civil disobedience during the latter half of the 1950s offers an appropriate and fitting metaphor for the movement that she and Peter Maurin (a wandering French philosopher/visionary) had founded on May Day in 1933, a movement to live out the Catholic, "personalist" ideas of Emmanuel Mounier and Jacques Maritain by working with and for the poor, whom Day and Maurin always called "the first children of the Church."[7]

After her tutelage under Peter Maurin in the finer points of philosophical personalism, Day always saw "the Movement" as God's providential opening, allowing her to live out her life with the poor. As late as 1973, she continued to insist that "I first became a Catholic because I felt that the Catholic Church was the church of the poor ... the church of all immigrant populations that came over or were brought over for prosperous Puritan, money-making developers of this country, ravishers of it, you might say." Day herself variously described their movement with and for the poor as personalist, anarchist, communitarian, pacifist, and radical, and it probably *was* at least all of those things at different times and locations.[8]

The "houses of hospitality" (twenty-two nationally at the movement's apogee in 1939) founded by Day and Maurin to feed and care for the destitute and the confused — where food was served and beds were provided without a sermon or demands for repentance from a life of sin — probably came closest to defining the day-to-day discipline and rhythm of their communitarian, socialist experiment, although the "glue" that held the various Worker Houses together was probably its weekly newspaper, itself named the *Catholic Worker.* In Day's editorial in the first issue of that quietly radical paper, she had set out to explain its and her purpose in living out a life on what appeared to be the margins of society in the depth of the Great Depression:

> For those who are sitting on park benches in the warm spring sunlight. For those who are huddling in shelters trying to escape from the rain. For those who are walking the street in the all but futile search for work. For those who think there is no hope for the future, no recognition of their plight — this little paper is addressed. It is printed to call their attention to the fact that the Catholic Church has a social program — to let them know that there are men of God who are working not only for their spiritual, but for their material welfare.[9]

Thus the "Worker" — as Catholics "on the left" from the 1930s to the present familiarly refer to it — was a spirituality and a worldview more than a newspaper or a food line: Day and Maurin viewed the "corporal works of mercy" performed by their houses of hospitality — feeding the hungry, clothing the naked, etc. — as well as their paper, as proceeding from a profoundly *spiritual* impulse more than from an awakened social concern or from any political commitment to the proletariat. The Catholic radicalist tradition that the Worker movement defined thus flowed from a quite overt and unapologetic "supernaturalist" perspective on both political and economic theory — a tradition that represents a quite distinct alternative stream from that of both the American mainstream and Catholic social ethics traditions.

Unlike the mainstream American understanding of the nature of the *polis,* which identified the public sphere and the common good with the centralized and bureaucratic modern state, Day and Maurin, sharing many of the same views as English distributists like G. K. Chesterton and Eric Gill, simply denied that the primary political mechanism for the implementation of justice and the meeting of basic human needs was the government on any level — city, state, or federal. Rather, seeing a profound and intimate relation between the insights of theology and the demands of politics and economics, they sought to recapture the small-scale character of ancient and medieval understandings of the public sphere through "localist politics": decentralized, person-to-person interaction proceeding from Christian motives as the best answer to both the economic crises of the Depression and the political concerns of American democracy. What has been labeled the "christologically shaped politics" of Day and Maurin called for selective engagement with the modern state, cooperating with the government on their own, profoundly spiritual, terms rather than on the state's. Thus, as Day herself so trenchantly observed, "We are not denying the obligations of the State. But we do claim that we must never cease to emphasize personal responsibility. When our brother asks us for bread, we cannot say, 'Go, be thou filled.' We cannot send him from agency to agency. We must care for him ourselves as much as possible."[10]

Herself profoundly influenced by the writing of the Russian author Dostoevsky long before she seriously considered being a Catholic, Day loved to quote to idealistic and wide-eyed young recruits who regularly appeared on her doorstep from a passage that Dostoevsky had put into the mouth of Father Zossima in *The Brothers Karamozov*:

> Love in action is a harsh and dreadful thing compared to love in dreams. Love in dreams is greedy for immediate action, rapidly performed and in the sight of all. Men will even give their lives if only the ordeal does not last long but is soon over. . . . But active love is labor and fortitude.[11]

From the afternoon on which she found Peter Maurin waiting on her doorstep in December 1932 — having been sent to seek her out by *Commonweal* editor George Shuster, a meeting that she consistently called "an answer to my prayers" until her death — Day resolved to live a life of discipleship and service at the "harsh and dreadful front of active love," a life that would earn her the designation of being "the most significant, interesting, and influential person in the history of American Catholicism."[12]

This harsh and dreadful front line became clearer and more lucid as a result of the lessons she learned from Maurin who (quite literally) would follow her around the apartment — and later around the Worker house — preaching to her while she was performing her chores. Maurin would talk to her from three in the afternoon until sometimes ten or eleven at night, explaining the history of the church and its social teaching, and then interpreting the significance of contemporary events in light of that history. In Maurin's distillation of Catholic teaching and personalist philosophy, Day discovered the bridge between the promptings of her faith and the needs of the poor around her; indeed, one can safely argue that it was his teaching, more than any other influence, that led her to believe that mass political action aimed at social reconstruction — mass action of the type envisioned by the American Communist Party no less than FDR's New Deal — that ignored the immediate, tangible poor at one's door was simply and always false. There would be, and could be, no quick or revolutionary "leap" to a socially strategized good society that put aside what Maurin called "personalist action," that is, that ignored the duty of individuals to perform the "corporal works of mercy" to the people in need around them.[13]

Modeling his teaching and writing styles on the "Easy Conversations" of the most popular saint of the Catholic Reformation, Philip Neri, Peter Maurin offered Dorothy Day an astonishing (and for our purposes, quite ironic) view of Catholic Christianity:

> If the Catholic Church
> is not today the dominant social, dynamic force,
> it is because Catholic scholars have failed
> to blow the dynamite of the Church.
> Catholic scholars have taken the dynamite of the Church,
> have wrapped it in nice phraseology,
> placed it in an hermetic container
> and sat on the lid.
> It is time
> to blow the lid off
> so that the Catholic Church
> may again become the dominant social dynamic force.[14]

And blow the lid off — in her own quiet but determined way — Day did. But contributing to that explosion other (even more unlikely) influences than Maurin's easy conversations can be discerned. Perhaps most unlikely of all among those influences are the powerful influence of the "Little Way" of St. Therese of Lisieux (the "Little Flower") and a sure if intuited understanding of what Sacvan Bercovitch has called "the Puritan origins of the American self." The ironies of this dual in-

fluence are profound and arresting and uncover significant impulses in
the story of American Catholicism at mid-century.

As others have so keenly observed, St. Therese and Day make a
most unlikely pair: the one an icon of nineteenth-century French sac-
charine piety and the other the doyenne of Catholic radicalism in
America. But the rich irony here is that Day the activist recognized in
St. Therese's mystical "Little Way" of piety — focusing on everyday,
mundane acts of selflessness and charity as the truest path to holiness over against "heroic" corporate activity — an undermining of the
duality of mysticism and politics. Indeed, even to understand Day's
reading of Therese requires a "transformation of our notions of *both*
'mysticism' and 'politics' — a transformation that entails a willingness
to acknowledge the risks involved in speaking of the 'politics of the
Little Way.' "[15]

Likewise, Day, as one to the culture born and bred, discerned more
clearly than many of her American Catholic co-religionists so eager
for acceptance and adaptation that "antinomianism" came as close as
anything else to being the true inheritance of the Puritan founders of
the culture. Over against much of the rest of the adaptationist story
of American Catholicism in the 1940s and 1950s, Dorothy Day might
very well stand as "the first American to exploit fully Catholicism's potential as a sign of contradiction" in a culture that loved and rewarded
conformity, a sign of contradiction that made both those inside no less
than those outside the Catholic Church uncomfortable and even suspicious of her. Day loved to recount how she and her Workers had
been "investigated by the Detective Bureau at Center Street on complaints that we were Communists masquerading as Catholics," no less
than by the chancery of the Roman Catholic archdiocese of New York
itself.[16]

The "downward path" offered by Day and the Catholic Worker
movement in the postwar years — a path witnessed to in their quiet
but determined opposition to all talk of compliance during air-raid
sirens — had as its purpose, however, an even larger object than simply protesting the conformity and accommodationism of post–World
War II American culture. Indeed, as one of the canniest students of the
Catholic Worker movement has observed, Day envisioned her path,
far more radically, as a "counter-claim to a ubiquitous post-Protestant
cultural order that couldn't be named." Over against both the Protestant and post-Protestant "guardians" of American culture, no less than
against the heavily clerical champions of Catholic accommodation and
adaptationism to the American circumstance, Day and Maurin uttered

a loud and resounding "no." The sons and grandsons of Irish and Italian Catholic immigrants

> were much less able than a formerly Protestant woman to turn the most cherished of national myths — especially those involving the primacy of autonomous self-hood in American thought — to their own advantage. These "Americanists" often seemed *too* self-conscious, too intent on bold pronouncements [of their loyalty] that only seemed to heighten their sense of uncertainty. They *were* both Americans and Americanists, and the more fervently they claimed to reconcile the two the less convincing they became.[17]

Thus, it can (and will) be argued that over against Catholic accommodationists no less than defenders of the Protestant culture religion for whom she and her movement offered a "sign of contradiction" in the middle years of the century, the radicalism of Day and the Catholic Worker was far more *American* than the vision of an unexceptional and "mainstreamed" Catholicism offered by her "Americanist" co-religionists like Cardinal Spellman and the "positive thinking" and suburban piety proffered by the leaders of the Protestant postwar revival like Norman Vincent Peale. And it is here that the seminal distinction between "structure" and "anti-structure" discerned by the great cultural anthropologist Victor Turner offers some aid in understanding Dorothy Day's importance for twentieth-century American Catholicism.

"Structure" and "Anti-Structure"

Victor Turner has argued that there are two major "models" for understanding how human beings interact in society, models that operate in a dialectical fashion. The first model he labeled "structure," referring to the hierarchical, bureaucratic organization of society on a vertical scale which distinguishes between persons in terms of "more" or "less." The formal organization of the Roman Catholic Church, in which "power" descends hierarchically from the pope to cardinals and bishops, then to priests and finally to lay persons, offers a classic instance of such "structure." Inequality, hierarchy, status, rank, complexity, and "sagacity" mark this structured model of society, and obedience to law and subservience to "duly constituted authority" rank among its most cherished virtues. Over against this first model, Turner offered a second vision of social organization, which he labeled *communitas* or "anti-structure." In this second, anti-hierarchical form of social organization, the "good society" is seen as an unstructured or rudimentally structured community, or even as a communion of equal individuals dedicated corporately to the common good. This second model, according to Turner, assigns an almost mystical quality to "humankindness" and concern for the marginalized and impugns any socially defined identity whose power derives from holding an office or position in the social structure. The virtues of this second model, over against the hierarchical ones noted above, are equality, absence of status, simplicity, humility, and "foolishness." Perhaps the classic locus of such anti-structure in Western culture has been the monastic/mendicant tradition of the Roman Catholic Church, in which men and women turn their backs on the world and its values of property acquisition, sexual fulfillment, and self-determination by taking the classic vows of poverty, chastity, and obedience.[18]

Turner noted that all human societies operate under *both* of these models in a dialectical fashion, looking sometimes to one model and then to another, depending on the stresses of the social organization, as they are mutually indispensable for a healthy community:

> From all this I infer that social life is a type of dialectical process that involves successive experiences of *communitas*/anti-structure and structure, homogeneity and differentiation, equality and inequality. In the passage from one to the other, the opposites constitute one another and are mutually indispensable.[19]

The detachment of any group in a society either from an earlier fixed point in the social structure or from an outmoded identity within an earlier hierarchy forces it into a "liminal" condition — that is, into an ambiguous and fluid social situation; and this "liminal condition almost always opens the group up to anti-structural, "radical" impulses that critique the older structure and offer a new vision of social interaction. Turner labels this ambiguous period of group movement from one social location to another the *rites de passage,* and notes that these "rites" always generate a new set of social values which provide the group undergoing social relocation with a set of models or templates that are really "reclassifications of reality and [the human] relationship to society, nature, and culture."[20]

Turner's anthropological concerns in adumbrating this distinction between "structure" and "anti-structure" were focused on certain "women's rituals" among Ndembu tribesmen in northwestern Zambia; but his insights can be applied to mid-century American Catholicism with equal success in uncovering some quite important dialectical impulses in the mid-century cultural circumstance. In such an application, the place of Dorothy Day and her "Movement" take on an importance and singularity that warrants some attention from the student of American culture. For more than any other American Catholic at mid-century, Dorothy Day recognized that the newly triumphant "accommodationist" vision of her faith in the brave new world — pressed by American bishops and priests within the "power structure" of American Catholicism, no less than by lay Catholics very much at home in the "suburban captivity of the church" — had to be rethought, and a more radical (and, ironically enough, more "American") vision had to be posed against it.

In the best tradition of those antinomian Puritans who founded the culture in the seventeenth century, Day believed that the only American society worth the bother was one built on the solid foundations of individual religious experience and personal commitment, a society in which the "godly" gathered into communities of prophetic witness and common concern, making significant claims on the culture precisely by serving it "on the margins" of power and prestige. How odd that it may very well turn out that the pacifist and personalist "Lady of Chrystie Street" — who had such disdain for concerns about cultural acceptance and national identity — was the most American of all Catholics at mid-century.[21]

The *Rites de Passage*

On December 8, 1932, a young journalist who had been received into the Roman Church five years previously made her way to the crypt of the National Shrine of the Immaculate Conception in Washington, D.C., offering there a heart-felt and tearful prayer for direction in a life still unfulfilled and incomplete. As she recounted it a year later in her column in the *Catholic Worker*, Day confessed that part of her confusion at that time came from her recognition that the demands for social justice made on behalf of the poor by the communists and radicals who had been her former comrades at the socialist *New York Call* and *The Masses* were holy demands — demands in keeping with the best traditions of the Christian gospel:

> They were among the ones Christ was thinking of when he said, "Feed my sheep." And the Church had food for them, that I knew. And I knew, too, that amongst these men were fallen-away

Catholics who did not know the teachings of their Church on social justice — that there was a need that this message be brought
to them. So I offered up my prayers that morning that some way
be shown to me to do the work that I wanted to do for labor.[22]

In a dramatic response to prayer usually found more often in Holly-
wood grade-B pictures than in what many so blithely if confusingly
call the "real world," Day received her answer just days later upon
her return to New York City: when she returned to her apartment
in Greenwich Village she found a singular and slightly wild-looking
Frenchman lecturing her brother and his astonished anarchist wife on
the Roman Catholic Church's social teaching. The Frenchman then
turned his attention to Day herself, explaining to her that it was
her divinely appointed vocation as a journalist to popularize his program for Christian social reconstruction based on three components:
"roundtable discussions" with the poor to clarify both the issues and
the Catholic Church's answers to them; hospices, or "houses of hospitality," in which the ancient Christian tradition of offering food and
shelter to the poor could be undertaken by everyone; and a back-to-
the-land agrarian scheme that Maurin called "the Green Revolution."
Day was hooked from the first, and recognized in Maurin the "sign"
she had asked for in the crypt of the National Shrine. While it would
be months and even years before the various components of Maurin's
scheme was in place, in a real sense the Catholic Worker movement
was born on that December afternoon in Day's apartment, in the
presence of her undoubtedly still-astonished sister-in-law.[23]

Day's own pilgrimage to that moment in her cramped apartment
had been a mixture of idealism, hard-nosed journalism, and romance.
She was born on November 8, 1897, in Brooklyn to a sportswriter
father, and three of her four siblings would devote their lives to newspaper work. Raised in California and then Illinois, Dorothy attended
the University of Illinois in Urbana for two years before she followed
her father back to New York, where he had found a job as racing
editor for the *Morning Telegraph*. Once there, she cajoled the editor
of the (socialist) *New York Call* to hire her on a "let's see" basis for
$5.00 a week. From there she moved on to a staff position on the
even more radical newspaper, *The Masses,* and finally to an assistant
editorship of *The Liberator* in 1923. Whether writing about imprisoned prostitutes weeping for their children or birth control crusaders
enduring hunger strikes for the advancement of the race, Day's "ur-
gent tone" during these years — according to one of the most astute

students of her movement — indicates that by the time she was twenty years old, "the mystery of human suffering had become her consuming passion."[24]

Day became a central figure in the "drama of Village life" during these years, years that were defined by an idealistic commitment to "left of center" journalism focused on workers and the poor, a social life that centered on debating economics and politics in the taverns and apartments of the West Village with a number of the "major leaguers" of the New York intellectual Establishment and a constant search for a larger meaning and pattern in her life. Even without any kind of articulated religious faith during these years on the front lines of progressive journalism, Day would find her way to the early morning Mass at St. Joseph's Church in the Village, after sitting up all night in taverns debating ideas with her friends and colleagues, where she "knelt in the back, not knowing what it was about but feeling comforted."[25]

In 1924, after several months in Europe, Day published a semi-autobiographical novel, *The Eleventh Virgin*, a publication that showed that she was not a novelist but that netted her $5000 from the movie rights her publishers had bartered for the book. With that money she bought a modest bungalow on Raritan Bay on Staten Island, where she moved in the spring of 1925 with her common-law husband, Forster Batterham, who spent much of his time boating on the bay and investigating marine life. On March 3, 1927, a child, Tamar, was born of the union. As Day herself recalled in her account of her conversion, *From Union Square to Rome,* the birth of her daughter brought about a crisis that would change her life forever. For at some indistinguishable moment after Tamar's birth she resolved to have the baby baptized in the Catholic Church, an action that she knew would cause a separation from Batterham, an anarchist and naturalist who despised religion and especially the Catholic Church as a hypocritical ruse that had enslaved the poor for millennia. But Day had decided that she did not want her daughter "foundering through many years as I had done, doubting and hesitating, undisciplined and amoral." Encountering a Sister of Charity while taking Tamar for a walk in their neighborhood, the woman known in the Staten Island neighborhood for her "Bohemian" lifestyle asked the startled nun if she could have the child baptized, and the baptism occurred a short time later.[26]

Day's desire for Catholic baptism for her daughter was, on one level, an extraordinary break with her previous life and the world she shared with her common-law husband; it has, in fact, spawned a cottage industry among students of the Catholic Worker movement attempting to make sense of this seemingly anomalous decision in an otherwise secular "progressive" life. But one of the most astute students of Day and her movement has discerned a pattern in her "preregenerate" years that makes her decision appear far less dramatic than it appears at first glance. James Fisher has noted that interpretations of Day's conversion "have suffered from a tendency to search for causes rather than meaning." As Fisher has lucidly argued,

> Day's "turning" was — given her lifelong religious experience — an illustration of [the] theory that "an individual who 'converts' from one orientation to its exact opposite appears to himself and others to have made a gross change, but it actually involves only a very small shift in the balance of a focal and persistent conflict."[27]

Fisher thus records the recollection of Day by Agnes Boulton — Eugene O'Neill's second wife and onetime rival with Day for the playwright's affections — who recalled that a dramatic instance of Day's legendary "desperate quality" during her Greenwich Village years as a young journalist had been her inability "to resist those sudden and unexplainable impulses to go into any nearby Catholic church." Catholicism, in many ways, offered itself as a resolution to many of Day's deepest demons — to her passionate interest in and commitment to the poor and suffering, to the middle-class Protestant sterility that she rejected in her early journalistic career, to her profound need for a spirituality that would consume and fulfill her. Not least among its attractions, then, was Catholicism's very identity as the "religion of the despised."[28]

Day's later recollections of her own conversion process following the baptism of her daughter strike the reader as surprisingly joyless and dogged — hardly the stuff of spiritual triumph and fulfilled searching that one so often finds in the literature of the time. The nun who guided her through the catechetical preparation for the sacrament fits the profile of the celibate "spiritual bully" so beloved of anti-Catholic literature: "And you think you are intelligent," the nun scolded her world-wise candidate; "my fourth grade pupils know more than you do." Further, Day recognized from the first that the Roman Church in America too often sought the patronage of its wealthy and privileged members in a sea of immigrant poor, as well as often seeking a venal accommodation with a culture that was indifferent to its claims. But this only whetted her growing attraction to Catholicism as a healthy "sign of contradiction" to sterile middle-class culture: she "intuitively sought a means of turning Protestant-secular America inside out, aware that this demanded that the nation's middle-class mythology be challenged where it really counted — on the altar of the self."[29]

Day acted with dogged resolution on the very morning after she finally broke off her long relationship with a Batterham now profoundly embittered by the executions of Sacco and Vanzetti. She took the ferry from New York City to Tottenville, on Staten Island, walking to a small Catholic church overlooking Raritan Bay near her cottage, and was baptized into Holy Mother Church. That morning — December 18, 1927 — turned out to be a date that would forever change American Catholicism. But the import of that baptism hardly appeared auspicious at the time, even to Day herself. As Day later recounted,

> I had no particular joy in partaking of these three sacraments, Baptism, Penance, and Holy Eucharist. I proceeded about my own active participation of them grimly, coldly, making acts of faith, and certainly with no consolation whatever. One part of my mind stood at one side and kept saying, "What are you doing? What kind of affectation is this? Are you trying to induce emotion, partake of an opiate, the opiate of the people?"[30]

What she could not know on that blustery December morning was that her new faith would indeed prove fruitful for living out a "sign of contradiction," for both those within and outside "the Faith." In a richly ironic way analogous to the story of Therese of Lisieux — a sheltered contemplative nun who was to be named the "Patron Saint of Foreign Missions" — Day's vision of Catholicism as the "downward path" challenging the complacency of her culture would place her in one of the oldest and most revered of American traditions: that of the "outsider" witnessing to the ideals that the "inside" still claimed but fell short of implementing. Day's witness to those ideals, especially after meeting Maurin in 1932, extended to her newfound ecclesial family no less than the bourgeois culture she had renounced. As she would later observe with a fierce honesty that would have bordered on the sacrilegious if it had not proceeded from such devotion and loyalty: "I love the Church, not because it is perfect, but because it is the Cross on which Christ is crucified."

The "sign of contradiction" that Day had sought throughout her adult life, and believed that she had found in December 1927, achieved material form on May 1, 1933, when she paid $57 to a printer for twenty-five hundred copies of the first issue of the *Catholic Worker,* a paper that she and Maurin had conceived shortly after their meeting. The money for the printer had been cobbled together from her rent and gas money, as well as from some small contributions by friends.[31]

Day, along with a sickly convert named Joe Bennett and two volunteers from a nearby parish, walked from her apartment at 463 East Fifteenth Street to Union Square on that fateful morning and proceeded to sell her paper for a penny a copy to the fifty thousand workers who had gathered there for the annual "rites of the workers." Day, moreover, stayed on in the park after the others disappeared after hearing the taunts of the communists gathered there, communists who undoubtedly shared the opinion of Emma Goldman — one of the stars of the American communist pantheon — who remarked after hearing of Day's Catholic radicalism, "I must confess that [this] is a new one on me, for I have never heard of Catholics being radical."[32]

From that first issue, the paper would remain anti-socialist, anti-Fascist, and anti-communist in its editorial policy. Day saw the crimes of both Stalin *and* Hitler, Tito *and* Franco, with "a clearer eye, and sooner, than most of her generation." Day would have few illusions about the monstrous crimes committed by the Loyalist Left in the Spanish Civil War — the "defining conflict" for 1960s radicals — just as she would have few illusions about the crimes committed by the object of American Catholic support during that same war — Franco's right-wing rebels.[33]

The second issue of the paper was primarily Maurin's, outlining his three-pronged "personalist" revolution of round-table discussions, hospitality houses, and "agronomic universities." After the second issue of the paper, Maurin regularly had a column on the front page of the paper for his "Easy Essays," which blended Christian anarchism and pacifism with papal social teaching in a mix that most American Catholics had never witnessed before (and maybe since). From the first, the paper's editorial slant privileged Maurin's personalism, which consistently protested the twin phenomena of the "bourgeois period of history": military nationalism and capitalism. Over against these two cardinal sins of the modern era, Maurin proposed a form of Christian anarchism: social decentralization and social simplification ("decent poverty" — going without superfluities that all might have the necessities).[34]

Day herself had wondered how ready American Catholicism was to hear such radical ideas "on the front line against communism." But, in the event, her private fears proved groundless: by 1934 the monthly newspaper had a circulation of twenty-five thousand; by 1935 it was sixty-five thousand. By May 1935, when the circulation hit a hundred thousand, Day believed that she had received the blessing of God on her effort to present the Catholic position with the same tactics that the communists used in reaching workers and the homeless, for "heaven knows that Communist literary fare was dull often enough."[35]

From the first, the *Catholic Worker* addressed social problems that had been either ignored or unpopular in American Catholic journalism: the status of blacks in the work force, in the culture, and in the Catholic Church; the inequities and injustice of laissez-faire capitalism seen in the plight of the urban poor and of farmers, unable to feed their children or keep their jobs; the growing anonymity and bureaucratization of a government that appeared to claim ever larger sections of the commonweal as its preserve with ever decreasing accountability to the common person — the "little ones" loved by Christ whom the *Worker* claimed as its special object of concern.

One of Day's greatest charisms as both a journalist and as the center of the movement was her ability to discern, to describe, and to get others to love the human face behind the story of poverty, injustice, and discrimination that formed the backbone of her ongoing column in the *Worker,* "On Pilgrimage": a migrant mother in the southwest worrying about where the next meal for her children could be found; a transplanted black laborer in New York City, recently arrived from the South, without friends, without prospects, without hope; a Polish Catholic miner in central Pennsylvania who had worked sixteen hours a day to feed his family, beaten almost to death by strike-busting thugs who accused him of being a communist for participating in union activities. Day's journalistic approach to these stories, like her piety, was direct, concrete, and took few prisoners. Catholics, she consistently argued, had *personal* as well as political obligations to care for these people, as Christ's commands were binding on *all* of his disciples, not just on the "professionally religious" or on government bureaucrats:

> We claim that as Catholics we have not sufficiently cared for our own. We have not used the material, let alone the spiritual resources at our disposal.... It is sad that it is always the minimum that is expected of lay people. On the other hand, we get too

much praise from some for performing work which is our plain duty. If we have a vocation for the work (and the joy we take in it is one of the proofs of our vocation) then we deserve no credit. Indeed, we deserve censure for not having done more.[36]

And as the *Catholic Worker* honed its radical personalist position more clearly during its first few years, it likewise unleashed a "rolling wave of reaction" among many Catholics at home in bourgeois culture to whom such ideas sounded foreign, or worse. To these American co-religionists, the anarchist ideas of Day and Maurin appeared so bizarre and radical that some came to believe that they *must* be rooted in some demonic heresy, usually stated as either communism or atheism, although sometimes both. Day recounted receiving one letter that announced "your entire production is a hoax and camouflage. It is the most poorly and thinly-disguised sheet of communistic rabble-baiting literature it has been my misfortune to see."[37]

By the late 1950s, then, after several decades of radical journalism and direct social action, the Catholic Worker had already earned a reputation of being "as far left as you could go and still be in the Church." Dan Wakefield, in his chatty but insightful memoir of New York in the 1950s, noted that by the latter half of that decade the Worker movement served as an "intellectual and spiritual base" for many young people who came to New York. By the early 1950s, the house of hospitality on Fifteenth Street had become a "cynosure for Catholic intellectuals," and visitors from all over the Catholic world dropped by to participate in the nightly discussions, including the great French philosopher Jacques Maritain, Jesuit journalist and early promoter of racial justice John LaFarge, and the British writer Hilaire Belloc.[38]

Wakefield recalls being introduced at one point during that summer of 1955 to a "quietly imposing woman," without makeup, who wore her grey hair in a braid around her head "like a peasant or one of those strong Midwestern farm women painted by Grant Wood." He immediately intuited, like others before him, that this short and spare woman was a person to be reckoned with. Quoting writer and one-time Worker Michael Harrington, he noted that "she looked like a mystic out of a Dostoevsky novel. She was a presence, the sort of person a stranger who had never heard of her would know as significant as soon as she entered a room."[39]

By the mid-1950s, Day's headquarters on Manhattan's Lower East Side was feeding upward of three hundred people daily; but unlike the other religious shelters for the poor in their neighborhood, Day's operation refused to call itself a mission, but rather a "hospitality house." Likewise, unlike other shelters in the neighborhood, the Catholic Worker did not demand any declaration of faith or hymn singing from its clients in return for food: "they only had to be hungry."[40]

In 1955 the Catholic Worker's newspaper circulation stood at around sixty-five thousand, despite its loud and consistent opposition to the Korean conflict, a conflict supported by New York's Francis Cardinal Spellman, who had (literally) sprinkled holy water on the guns of the troops during his December tour in southeast Asia. But Day and her bishop had a cordial if wary relationship, she being a dutiful "daughter of the Church" and he (being a consummate politician as well as powerful churchman, if there was a difference) recognizing a prophet when he saw one. For all of her social radicalism, Dorothy Day remained on many levels a conservative Catholic, fingering her rosary during her prayers at daily Mass and sprinkling her columns with reverential quotes from popes and saints. Perhaps like Rocco Parilli, the "innocent" arrested with the Workers during their first air-raid protest in 1955, the cardinal archbishop of New York was hard-pressed as to what to make of her.[41]

But the relationship between Day and Spellman was haunted by the issue of war and the question of the necessity of pacifism, especially in light of the atomic threat. If the 1930s had represented a crisis of poverty and economic destitution that Day felt the Worker must address — and thus the founding of several dozen hospitality houses around the country — and the 1940s the threat of militarism and fascism, Day saw the great international crisis of the 1950s as residing in the horrific threat of atomic warfare and the social anesthesia and false security that "atomic bomb drills" threatened to spread over the land. When word of the dropping of the atomic bomb on Hiroshima first reached her, Day immediately penned her outrage at the "tribal morality" that celebrated the victory in an editorial entitled "We Go on Record." In it, Day lamented that "they are vaporized, our Japanese brothers, scattered, men, women and babies, to the four winds, over the seven seas. Perhaps we will breathe their dust in our nostrils, feel them in the fog of New York on our faces."[42]

Day's outrage would prove to be both long-lived and contagious. At their hearing following the 1955 protest, one of Day's fellow protesters, Ammon Hennacy, was given permission by Judge Hyman Bushel to read a short statement before being sentenced. Deeply devoted to Day and her ideals, Hennacy read a brief credo that expressed her and the movement's position in relation to its dual Catholic and American heritage:

> As a Catholic, I [refuse] to take part in air-raid drills in accordance with the practice of St. Peter, who was arrested twice for speaking on the street, and he and all the Apostles said to the state that they should obey God rather than man. As an anarchist, I follow the practice of William Lloyd Garrison, the first American Christian anarchist.[43]

The Catholic reaction to the 1955 protest was modest and largely hostile: *Commonweal* magazine, a weekly that was generally considered "left of center" but certainly more mainstream than the *Catholic Worker,* was the only Catholic publication that explained and defended their action. The response from most of Day's co-religionists was either silence or hostility: more typical than *Commonweal* was the response of a priest who wrote in shortly after the affair requesting that he be removed from the subscription list, as the Workers had embarrassed the church by their "extremist" fuss over air-raid drills. Fulton Lewis, Jr., a well-known radio commentator of the day, publicly declared it reprehensible that a group like Day's — which appealed to public money to help it support the poor — would use that same "charity money" to hire lawyers to defend themselves for breaking the law. But Day and her Workers were unbandaged and unbowed by the lack of Catholic support: in the months that followed the paper mounted a barrage of news articles and extended philosophical essays on the atomic threat and the need for widespread — and specifically Catholic — protests against that threat. By March 1956, the paper was publishing editorials advising readers to withhold payment of their income tax, as that tax constituted "war's chief supporter."[44]

By the time of their 1956 "action," Day had come to see nuclear testing as a symbol of "utter atheism" — human beings attempting to shut off earth from heaven. Day herself felt profoundly ambivalent about the media coverage that these Worker protests were beginning to elicit in their second year, recognizing their importance in spreading their message but also seeing the circus atmosphere that came in their wake. Thus, in her account of the arrest that year, Day bewailed the fact that "even before the sirens began their unearthly noise at 4:10 p.m., newspaper reporters and photographers and a television camera were on the scene, which of course added to the confusion."[45]

During her thirty-day jail sentence for their refusal to "play war" and to plead innocent at their hearing in July 1957, Day wrote back to the Worker house of hospitality on Chrystie Street giving instructions to the staff there about putting out the next issue of the paper and announced that she had no complaints about the way the protesters were treated in jail: "Certainly Holy Mother City tries to do right by everyone here." Never one to play the martyr, Day saw the acts of civil disobedience undertaken by the Workers throughout the late 1950s as mandated by a simple and common-sense reading of Catholicism, not by any heroic call to sacrifice; indeed, she consistently feared that her little band was not doing enough to arouse her fellow believers into action against the "sham precautions" in preparation for an unspeakable and profoundly anti-Christian nuclear war. She consistently and movingly described her commitment to the Little Way of Christian witness — evinced in her "annual little war games" throughout the late 1950s — not because she believed that she would ever win over a majority of fellow Catholics to her movement, or because she thought she had a reasonable chance of affecting America's Cold War strategy of *Realpolitik,* but because she saw clearly that such activities constituted the "downward path that leads to salvation." She and her Workers constituted a "spectacle unto the world," which is just what she believed God wanted them to be.[46]

The "Most Interesting and Influential Catholic at Mid-Century"

What is one to make of this fervent but numerically modest movement in the latter half of the 1950s, led by a spare but clear-sighted journalist and a French mystic to protest "nuclear preparedness" and *Realpolitik?* How to interpret the annual "little war games" that drew the anger and suspicion of fellow citizens and the confusion of fellow Catholics during the unsettled and unsettling heyday of the Cold War? How is it, exactly, that Dorothy Day might very well be the "most significant, interesting, and influential" American Catholic at mid-century?

Certainly, in terms of numbers, the Catholic Worker movement remained (and remains) quite marginal: in the nation's largest and most powerful denomination, claiming the religious allegiance of a fifth of all Americans, Day's followers never numbered more than several thousand. Further, in terms of institutional strength, the Catholic Worker's several dozen hospitality houses and farms were dwarfed by the hundreds of hospitals, orphanages, and food kitchens operated by diocesan departments of "Catholic Charity" and parochial

Vincent de Paul Societies. Likewise, while the *Catholic Worker* has maintained a devoted and fairly sizeable readership in the tens of thousands over six decades, it never achieved the canonical status of being the "voice" of American Catholicism in ways that the massively larger *Our Sunday Visitor* or the smaller but more intellectually mainstream *Commonweal* did. And while Day's and the Workers' protests against nuclear bomb drills were consistently noted and written about, they never drew more than several dozen people annually between 1955 and 1960: how is it, then, that Dorothy Day and her "marginal" movement might be the most "American" of all Catholic groups at mid-century? Why the consistent recognition from pundits as diverse as Robert Coles and Dan Wakefield that something significant — even defining — occurred in American Catholicism because of the works centered in a ramshackle house on Manhattan's Lower East Side?

It is here — in interpreting the meaning of Day and her followers — that the insights of Victor Turner help to uncover deeper patterns in the story. For American Catholicism at mid-century was most assuredly undergoing what Turner would call a *rite de passage:* viewed from the outside, American Catholicism was no longer the nineteenth-century church of poor and uneducated immigrants, but certainly not an "establishment" faith either. As Thomas Merton, Leonard Feeney, and Fulton Sheen witnessed, Catholicism was moving, ecologically, from its niche in the American religious landscape, and its destination appeared uncertain. Ultramontanists called for continued allegiance to the "ministate" model — in which Catholics lived in a network of parochial and diocesan institutions from cradle to grave parallel to American "secular" ones — while Americanists called for adaptation/ immersion in the culture. But all the parties to the debate recognized that a seismic redefinition of Holy Mother Church's relation to the culture was underway. American Catholicism's "structured" identity, then, was adrift and undergoing radical redefinition in the decades after World War II. Students of Turner would say that American Catholicism between 1955 and 1960 was in a "liminal phase" of identity.[47]

Building on the insights of the seminal cultural anthropologist Arnold van Gennep, Turner has argued that cultural *rites de passage* — like that defining American Catholicism in the late 1950s — are marked by three identifiable phases: separation, margin, and aggregation. The first, "separation" phase can be identified by "symbolic behavior signifying the detachment of an individual or group either from an earlier fixed point in the social structure or from a set of cultural conditions." The Boston Heresy Case, with the eventual ex-communication of Leonard Feeney, might appropriately stand as an example of such "symbolic behavior," detaching a group from an "earlier fixed point in the social structure." As much as anything else, that event had proclaimed, both to Catholics and non-Catholics, that the older Catholic ministate within America was in the process of dis-solution, and that Catholics *could,* in fact, "resort with impunity" with Protestants.[48]

But in Turner's second, "marginal" phase — the liminal period when a group's identity has separated from its previously fixed loca-tion in the social landscape and before "aggregating" into a new social location — the characteristics of the "pilgrim" are ambiguous. There is an unsettling blend of "lowliness and sacredness" in this phase, ac-cording to Turner, a blend that gives rise to radical, "anti-structural" experiments in limning the possibilities of the group's future. These experiments attempt to replace the older social location — a loca-tion marked by hierarchy, differentiation, and "structured" identity — with a charismatic, egalitarian emphasis on community and prophetic models of social interaction.[49]

It is precisely in this second, charismatic liminal phase of the *rites de passage* that "young men see visions and old men dream dreams." The "sacred component" of this anti-structural phase consists precisely in the vision of a radically different style of community in which "the underling becomes uppermost, the supreme authority is portrayed as a slave, recalling that aspect of the coronation of a pope...when he is called upon to be the *servus servorum Dei.*" The vision offered allows the possibility that the poor will, indeed, inherit the earth, and the peacemakers will be recognized as children of God.[50]

In most structured societies undergoing this rite of passage, accord-ing to Turner, it is the marginal group or the outsider who most often comes to symbolize the "sentiment for humanity" that questions the viability or even morality of the structured reality on what are often perceived as unrealistic principles, like the Golden Rule. Over against the norm-governed, institutionalized, and abstract justifications vin-dicating the foundations of "structure" (the balance of power, the "nuclear umbrella," *Realpolitk*), the proponents of *communitas* offer immediate and concrete remedies for social dis-ease that involve in-dividuals in concrete and deeply satisfying experiences (feeding the hungry, sheltering the homeless, etc.) attached to a utopian vision of community and fellowship.[51]

The charismatic and prophetic questioners of the finality and durability of the official structure usually attack the received worldview "through the interstices of structure...at the edges of structure, in liminality." The attack on the wisdom and reality of the received worldview is sometimes even considered sacred or holy, possibly because such an attack "transgresses or dissolves the norms that govern structured, institutionalized relationships, and is accompanied by experiences of unprecedented potency."[52]

From the viewpoint of those charged with maintaining the "structure," however, any and all such manifestations of charismatic anti-structural activity appear as dangerous: they constitute anarchical attacks on the good order of society and must be resisted or (at the very least) hedged in with prescriptions, prohibitions, and conditions.

Dorothy Day and the movement sustained by her and Maurin's vision of a "hospitable" world — a world of voluntary poverty, pacifism, and the corporal works of mercy — offered just such an anti-structural vision of what American Catholicism might be during a period of great uncertainty and flux, when Catholic group identity was fluid and ambiguous and its new corporate "niche" in the religious landscape remained unclear. Building on some of the richest traditions of modern Catholicism — the papal social teaching of Leo XIII and Pius XI, the French personalism of Mounier and Jacques Maritain, the thought of English Catholic distributists like G. K. Chesterton and Eric Gill, the deeply mystical but concrete spirituality of Therese of Lisieux — they crafted a corporate "no" to *both* the older "Catholic ministate" model of immigrant religion and to the emerging suburban captivity of the church. Catholicism, in Maurin and Day's vision, would neither stand above nor completely acculturate to American society: it would, rather — much like the pope — become the *servus servorum Dei* to the first children of the church, the poor, thereby (strangely enough) becoming a foundation of society.

But Day drew, significantly, on more than just Roman Catholic sources for her inspiration: borrowing from the revered *American* philosophical and political radical traditions — the Puritan, Congregationalist tradition of "localism" and personal responsibility over against centralized, corporate power structures, the transcendental "self-reliance" of canonical figures like Emerson and Thoreau, the respected but largely ignored pacifist and "immediatist" tradition of abolitionists like William Lloyd Garrison — Day fashioned a resolutely American movement that made no apologies to the culture. With a sure instinct granted to the children of the land, who grow up never thinking of themselves as other than the heirs of the place, Day offered a thoroughly American vision of what Catholicism might be in a popular (and populist) democracy.[53]

Most presciently of all, Day recognized with the clarity of a native that "outsidership" was itself a revered (quite possibly the most revered) form of claiming American "insidership." As R. Laurence Moore has so convincingly argued, the American experiment from its inception at the hands of "nonseparating nonconformists" in Massachusetts has "encouraged people to express their most cherished convictions in the language of dissent." *Protestants* — quite literally, "protesters" — provided, after all, both the foundation and the mainstream of the cultural experiment, and the pantheon of cultural heroes — William Brewster and Roger Williams, Tom Paine and Ralph Waldo Emerson, Frederick Douglass and Martin Luther King — appears more full of nonconformists for righteousness' sake than any other category. Many of the culture's most important "holy days" — Thanksgiving, the Fourth of July, Martin Luther King's birthday, etc. — celebrate those who refused to settle for the status quo, who protested against the oppression and inequality of the "establishment." Thus, religious and political "protest," at least as much as any other form of cultural expression, has served as one of the most revered paths of "Americanization." Moore's study of various "outgroups" in America — Catholics, Jews, Mormons, African Americans — illustrates how their protest against the mainstream cultural Establishment "did a great deal to expose the shabbiness and the arrogance of the culture surrounding them and contributed a fair measure to whatever success the American system has had."[54] Dorothy Day appears to have sensed in the American anarchist, radicalist tradition of William Lloyd Garrison, Mother Jones, and Emma Goldman, and in the mystical/social tradition of Chesterton, Maritain, and St. Therese introduced to her by Peter Maurin, the answer to the dilemma of Catholicism in the brave new world. Especially in the self-satisfied but anxious years after World War II, when American Catholicism had yet to "aggregate" in a new social location, the Catholic Worker's resolutely anti-structural gospel offered to Day's ecclesial community an answer that was "radical" in its root sense: American Catholics were called by Day's movement to return to their *roots* in living out a life of prophetic liminality over against the comfortable accommodation represented by Cardinal Spellman's "Power House" and the concerns over suburban crabgrass.

To be true to their dual heritage of religious and political nonconformity handed on by both Puritan founders and immigrant forebears — to work in the service of the millennial vision of a "Citie upon a Hill" outlined by John Winthrop and the social concern for the poor preached by every pope after Leo XIII — Day called American Catholics to keep their feet firmly planted "at the door," on the margins, in liminality, because it was precisely there, in the Little Way, that God was to be found. But in issuing such a radical call, ironically enough, Day stood not at the margins at all, but rather very much at the center of both the American and Catholic traditions: it was *because* Day was so committed an American and devout a Catholic that she demanded both traditions to make good on their promises about the poor and the marginalized, about feeding everyone at the table. Day discerned the radical core of both the American and the Catholic worldviews and held them to account for their rhetoric. As David O'Brien recognized so well in penning his subtitle to Day's eulogy in the pages of *Commonweal* in 1980, Day stood "Not on the Fringe, but at the Church's Center."[55]

While Day probably contributed more than any other individual to the emergence of a distinguishable "Catholic counter-culture" in the 1960s and 1970s (led by brother priests Dan and Phil Berrigan) she herself consistently denounced "parties" in the church. Her consistent and powerful voicing of the needs of the poor "cut directly to the heart of the matter, to the mysteries of good and evil, to the clarity of most moral issues and the ambiguity of our response." And she did this, moreover, "without arrogance or self-righteousness."[56]

Day's vision, of course, was the road not taken by American Catholicism in the late twentieth century. Traditionalist calls for a return to a distinguishable "Catholic culture" in but not of the naked public square in the late twentieth century, and accommodationist visions of a faith in, of, and for the culture have riven American Catholicism in the decades since Day's death in 1980. American Catholicism's mid-century migration to a new ecological niche in the American religious landscape appears, in fact, to mirror the location of the Protestant mainstream itself at the beginning of the century — divided into pitched camps of liberals, moderates, and conservatives, however new and strange such adjectives may sound to older Catholic ears. When Day entered the church in 1927, after all, there was no such thing as a "liberal" or a "conservative" Catholic. But to the surprise of everyone — perhaps even to Day herself — the third, "aggregation" stage of American Catholicism's *rites de passage* in the latter half of the century eschewed the older fortress model of immigrant Catholicism, the "progressives' " call for a totally inculturated faith, and Day and Maurin's own personalist and anarchist vision of a harsh and dreadful love committed to localist decisions and the corporal works of mercy. It simply settled for reflecting the political/social divisions of American society itself.

Dorothy Day never considered herself as other than a dutiful daughter of the church: it would never have occurred to her that she was crafting a "radical" or "left-wing" brand of Catholicism. She was simply implementing the commands of the gospel and of every pope since 1891 (the year of Leo XIII's great social encyclical, *Rerum Novarum*). One can, however, speculate about how the story might have evolved otherwise had her religious community heeded Day's prophetic call to take the downward path, which leads to salvation.

Chapter 6

A Catholic for President?

JFK, Peter Berger, and the "Secular" Theology of the Houston Speech, 1960

> "I want a chief executive whose public acts...and whose fulfill-
> ment of his Presidential office [are] not limited or conditioned by
> *any* religious oath, ritual or obligation."   —JOHN F. KENNEDY[1]

JFK among the Ministers

At 8:55 on the evening of Monday, September 12, 1960, John
Fitzgerald Kennedy, the youthful but somewhat weary Democratic
candidate in that year's closely fought presidential race, sat down on
the dais of the ballroom of the Rice Hotel in Houston, Texas. "We can
win or lose the election right there in Houston on Monday night," Ted
Sorensen, one of Kennedy's closest political advisers, had told a friend
the previous weekend in Los Angeles, and Kennedy had flown back
"east" from barnstorming on the Pacific coast just for that evening's
event. That "event" was an invitation to address the Greater Houston
Ministerial Association, three hundred evangelical clergymen strong,
who had been gathering for close to an hour when Kennedy sat down
next to the evening's moderator (a Presbyterian pastor) five minutes
before the meeting was to begin.[2]

Kennedy's address to the assembled clergymen that evening — ostensibly about the role of religion in American politics, but actually
about Kennedy's own "religious affiliation" (as he so singularly put
it for a Roman Catholic) — represented *both* an unexceptional instance of American political rhetoric ("I believe in an America that
is officially neither Catholic, Protestant, nor Jewish"), and a rather
extraordinary "theological" reflection on the role of religion in American public life ("I want a chief executive whose public acts are...not
limited or conditioned by any religious oath, ritual or obligation").
Indeed, within a very short time of the address itself, both Catholic

and Protestant commentators, no less than hard-nosed secular political pundits who cared not a whit for theology, opined about the nature of the "theology" informing Kennedy's speech.[3]

Kennedy, of course, was attempting to address the neuralgic "religious issue" in the 1960 presidential campaign that September evening in Houston, and, to judge by the results of the November election two months later, he had offered a reasonably cogent answer to the question of "how can a Catholic live in the White House?" Like Al Smith in the 1928 presidential campaign, Kennedy had found his Catholicism to be a troublesome and recurrent issue in his bid for the presidency, and had reiterated in the Houston Speech the hardline "separationist" position on church and state that had marked his political career from its inception.[4]

On one level, the very issue of Kennedy's religion in the campaign could easily be seen as ironic, as Jack Kennedy had never been accused of being overly pious at any point in his life. His wife, Jacqueline, had reportedly told journalist Arthur Krock that she was mystified over the religion issue, as "Jack is such a poor Catholic." Likewise, close advisers to JFK would later report that, while Kennedy resented his portrayal in the press as not deeply religious, "he cared not a whit for theology, [and] sprinkled quotations from the Protestant Bible throughout his speeches." Indeed, Ted Sorensen, arguably JFK's most intimate counsel in public life and himself a Unitarian, recalled that "during the eleven years I knew him I never heard him pray aloud...or, despite all our discussions of church/state affairs, ever disclose his personal views on man's relation to God."[5]

But Kennedy's Catholicism *was* in fact a key if diffuse issue in the campaign: the religious distrust that Kennedy had to address in order to be a viable candidate for the presidency in 1960 spanned the cultural spectrum from a crude prejudice against "micks," pressed by hooded "patriots" who burned crosses in the night, to highly literate, liberal concerns, voiced by some of the most respected seminary professors in the nation, about the hegemonic designs of a religious institution that had held, for many centuries, that "error has no rights." The Houston Speech was the Kennedy team's most organized effort to address the entire spectrum of doubters — from "mick-haters" to bureaucrats in the National Council of Churches' "God Box" on Morningside Heights — and to, finally and permanently, put the issue to rest.[6]

Much has been made, both at the time and since, of a Catholic being successfully (albeit closely) elected to the presidency in 1960. Some have seen in Kennedy's election one of the most visible signs of the Catholic "coming of age" in American culture — the public event that marked the movement of the Catholic community from the cultural ghetto into the mainstream of American life. Others have portrayed the 1960 election as the public funeral of what Arthur Schlesinger, Jr., termed "America's oldest prejudice": with Kennedy, the three-centuries-long tradition of anti-Catholicism in American culture appeared at an end, and a genuinely "post-Protestant America" appeared (finally) to be abirthing. Still others have analyzed the Kennedy victory and presidency as the moment when the twentieth century came "into its own" in American public life: as the first president born after 1900, JFK seemed to be the perfect icon for a generation that had left behind the "bogeys" of the nineteenth century, ethnic, racial, and religious prejudices among them. The intellectual and moral "toughness" called for in the sobering game of *Realpolitik* that defined the post-1960 "New Frontier" appeared to have little time for religious (or any other kind of) bigotry.[7]

Further, it is possible to read the theological vapidity of Kennedy's "religious affiliation" — at least as expressed in public pronouncements like the Houston Address — as the legitimate child of what has been called the "Religious Revival" of the 1950s. Whatever one thought of the putative "revival" of religion that marked the opening years of the Nuclear Age — and scholars of American religion have portrayed it as fostering everything from the "suburban captivity of the churches" to the cult of "social anesthesia" — one could not deny that one of that revival's most important effects was both the high visibility *and* the almost contentless theology of the "Piety on the Potomac" that had marked the Eisenhower years in the White House. Monsignor (later Bishop) Fulton J. Sheen had played an unwitting and ironic role, along with the Reverend Norman Vincent Peale and Rabbi Joshua Liebman, in making the "Judeo-Christian tradition" (a religious tradition that now included Catholics and Jews along with Protestants) the now agreed-upon basis of public rhetoric. This new religious piety — its appeal to a three-thousand-year-old tradition notwithstanding — had found its most popular and visible high priest in Eisenhower himself, who had opened his presidency (and stunned the Washington Establishment) with reading his *own* prayer during his inauguration ceremony, and who thereafter punctuated his public addresses with transcendent if vague references to the "Supreme Being." If "vagueness" was thus a theological virtue in presidential rhetoric after the Eisenhower years, then John Kennedy certainly had done his divinity homework well.[8]

All of these interpretations offer important insights into the political events of November 1960, as well as into the "theology" of Kennedy himself. But the Houston Speech, and the theological agenda informing it, might also offer other, more ironic, lessons for understanding the role of religion in the brave new world of late twentieth-century American life, quite apart from the depth of piety felt or expressed by the young senator from Massachusetts. These lessons have less to do with the demise of religious prejudice in American culture or with the new post-Eisenhower religious inclusiveness in "the American Way of Life" than with a "naked public square" in which religious impulses were marginalized in public discourse.

Precisely *because* John F. Kennedy was a Roman Catholic — an adherent (however selectively) of a religious tradition that had been successfully excluded from the "high priesthood" of American politics for almost two centuries — it might be argued that he *had* to "secularize" the American presidency in order to win it. Indeed, it is the contention of this chapter that Kennedy's Houston Speech can be fruitfully seen as a key moment, not only in American Catholicism's "coming of age," but also of the articulation of the *terms* of that rite of passage.

The Houston Speech — and the "theology" that undergird it — is the more dramatic when considered in the context of the traditional role of the American presidency in fostering devotion to the American "civil religion." At least since Lincoln's mytho-religious musings about the "almost-chosen people," through Woodrow Wilson's millennial perceptions of America's role during and after the First World War, to Dwight David Eisenhower's famous regular but vague incantations as the "pontifex" of the American public cult, American presidents had regularly and clearly elucidated the Christian foundations of the American experiment. Indeed, just a few years before Kennedy's campaign, President Eisenhower had announced that the American experiment made no sense without a "deeply felt religious faith — and I don't care what it is." Thus, Kennedy's stark new vision of an exceedingly high and solid wall of separation between church and state elucidated at Houston was the more dramatic and noteworthy — and was noted as such at the time — precisely because he appeared after one of the more willing practitioners of the national religious cult.[9]

Kennedy's "secularizing" of the presidency was not aimed at the disappearance or denigration of religion or religious impulses; rather, it took the form of the *privatization* of religion as described by sociologist Peter Berger. In Berger's theory, the social and epistemological pluralism endemic to "complex modern societies" like that of the United States after World War II almost inexorably leads to the removal of religious impulses from the public to the private spheres; but such removal, while gaining social comity and political order, also comes at a price:

> Private religiosity, however "real" it may be to the individuals who adopt it, cannot any longer fulfill the classical task of religion, that of constructing a common world within which all of social life receives ultimate meaning binding on everybody. Instead, this religiosity is limited to specific enclaves of social life that may be effectively segregated from the secularized sectors of modern society.... The world-building potency of religion is thus restricted to the construction of sub-worlds, of fragmented universes of meaning, the plausibility structure of which may in some cases be no larger than the nuclear family.[10]

In such a reading of the events of 1960, the Houston Speech of September 12 represented a landmark in the "secularization" of American politics, no less than in the (highly ironic) "mainstreaming" of American Catholicism. The "privatization" of transcendent impulses that Kennedy's address represented, however understandable on the level of political reality, represented a "severe rupture of the traditional task of religion, which was *precisely* the establishment of an integrated set of definitions of reality that could serve as a common universe of meaning for the members of a society." If, indeed, Kennedy understood and meant what he stated at Houston — that he represented a vision of the presidency "not limited by any religious obligation" — then he built better than he knew. Presidential discourse between Kennedy and Jimmy Carter — that is, until the rise of what the secular press christened "the New Religious Right" — would be marked by a singular and new absence of religious metaphors and Christian imagery.[11]

But there is an irony to the story as well: the Houston Speech, which marked an America well on its way into the secular city no less than marking Jack Kennedy on his way to the White House, was itself the logical end result of Protestants like Billy Graham and Norman Vincent Peale highlighting Kennedy's religion as a problematic issue in the 1960 presidential campaign. The very issue that *they* made of his Catholicism helped to insure the "privatization" of religion in public rhetoric.[12]

The Making of the (Catholic) President, 1960

At least since the famous — or infamous — presidential election of 1928, when the "wet" Democratic governor of New York, Al Smith, had lost the election by a landslide, many in the Democratic Party leadership had believed that a Catholic candidate for the presidency would lose more votes than could be gained by adherence to that faith. This common wisdom, in fact, represented one of the most discussed and debated issues in the Democratic Party — especially given Roman Catholicism's status as the largest religious body in the nation and its "majority status" in key presidential electoral states like New York, Pennsylvania, and Illinois. Indeed, this party discussion had reached a critical point by 1956, when two Roman Catholics, along with two "Dixiecrats," were being considered by the Democratic Party leadership for the number two spot on the presidential ticket: New York City mayor Robert Wagner and the young senator from Massachusetts, John Fitzgerald Kennedy.[13]

Kennedy himself (and a number of politicos who supported his bid that year) believed that his religion would help defend his party's ticket against Republican charges that the Democrats were "soft on communism," as well as help counter the divorced status of the party's presidential contender, Adlai Stevenson. Further, the Kennedy camp based their argument in favor of the young Massachusetts senator on more than just bravado.[14]

John Bailey, state chairman of the Connecticut Democratic party and a fervent Kennedy supporter, had sent around to party officials a report subsequently known as the "Bailey memorandum," although it had, in fact, been written by Kennedy's chief aide, Ted Sorensen. The Bailey memorandum contended that millions of Catholic Democrats who had voted for Eisenhower in 1952 would return "home" to the Democratic Party if a Catholic were chosen as Stevenson's running mate. The memorandum likewise challenged the so-called "Al Smith Myth" within the party by presenting statistical and historical arguments to show that the 1928 candidate had lost not because of anti-Catholic bigotry, but rather because 1928 was a "Republican year" due to prohibition, distrust of Democratic Party "bossism," and a host of other concerns completely unrelated to Smith's religion. Indeed, the memorandum asserted that Kennedy would be an ideal candidate to shoo away any lingering shadows of Smith and bring into the party fourteen pivotal "Catholic states" which carried, between them, 261 electoral votes.[15]

As Sorensen himself later observed, the Bailey memorandum — aimed at convincing Protestant no less than Catholic stalwarts of the party — "made no pretense of being a comprehensive and objective study. It was a political answer to sweeping assertions made against the nomination of a Roman Catholic for vice president." In the event, the memorandum failed to galvanize party support for Kennedy: several political scientists on the party's payroll claimed to have discredited its statistical data, while others observed that it had made no ethnic distinctions among Catholic Democrats, thus raising questions about the veracity of its conclusions. Further, liberal Protestant journals (to the "left of center" politically and sympathetic to the Democrats' social agenda) voiced their lack of conversion to the Kennedy cause after the Bailey memorandum: the issue, the *Christian Century* opined in an editorial just days before the party's convention, had more to do with the *style* of Wagner and Kennedy's religion than its brand. Neither had manifested much independent thought, religiously or otherwise, during their political careers, so that Protestant worries about either Catholic in the Oval Office — even in so progressive a journal as the *Christian Century* — were hardly put to rest. Neither Kennedy nor Wagner was nominated for the Democrats' number two spot in 1956.[16]

Thus Kennedy supporters within the party turned their eyes to the 1960 race. In preparation for that campaign, Kennedy himself began to reiterate his rather "strict constructionist" reading of separation of church and state questions in a number of interviews and speeches, perhaps most famously in a March 1959 interview with Fletcher Knebel in *Look* magazine. In answering a question put to him during that interview about possible conflicts between his (Catholic) conscience and the presidential oath to uphold the Constitution — a somewhat tendentious and insulting question, given Kennedy's by then well known views about public aid to parochial schools, an ambassador to the Vatican, and other "Protestant fears" — Kennedy had answered, in what would later be termed an "unvarnished" way, that "whatever one's religion in private life may be, for the officeholder, *nothing* takes precedence over his oath to uphold the Constitution in all its parts — including the First Amendment and the *strict* separation of church and state."[17]

However understandable Kennedy's political concerns may have been to allay Protestant fears about a candidacy that was yet to be formally announced, the Catholic press took immediate and hostile exception both to the questions asked in the *Look* interview and to

Kennedy's answers to them. Why, they asked, should Kennedy have submitted to a "loyalty test for Catholics only"? The diocese of Baltimore's *Catholic Review* stated that it felt Kennedy "appears to have gone overboard in an effort to placate the bigots," while John Cogley, in his column in the liberal Catholic weekly *Commonweal,* intimated that Kennedy had perhaps leaned a little *too* far in the direction of accommodation to Protestant fears and that a Catholic president "would have to acknowledge that the teachings of the Church are of prime importance to him." The Jesuit-edited *America* magazine likewise noted on its editorial page that "we were somewhat taken aback by the unvarnished statement that 'nothing takes precedence over one's oath.' Mr. Kennedy doesn't really believe that. No religious man, be he Catholic, Protestant, or Jew, holds such an opinion."[18]

James Pike, one-time Catholic himself and Episcopal bishop of the diocese of California in 1959, offered one of the most perceptive readings of the entire *Look* affair in his book published a few months later. Pike, writing by his own admission to separate "legitimate concerns" about a Kennedy presidency from anti-Catholic fears arising from prejudice, observed that Kennedy's statement in *Look,* "far from posing the threat of ecclesiastical tyranny, would seem rather to represent the point of view of a thorough-going secularist, who truly believes that a man's religion and his decision-making can be kept in two watertight compartments." For Episcopal Bishop Pike, Kennedy's problematic "religious" values thus had little to do with his Catholicism.[19]

Further, the *Look* interview had certainly done little to put to rest fairly consistent rumors of widespread opposition to the Kennedy ticket among the hierarchy of the American Catholic Church itself. Such opposition among Catholic bishops only rarely manifested itself in a public way — as when New York's Francis Cardinal Spellman publicly (and warmly) welcomed the Republican candidate, Richard Nixon, to his city. But whether the American Catholic bishops considered Kennedy's political or religious views too "liberal" (usually meaning "accommodationist"), whether they feared a revival of anti-Catholic hostilities that a Catholic candidate would engender, or whether they felt that a Protestant candidate would be more likely to "woo" their support than a Catholic, the hostile silence of many American Catholic bishops to the Kennedy ticket clearly belied Protestant fears of an organized "clerical plot" behind Kennedy's campaign.[20]

On Saturday, January 2, 1960, the forty-two-year-old Kennedy announced his candidacy for the presidency and was challenged forthwith by Hubert Humphrey, the other likely contender for the Democratic ticket, to match political "gospels" in the Wisconsin and West Virginia primaries. Kennedy immediately (and correctly) recognized the gauntlet thus thrown by Humphrey as the crucial test of the "religion issue" in the 1960 election: in neither primary would he be running as the "favorite son" as he would in states (like New York and Illinois) where the Catholic vote guaranteed him a good showing. Wisconsin represented a campaign field where Protestant and Catholic voters were about evenly divided, while West Virginia represented a state in which 95 percent of the voters were Protestants — and heavily evangelical Protestant at that. Kennedy had recognized that "I had to prove that a Catholic could win in heavily Protestant states. Could you imagine me, having entered no primaries, trying to tell the [party] leaders that being a Catholic was no handicap?"[21]

By the end of the Wisconsin primary, Kennedy felt that he could say that, whatever other qualifications he might bring to the White House, "I knew Wisconsin better than any other President." And while Kennedy had systematically attempted to avoid the religion issue in the campaign, the local and national press would not let it go: pictures of Kennedy greeting groups of nuns were printed across the nation, while other pictures were left on the newsroom floor; frequent questions from student audiences regarding his religion were invariably and extensively reported, while other questions about labor and agriculture went unnoticed. As Kennedy himself noted in amazement and anger, voters at his rallies were beset by reporters outside the hall and asked their religion — "not their occupation or education or philosophy or income, only their religion." One newspaper's political analysis of his campaign, he noted, mentioned the word "Catholic" twenty times in fifteen paragraphs.[22]

The Wisconsin primary results confirmed *both* Kennedy's hopes and fears: he had won the April 5 footrace with more votes than any candidate in the history of that state's primary. But pollsters (especially at CBS) — hard pressed to explain how his reception of 56 percent of the Wisconsin vote exceeded the 53 percent they had predicted — attributed his win to Catholic Republicans "returning home" from Ike's party, and his losses to Protestants and farmers. Humphrey had run best in the least Catholic areas, it was correctly reported, but few pointed out that those areas were near the Minnesota border (Humphrey's home turf). Wisconsin thus (ironically enough) threatened to make religion *the* issue in the campaign, despite Kennedy's resounding victory in the primary. Indeed, a Lou Harris poll taken immediately after the Wisconsin race showed a sharpened new awareness of the religion issue among voters in the state hosting the next crucial primary, West Virginia.[23]

It was the ironic highlighting of the "religion issue" after the Wisconsin primary (despite Kennedy's more than respectable showing there), as well as the prospect of campaigning in (Protestant) West Virginia, that led Kennedy to a "switch of tactics" regarding religion: if he were going to be felled by the "Catholic question," then he would go down fighting. And Kennedy's conversion to new tactics on the religion issue entailed three immediate decisions: he would switch the topic of an upcoming address at a national meeting of newspaper editors from foreign aid to religion; his staff would organize a group of nationally prominent Protestant clergy to issue a public letter to their colleagues, calling for an end to religious prejudice and "insinuation" in political ads; and, unlike his strategy of silence on the religion issue in Wisconsin, he would make a direct and open appeal in West Virginia for "fair play" regarding religion.[24]

His address to the American Society of Newspaper Editors in Washington, D.C., represented one of Kennedy's most direct expositions of his views on church and state, birth control, and diplomatic relations with the Vatican. In it Kennedy emphasized, yet again, what he felt had been his position since the outset of his campaign:

> There is only one legitimate question.... Would you, as President, be responsive in any way to ecclesiastical pressures or obligations *of any kind* that might *in any fashion* influence or interfere with your conduct of that office in the national interest? My answer was — and is — no.... I am not the Catholic candidate for President. I am the Democratic party's candidate for President who happens to be a Catholic. I do not speak for the Catholic Church on issues of public policy, and no one in that Church speaks for me.[25]

When he concluded his address, Kennedy called for questions, but there were none from the assembled newspaper editors — a silence, in fact, that made Kennedy both disappointed and suspicious: many of the editors present would continue to print stories about Catholic voting blocs and Kennedy's "cold-blooded" utilization of them. Likewise, the second plank of his revised tactical approach to the religion issue — an open letter from nationally prominent Protestant clergy — proved a more difficult project than initially perceived.

Evangelist Billy Graham was approached by Kennedy staffer Pierre Salinger, who asked the revivalist to consider organizing a "fair play" letter to fellow ministers. Graham promised to give the idea "prayerful consideration," but shortly thereafter decided that such a letter would itself make religion an issue in the campaign, and declined. Both Kennedy and Salinger had reason to question the real motive(s) for Graham's "prayerful" declining of Salinger's proposal later that spring, however, when Graham declared that religion would definitely be a *legitimate* major issue in the campaign "whether we like it or not," and proceeded that fall to lead a Nixon rally in prayer.[26]

Finally, on May 3, one week before the West Virginia primary, Francis Sayre (dean of the Washington Episcopal Cathedral), Methodist Bishop Bromley Oxnam (whose long years of opposition to the American Catholic hierarchy as a leader of the lobbying group Protestants and Other Americans United for the Separation of Church and State gave him "impeccable" credentials for the task), and eleven other Protestant leaders issued an open letter to their "Fellow Pastors in Christ." "Quite apart from what our attitude toward the Roman Church may be," the letter said, "we think it unjust to discount any one of [the candidates] because of his chosen faith."[27]

Likewise, shortly after the Episcopal bishop of Wheeling, West Virginia, announced his opposition to a Catholic candidate for the presidency on religious grounds alone, Kennedy launched into the third of his reconsidered tactics: if religion were a valid issue in the presidential campaign, he told a West Virginia audience, "I shouldn't now be serving in the Senate, and I shouldn't have been accepted into the U.S. Navy," for the oath of office was essentially identical in each case: an oath sworn on the Bible to defend the Constitution.[28]

The response to Kennedy's new tactics on the religion issue, especially in the national press, was mixed: some accused him of fanning the controversy and "running on the religious issue" in West Virginia, while others opined that he had acquitted himself honestly and fairly in an issue not of his making. Kennedy held his own counsel as to the success or failure of the new tactics, but steeled himself for defeat in a primary state so overwhelmingly Protestant. The returns late on the evening of May 3, 1960, however, must have outshown his rosiest hopes: Kennedy had carried the state by a 61 percent to 39 percent margin, winning in all but seven of the state's fifty-five counties. He had carried districts dominated by the United Mine Workers, in both farm and urban areas, and, most significantly, he had carried the white Anglo-Saxon Protestant vote. That very evening, Kennedy accepted Hubert Humphrey's gracious withdrawal from the presidential race. The religious issue, he announced a tad too precipitously, had been "buried here in West Virginia."[29]

Kennedy continued his nonstop campaigning in the primaries that summer, although the results seemed no longer uncertain. Indeed, by July 9 — two days before the opening of the Democratic National Convention in Los Angeles — Kennedy told an interviewer on *Meet the Press* that he was fairly certain of winning the convention's nomination. But to many Kennedy's confidence appeared arrogant, and even foolhardy: Eleanor Roosevelt, echoing the sentiments expressed in a famous column by Walter Lippmann, expressed the hope that Kennedy's "unselfishness and courage" would lead him to take the *vice*-presidential position, in which he would have "the opportunity to learn and grow," while Hubert Humphrey — so gracious in West Virginia — announced that he was supporting Adlai Stevenson for the presidential nomination, "out of concern for my country." But to the delight of the Kennedy forces and to the dismay of all the political pundits predicting a convention deadlock (in part over the question of Kennedy's Catholicism) Kennedy won on the convention's first ballot.[30]

The "religion issue" thus appeared over after the dramatic victory in West Virginia as well as Kennedy's first-ballot nomination in Los Angeles. Indeed, by the end of the summer — after the Republicans had met to nominate Richard Nixon as their candidate — the *Christian Century* offered an editorial that seemed to bury the issue by deprecating the faith of both candidates. How to choose between Nixon and Kennedy on religious grounds, the editorial asked, as

> Mr. Nixon is a Quaker who works at Quakerism so little that he could be a naval officer in World War II. Mr. Kennedy is a Catholic who has repudiated so many of the official positions of his church that he has been attacked repeatedly in the Catholic press. So the country will have to choose between two men who have much in common, yet differ at crucial points.[31]

This "burial" of the religion issue by the end of the summer, however — much like the reports of Mark Twain's death — was revealed yet again as being somewhat exaggerated on September 7, 1960, when a new organization of prominent Protestant clergy, the National Conference of Citizens for Religious Freedom, flung a gauntlet to the Kennedy ticket after a day-long meeting presided over by the "king of mind cure," the Reverend Norman Vincent Peale. Peale, the nationally

famous pastor of "America's hometown church" and the author of the
self-help "bible," *The Power of Positive Thinking,* as well as a close
personal friend of Richard Nixon, had already marked out his "turf"
on the Kennedy ticket a month before the West Virginia primary: in
a speech in Charleston, West Virginia, on April 14, 1960, Peale had
argued that not only was it relevant to raise the religious issue in the
campaign, but it was *essential* to do so. Indeed, Peale (who counted
Nixon and his wife among his parishioners at the Marble Collegiate
Church when they were in New York) opined that *the* basic issue in
the primary to be held in West Virginia was whether, if Kennedy were
president, he would be "as free as any other American to give 'his first
loyalty to the United States.' "[32]

The September 7 meeting of the "Peale Group" (as "Citizens for
Religious Freedom" quickly became known in the press and among
politicians to the distress of Peale himself) had been planned the pre-
vious summer in Europe, when the vacationing Peale had met with
Billy Graham, Harold Ockenga (charter member and strategist for the
National Association of Evangelicals), and twenty-five other American
evangelicals in Montreux, Switzerland, to discuss how they might or-
ganize Protestant support for the Nixon campaign. By the time of the
September meeting in Washington, D.C.'s, Mayflower Hotel, the Peale
Group included Dr. Glenn Archer (head of Protestants and Others
United for Separation of Church and State), Dr. Clyde Taylor (an
officer of the National Association of Evangelicals), and 150 other
"representatives" of the Southern Baptist Convention, the National
Council of Churches, and "other groups not related to any of these."
The concern of them all, it was announced, was to be "fair, factual,
and candid in expressing Protestant concern."[33]

At the conclusion of the day-long conference, Peale met with the
press and made available copies of the group's statement, which
consisted of a five-point indictment of the "politics" of the Roman
Catholic Church, which had served as the focus for the day's discussions. The statement charged the Catholic Church with being a
political as well as a religious organization, a fact seen most clearly
in countries (as in South America) where it constituted the majority of
citizens. And the statement concluded with the observation that, however sincere Kennedy himself might be regarding his commitment to
upholding the principles of the First Amendment, he could never be
free of his church's "determined efforts... to breach the wall of separation of church and state." Indeed, that there was a "religion issue"
at all in the campaign was "not the fault of the candidate. It is created

by the nature of the Roman Catholic Church which is, in a very real sense, both a church and also a temporal state." The Reverend Harold Ockenga, pastor of the resolutely evangelical Park Street Church at the corner of Boston Common (known to Bostonians as "Brimstone Corner" because of the dour preaching famous in that congregation), also met personally with the press and likened Kennedy to the Russian Premier Khrushchev in being a "captive of the system."[34]

It was thus both expedient and wearying (in about equal measure) that Kennedy should accept an invitation — not unlike that of the spider to the fly — from the Greater Houston Ministerial Association to address a group of Protestant clergymen five days after the meeting of the "Peale Group." Not surprisingly, the candidate elucidated a "separationist" position on church and state that evening that was aimed at strangely warming the heart of Peale and everyone else who had been at the Washington meeting five days before.

At the very outset of his remarks on the evening of September 12 in Houston, Kennedy observed that far more critical issues than his personal religious beliefs needed to be addressed in the 1960 presidential campaign:

> the spread of communist influence, until it now festers only ninety miles off the coast of Florida...the hungry children I saw in West Virginia, the old people who cannot pay their doctor's bills, the families forced to give up their farms — an America with too many slums, with too few schools, and too late to the moon and outer space. These are the real issues which should decide this campaign....But because I am a Catholic, and no Catholic has ever been elected President, the real issues in this campaign have been obscured — perhaps deliberately in some quarters less responsible than this.[35]

Kennedy then launched into his personal — and somewhat singular — credo: "I believe in an America where the separation of church and state is absolute...where no church or church school is granted any public funds or political preference." Indeed, the "absoluteness" of the separation between church and state that Kennedy envisioned was shortly outlined with breathtaking clarity: "I believe in a President whose views on religion are his own private affair, neither imposed on him by the nation nor imposed by the nation upon him as a condition to holding that office." These resolutely "private" views of the highest office-holder in the land represented "the kind of Presidency in

which I believe, a great office that must not be humbled by making it
the instrument of any religious group."[36]

But Kennedy's speech that evening adumbrated a "wall of separation" between religion and public service that went considerably
beyond what might be termed the allaying of bigoted fears; indeed,
Kennedy's "theology" appeared to outline a relationship between "private" belief and "public" action that social scientists and scholars of
religion have termed the "privatization of religion":

> I want a chief executive whose public acts are responsible to all
> and obligated to none — who can attend any ceremony, service
> or dinner his office may appropriately require him to fulfill —
> and whose fulfillment of his Presidential office is not limited or
> conditioned by any religious oath, ritual, or obligation.[37]

This was the kind of America Kennedy had fought for in the South
Pacific, "and the kind of America my brother died for in Europe." Indeed, Kennedy observed that "no one suggested then that we might
have a 'divided loyalty,' that we did 'not believe in liberty,' or that
we belonged to a disloyal group that threatened 'the freedoms for
which our forefathers died.'" This, in fact, was *precisely* the kind of
freedom for which "our forefathers [died] when they fled here to escape religious test oaths that denied office to members of less favored
churches."[38]

It was on *this* understanding of the church-state relationship that
Kennedy was running for president, not on the basis of pamphlets
that "carefully select quotations out of context from the statements of
Catholic Church leaders, usually in other countries, frequently in other
centuries." To all such half-baked historical accusations and scurrilous
insinuations, Kennedy announced: "I do not consider these quotations
binding upon my public acts — why should you?" Those who had repeatedly stressed Kennedy's "religious affiliation" during the campaign
had simply deflected serious attention away from more serious issues.[39]

Kennedy and the Secularization of the Presidency

Religious leaders and political pundits at the time (and since) Kennedy's "Houston Speech" have raised searching questions about the
implications of a faith "not limited or conditioned by any religious
obligation," about a theology that is one's "own private affair," and
about denominational membership in which one does "not speak for
[the] church, and the church does not speak for me." Indeed, a month

after the Houston affair, Winthrop Hudson, commenting in the *Christian Century,* observed that Kennedy as well as Nixon appeared to hold the "general cultural conviction that religion is a good thing but nonetheless a purely private affair which has few implications for the political order."[40]

A thoroughgoing *theological* analysis of such a resolutely private faith like that elucidated by Kennedy at Houston poses problems for the student of religion, as such a faith would appear to have very little social import or public manifestation. Indeed, such a faith might very well provide evidence for Bishop Pike's estimate of Kennedy as a "thoroughgoing secularist," or *The Nation's* famous portrayal of Kennedy as "close to being a spiritually rootless man." Catholic journalists at the time certainly remarked upon the singular expression of Kennedy's "take" on his faith.[41]

Ted Sorensen, recalling later the preparations for that evening in Houston, remembered reading the text over the phone to Jesuit theologian and church-state theorist John Courtney Murray, then teaching at Woodstock College in Maryland. Likewise, on the plane to Houston, the speech was reviewed by one-time *Commonweal* editor John Cogley. According to Sorensen, both men — Catholic intellectuals familiar with the Roman Church's theological tradition and with the American constitutional circumstance — apparently approved the main outline of the text. Indeed, several scholars have argued for Murray's role as intellectual preceptor to Kennedy on precisely this issue.[42]

But positing such a mentoring role for Murray demands a sophisticated understanding of the Catholic natural law discourse in which Murray was engaged — an understanding that would not have immediately furthered the political goals of Kennedy in any event, however conversant Kennedy may have been with scholastic philosophy (an unlikely eventuality). Murray's best-selling collection of articles published in 1960, *We Hold These Truths,* had sought to provide a "public space" for Catholicism in American society while also avoiding church-state entanglements. But one of the underlying themes of that collection had been a refutation of the "democratic heresy" that believed that "all issues of human life — intellectual, religious, and moral issues, as well as formally political issues — are to be regarded as political issues, and are to be settled by majority vote." This "heresy," a combination of what Murray termed "democratic monism" and secularism, was rampant in the modern West, and appeared to be especially virulent in postwar America.[43]

One of Murray's major agendas in his 1960 magisterial work had

been to offer a natural law reading of the American political circumstance that allowed the church to accomplish its mission — a resolutely
public mission, finally — while avoiding the traditional scholastic distinction between "thesis" and "hypothesis" that had been used by
earlier American Catholic theorists to justify the First Amendment.
While Murray offered a brilliant "end run" around this scholastic
position by arguing that the issue for the Catholic tradition was *not*
the establishment of the church but rather its freedom to accomplish
its social (public) mission, neither his nor the earlier scholastic reading of the situation would have gone far toward silencing the fears
of nervous Protestants like Peale and Ockenga. Indeed, Murray's argument might very well have been read as being the more insidious
because of the perceived republican clothing that hid the scholastic
wolf inside.[44]

Presenting either Murray or Cogley as the architects of Kennedy's
near-total privatization of his "affiliation" would thus appear to be,
at best, unlikely. Several years after the speech Murray himself opined
that Kennedy had been "far more of a separationist than I am," while
Cogley had been an open critic of Kennedy's "creed" as expressed
in the 1959 *Look* interview. Likewise, positing Kennedy himself as a
"thoroughgoing secularist" (his wife's observations to Arthur Krock
notwithstanding) presents problems for the historian, given Kennedy's
consistent claims to be a good Catholic, with a consistent record of
Mass attendance to prove it. A more neutral historical "take" on the
Houston affair — avoiding both "secret architects" and *ad hominem*
analysis — is that Kennedy's *Realpolitik* reading of the political and
social situation in the fall of 1960 mandated an almost-total privatization of his Catholic faith — a privatization that was politically
expedient, however theologically problematic it might be.[45]

And such a privatization, while offering a dichotomization that
poses significant *theological* problems, makes perfect *sociological*
sense, especially in light of Peter Berger's insights into the close relationship between social pluralism and religious secularization. Berger
has observed that "modernity plunged religion into a very specific
crisis, characterized by secularity to be sure, but characterized more
importantly by *pluralism*." For Berger, then, contemporary societies
like the United States are marked by a modernity that "pluralizes
both institutions and plausibility structures." This pluralistic cultural
situation, in "demonopolizing" any single religious tradition in a pluralistic culture, makes it progressively more difficult to maintain or
to construct anew viable religious "plausibility structures" — those

preconscious and epistemologically perspicacious "proofs" for the veracity of one's worldview:

> The plausibility structures [of any single religious tradition] lose massively because they can no longer enlist the society as a whole to serve for the purpose of social confirmation. Put simply, there are always "all those others" that refuse to confirm the religious world in question.... [Religions] become "subjectivized" in a double sense: their reality becomes a "private" affair of individuals. And their "reality," insofar as it is still maintained by the individual, is apprehended as being rooted within the consciousness of the individual rather than in the facticities of the external world.[46]

Thus, a key characteristic of all pluralistic situations that aim at social peace is the *voluntary* — and thus by definition *private* — nature of religious belief and observance. In these social situations, religion tends to become more concerned with the therapeutic needs of its adherents, and less concerned with offering a comprehensive worldview for the whole of culture. Such "privatization" of religious belief thus manifests itself in the prominence given to "private problems":

> the emphasis on family and neighborhood as well as on the psychological "needs" of the private individual. It is in these areas that religion continues to be "relevant" even in highly secularized strata, while the application of religious perspectives to political and economic problems is widely deemed "irrelevant" in the same strata. This helps to explain why the churches have had relatively little influence on the economic and political views of even their own members.[47]

Such a reading of the social and political world of "modernity" — when applied to the social circumstance of the United States in the fall of 1960 — goes a significant way toward explicating both Kennedy's Houston Speech and the "secularity" that it represented. Indeed, it might be argued that Berger offers a cogent reading for the "secularization of American politics" that emerged with such dramatic clarity during the turbulent 1960s: precisely *because* Kennedy was not an adherent of that mainstream Protestant religiosity that had created and buttressed the "plausibility structures" of political culture at least since Lincoln, he had to "privatize" presidential religious beliefs — including and especially his own — in order to win that office. A number of social and political factors abetted that privatization: his own party leadership's quite practical and nonideological concern about the chances of a Catholic in a presidential election after the sobering precedent set by Al Smith; the alacrity with which the press sought out and reported "the religion issue" as a key divisive issue in the campaign; his own less than missionary reception of his "religious affiliation." All of these factors played a role in shaping the "theological" statements in the Houston Speech. But these factors must also be placed within the larger picture of the "pluralization" of American culture along the lines spelled out by Peter Berger. The "secularity" that was emerging in mid-twentieth-century American culture rarely manifested itself as a frontal attack on religion or religious language, although both Madeleine Murray O'Hare early in the decade and the "Death of God" movement at the end of it represented numerically insignificant but culturally powerful impulses that did assault traditional religious belief. Likewise, the secularity expressed in the Houston Speech never denigrated the *personal* importance of religious conviction. Rather, the secularity that the speech *did* advocate represented a near-total privatization of religious belief — so much a privatization that religious observers from both sides of the Catholic/ Protestant fence commented on its remarkable a-theistic implications for public life and discourse.

But the irony of the cultural context that helped to shape the Houston Speech is often missed or ignored, and the irony here is rich and deep — whether one happens to be a student of Niebuhr or not. Cultural observers as diverse as Eleanor Roosevelt, Billy Graham, and Norman Vincent Peale had commented (in both overt and covert ways) on the problem posed by Kennedy's adherence to an ecclesiastical tradition outside the American religious mainstream for living in the White House. Whatever the validity of their concerns about Kennedy's religious and ethical principles for holding the highest office in the land — and even today there appears to be divided opinion on the question — their raising of the issue itself went a considerable way toward "secularizing" the American public square by privatizing personal belief. Their very effort to "safeguard" the religious aura of the presidency, in such a reading, contributed in significant ways to its secularization.

Democratic Party strategists, secular journalists, and Protestant religious leaders had all made the point that a "Catholic in the White House" was both historically unprecedented and (potentially) revolutionary because of the Protestant roots of the American "democratic faith." The pluralism of the postwar situation that made such an eventuality remotely likely — considered in the light of the recurrent harping on just this issue — made the privatization of religion the best political strategy for a pragmatist like Kennedy, whatever the theological problems posed by such a course. Considered in such a light, the Houston Speech may or may not witness to Kennedy's personal secularity, the shallowness of American public religiosity in the aftermath of the "Fifties Religious Revival," or the growth of religious tolerance in the United States. It *does* point to the pluralism of the American circumstance after World War II, and the (ironic) privatization of religion that occurred as a result of that pluralism.[48]

Chapter 7

"Into Uncertain Life"

The First Sunday of Advent 1964

"Something irreversible has happened
and been affirmed in the Church."

— YVES CONGAR, on the near-unanimous
passing of *Sacrosanctum Concilium*[1]

The Constitution on the Sacred Liturgy

On the damp morning of December 7, 1962, close to three thousand
bishops, curial functionaries, and "official observers" sat expectantly
in the vast nave of St. Peter's Basilica in Rome to vote formally on
the first decree to issue from the epochal church council convened
by "good" Pope John. John XXIII had been pope only ninety days
when — on January 25, 1959 — he had stunned both the legions of
clerical secretaries who constituted his "Curia" and bishops around
the world in announcing his intention to convene the church's twenty-
first universal ("ecumenical") council of bishops. After nearly four
years of preparation, the Second Council of the Vatican had opened
on October 11, 1962, to consider how the West's oldest Christian institution might bring about the renewal — *aggiornamento* in John's
own phrase — necessary to meet the challenges of the modern world.
The first fruit of those deliberations, focused on the church's worship,
was now about to be born.[2]

The Constitution on the Sacred Liturgy had been completely revised
three times by various subcommittees of theological *periti*, liturgists,
and bishops between October 22 and November 13, 1962, and when
the working text of the document had finally been presented to the
assembled bishops of the council, 328 oral interventions regarding
its contents and structure — surely some kind of in-door record in
the annals of church history — had been entertained on the floor of

St. Peter's. By the afternoon of that damp December day in 1962, the final, "official" version of that document (*Sacrosanctum Concilium*) was handily accepted by the council fathers by an astonishingly lopsided vote of 2162 to 46. Little did the council fathers then understand the implications of that overwhelming vote; for perhaps more dramatically than any other decree issuing from the council, the decree on church worship touched the "folks in the pews" in immediate and understandable ways: the "wars over the Mass" — the (literally) parochial version of the larger "wars over the church" — had been given permission to begin.[3]

The formal promulgation of the council's decree on liturgy, the act that made it universal church law, took place a little over a year later, on December 4, 1963, after even further "nuancing" and rewriting of the document that had been so overwhelmingly approved the previous December. That formal promulgation, however, remained purely a matter of theological interest, discussed primarily by theologians and liturgical scholars, for nine more months, until it was followed by an "Instruction" published by the Holy Office on September 26, 1964, which set out the *practical* implementations of the decree on the parochial level, that is, on the parish level, where the arcane language of theology took on flesh in a way that the ordinary Catholic could see and understand.

It was this Instruction of September 1964, which set the First Sunday of Advent 1964 (less than three months later) as the date by which the decree was to be "practically implemented," that revealed in detailed and practical ways the revolution in Catholic worship that would shortly take place: the priest would now celebrate the Mass facing his congregation rather than lead them in prayer with his back to the nave; significant sections of the Mass like the Gloria and the Our Father would now be recited in the vernacular rather than in the ancient and (more or less) universal language of "church Latin"; the laity would now be encouraged, and even expected, to respond corporately and uniformly to the celebrant rather than participate "mystically" in worship through the silent recitation of private prayers and devotions. In retrospect, John Henry Newman's famous observation after Vatican I — "there has seldom been a council without great confusion after it" — appeared an appropriate understatement to describe the reaction to the 1964 Instruction, although Newman had offered his observation over a century before.[4]

In many respects, the first decree of Vatican II to be popularly implemented was hardly anomalous or surprising, as it had been prepared for by a half-century of Catholic liturgical scholarship and praxis. In 1903, Pope Pius X, hardly a theological or liturgical innovator in any sense, had issued a *motu proprio* (*Tra le Sollecitudini*) condemning abuses in Catholic liturgy and music that isolated the laity from participating intelligently in the Mass. Pius feared that the elaborate but ill-suited use of classical music and a faulty understanding of the dynamics of the Roman Rite had allowed the celebration of the Mass to degenerate in certain places to an irrelevant concert. He thus called for a renewed study of the history of Catholic worship and for a return to the clean, uncluttered music of Gregorian chant for a more reverent and prayerful celebration of the Eucharist. Within a few years, the "Word Method" of plainchant and the "Pius X School of Church Music" — named after this unwitting liturgical prophet — were implementing the pope's liturgical "reforms" throughout the Catholic world.[5]

By 1909, largely in response to Pius's call for an informed Catholic reappraisal of public worship, the modern liturgical movement was born at the Benedictine monastery of Mont Cesar in Belgium, with a regular annual symposium on Catholic worship and chant; Mont Cesar's liturgical discussions, moreover, soon spread to other Benedictine abbeys under the leadership of the great Belgian cardinal and educational leader, Joseph Mercier. Within five years, Abbot Herwegan at Germany's Maria Laach Abbey had initiated a "liturgical week" for scholars interested in exploring the history and dynamics of Catholic worship, and in 1918 Maria Laach sealed its identity as the European intellectual leader of serious liturgical scholarship with the publication of the first volume of *Ecclesia Orans* — the first and perhaps most serious scholarly journal devoted to Catholic liturgics on the Continent.[6]

If the Benedictine monks at Mont Cesar and Maria Laach addressed themselves chiefly to Catholic intellectuals and scholars, however, Fr. Pius Parsch in Austria and Dom Gaspar Lefebvre in France began an enormously effective program of popularizing interest in Catholic worship and liturgical prayer "in the pews." Among the several tools that aided Parsch, Lefebvre, and their liturgical followers in generating popular lay interest in liturgy was the appearance in 1925 of a completely new Catholic devotional aid, the vernacular daily missal, which offered interested laity the opportunity to follow the actions of the Mass by setting out vernacular translations of the prayers of the Mass side-by-side with the Latin. While hardly revolutionary by post–Vatican II liturgical standards, the vernacular missal took the laity by storm and probably constituted the most significant grassroots influence on growing popular interest in liturgical issues.[7]

But the twentieth-century liturgical renewal was not just European in base: during the 1920s an American Benedictine monk from Minnesota's abbey of St. John's, Collegeville — Dom Virgil Michel — had undertaken something of a liturgical pilgrimage to Maria Laach, Mont Cesar, and Solemnes in order to gather ammunition against the "new paganism" that he felt was sweeping America in the years after World War I. What he found there strangely warmed his liturgically oriented Benedictine heart. Sharing with the European leaders of the new liturgical movement the realization that "liturgy" meant significantly more than "sanctuary etiquette," Michel came across what he later termed one of the greatest discoveries of his life — the idea of the church as the "Mystical Body of Christ" — a doctrine practically unheard-of in the United States at the time. As Michel would later promulgate it out of St. John's Abbey, the doctrine of the Mystical Body was expressed liturgically in the church's worship, as well as incarnated socially in the ecclesial community's "corporal works of mercy." In such an understanding of the ancient Pauline metaphor of the *mystici corporis,* then, liturgy, social action, and community were closely intertwined realities that should characterize the "work of Christ" in the world. By 1926, Michel had helped to found both Liturgical Press and the journal *Orate Fratres* at St. John's to implement his new insight of liturgy as the "work" of the Body of Christ. Both of these organs would help make St. John's Abbey the center of the liturgical movement in the English-speaking world. From Michel's abbey a small but influential group of Midwestern German-American priests — Hans Reinhold, Reynold Hillenbrand, Martin Hellriegel — took the lead as pioneers of liturgical renewal in North America. Catholic parishes on both coasts lagged behind the Midwestern parishes pastored by these men, parishes in which the "dialogue Mass" (referred to at the time as the *missa recitata*) was introduced immediately after the September 1958 "Instruction for American Pastors on Sacred Music and Liturgy." These Midwestern pastors, inspired by the ecclesial possibilities opened up by the 1958 Instruction, called on their congregations to resume their role in praying the common acclamations of the liturgy — in Latin, of course — while also sponsoring "Gregorian chant practice" for the congregation just before Mass. By at least 1958, what was called the "liturgical revival" was well underway — five years before Vatican II's first document.[8]

All of these liturgical reforms in the first half of the century notwithstanding, however, the Mass of the Roman Rite in mid-century America was perceived by most Catholics as a ritual not only of ancient provenance, but as something outside time altogether. As Garry Wills has recounted in his sweet (and often bitter) reminiscence of "Memories of a Catholic Boyhood," most American Catholics in 1964 still understood the celebration of the Mass to be defined by the "endless roll of *in saecula saeculorums*" that ended most of the prayers spoken by the priest:

> [This] was borne in on us by the unanchored, anachronistic style (or mix of styles) in all things the church did. Going into a Catholic church in our day, one might think history was a rummage sale, and this place had been fitted out after visits to the sale. Here one century, there another, and all jumbled together. In the drone of Latin, sudden gabbles of Greek. Ancient titles (*Pontifex Maximus*) and an ancient familiarity of address (*Paul* our Pope, and *Laurence* our Bishop).[9]

Most Catholics took it for granted that what they did on Sunday mornings looked like what the church had always done. The dramaturgy of High Mass, the seasonal Latin prayers accumulated over centuries, the complex Divine Office chanted in monasteries — "all these were things as tangible, for cherishing, as cathedrals or basilicas."[10]

The "September Instruction" of 1964 implementing the changes of Vatican II, therefore, represented innovation on an entirely new order of scale compared to anything seen in centuries — even more dramatic than the publication of Pius V's *Missale Romanum* in 1570, which had "standardized" the various styles in which the Roman Rite had been celebrated for a millennium into one "universal rite," concomitantly freezing Catholic public worship for four centuries. Indeed, if Vatican II can be rightly described as "the most important event in the history of the Roman Catholic Church since the Protestant Reformation," then the liturgical reforms mandated by that council can be cogently perceived as the most neuralgic issue facing Catholics on the parish level in modern times.[11]

The American Catholic bishops, under the progressive leadership of Detroit Archbishop John Dearden, worried about the effect of all of this even before the implementation of the changes began — worries expressed in a public manner unusual for the American hierarchy, which had attempted throughout its history to keep Catholic "family business" out of the public view. Thus, the resolutely progressive

National Catholic Reporter — still in its first year of published existence — reported about a month before the mandated changes were to go into effect that "the American Bishops' Commission on the Liturgical Apostolate has warned that there is the 'greatest possibility of scandal...' in the new English usage in the Mass." Similarly, *The Critic,* a sophisticated and informed Catholic "lay" journal that had followed the course of Vatican II with largely sympathetic reports, warned in its October/November 1964 issue that many American Catholics "will go to Mass next Sunday and see precious little evidence of the pentecostal revolution promulgated by the fathers of the Second Vatican Council.... I guess you don't 'promulgate' a revolution."[12]

Many Catholics, in fact, coming "home" to the Mass on the First Sunday of Advent 1964, "found it a strange house, cluttered with signs of alien occupancy." Centuries-old taboos and childhood memories of nuns' injunctions were suddenly — and traumatically — overturned: Catholics were now asked to do things against which elaborate inhibitions had been built up all their lives. A great part of the old liturgy had taken the form of "progressive obeisance" to a thing untouchable in ordinary ways, a hierarchic dance arranged around the eucharistic Host — "bowings, liftings, displayings, and hidings of it." All of that was now to be progressively banished to the sounds of guitars, the sudden appearance of banners, and an easy familiarity with the "bread of celebration" that left many Catholics reeling between confusion and feelings of betrayal. Thus, in an article in early 1965, a predictable range of complaints — aesthetic, devotional, theological — found voice. One woman complained that Catholic organists simply weren't accustomed to playing for congregational accompaniment, so that they "drag along and force the people to precede them or play so loudly that the people can't hear their own voices." Another discontented parishioner reported that his parish had

> a fellow who stands in front of the church and tells us when to stand, when to sit, when to kneel. It made me so mad I couldn't think about anything else.... I found another parish where they don't have an interlocutor saying, "Gentlemen, be seated."[13]

Father Gommar De Pauw, a Belgian-born priest in the Baltimore archdiocese, founded the "Catholic Traditionalist movement" in protest of the "new Mass" (sic) just eight weeks after the liturgy changes began to be implemented. De Pauw, destined to become the first and possibly most famous liturgical protester later in the decade, claimed that his conservative crusade had the backing of thirty American bishops as

well as high-placed Vatican officials. But De Pauw went considerably
beyond simply questioning the implementation or aesthetics of the
new rite: he denounced the "new Mass" introduced on Advent Sunday
1964 as the work of "extremist advisors to the bishops," a work that
threatened to "Protestantize the Catholic Church unless repudiated."
Among the "extremists" named by De Pauw in a news conference
on Easter Sunday 1965, were progressive theologians Gregory Baum,
Hans Küng, Bernard Häring, and John Courtney Murray — of a group
unlikely to agree on anything, much less the unified undermining of
the orthodox worship of the Western Church. Nonetheless, De Pauw
averred that the changes were extorted from the bishops by these theological traitors who "told the bishops that Catholics were tired of their
Catholic religion and have got to have something new." Against this
cabal of theological extremists, De Pauw called for an "Easter appeal
for theological sanity" — a massive national write-in through which
Catholics were urged to protest the new liturgy to their bishops: "This
is the American democratic way of freedom."[14]

The negative publicity generated by figures like De Pauw, of course,
made good copy in both the religious and the secular press, so that
the casual reader might very well infer that the First Sunday of Advent in 1964 unleashed a near-universal tide of complaints against the
new liturgy among the American Catholic faithful. But in fact many
Catholics — especially priests, liturgy enthusiasts, and "liberal" lay
people[15] — felt that the new "semi-reformed" Mass was well over-
due, and did not go far or fast enough. Thus, a letter published
during the spring during which the changes were being implemented
noted that "I fail to see anything in today's Mass worthy of the title
'changed.' It would seem more likely that the *other wing of the Church*
would rise in anger over the bones thrown to us after listening to the
pronouncements of the great new Mass which would revitalize our
worship." Likewise, Monsignor J. D. Conway, functioning as something like a clerical Ann Landers in his regular column in the *National
Catholic Reporter,* "The Question Box," answered an inquiry about
the changes from a distraught reader with a touch of impatience the
very week they were introduced: "My earliest memories of high Mass
center around the meaningless and threateningly endless repetition of
Latin words, sung to cheap and gaudy music by a mediocre choir
while the congregation sat in silent boredom. My earliest Communions were concerned more with the integrity of the fast than with
the joy of union with my savior." Father Joseph Nolan, answering
questions a month after "the changes" were introduced in an article

entitled "Questions and Answers by a Pastor Not at All Happy with
Half-Vernacular Mass," announced that the changes in the celebration
of the Eucharist were embarrassingly incomplete, as at least half of the
liturgy was still in a language most Catholics could not understand:

> I have always agreed with St. Paul that "I would rather speak five
> words which my mind utters for your instruction than ten thou-
> sand in a strange tongue." But I don't want to speak five lines in
> English which they understand and then five lines in Latin which
> they don't. It's like a runner going over hurdles. Every three steps
> there's a barrier.[16]

More dramatically than any other event in the postwar era (with
the possible exception of Pope Paul VI's 1968 encyclical condemning
all "artificial" forms of birth control), the new liturgy implemented
on Advent Sunday 1964 helped to shape new cultural nuances of
"being Catholic" in America on a number of fronts: for the first
time in their history, American Catholics could now be labeled as
"liberal" or "conservative" — prefixes largely unknown in the pre–
Vatican II Catholic world — based on (among other things) their
reception of the mandated liturgical changes; likewise, for the first time
since the condemnation of the "phantom heresy" of Americanism in
1899, American Catholics could now consciously address the question
of how "relevant" or inculturated their religious symbols and ritual
should be in the Land of the Pilgrims; for the first time in the lives
of most adult Catholics, questions of what "Eucharist" and "public
prayer" actually meant were presented as real, live issues that could
be asked and debated in print and in parish council meetings. The
harsh questions of modernity, so long seemingly held at bay outside
the strong fortress of Holy Mother Church, now pounded at the door,
and demanded attention.

Thus, while many Catholics welcomed the "reformed" liturgy introduced at the end of 1964 like water in an arid desert, other
Catholics used "betrayal" language to describe their new worship —
betrayal language often of a particularly fierce kind. Whole forests,
of course, have been decimated to provide books accounting for the
new "divide" over worship that emerged in 1964 and the fierce ex-
changes fired from both sides of the divide: some of these accounts
have attempted to situate the new liturgy as emerging seamlessly from
the liturgical impulses set in motion at the beginning of the century and pressed by Parsch, Michel, and Hellriegel and the *Nouvelle
Théologie;* others have lamented the liturgical changes as a hasty and

ill-thought-out "quick fix" for the perceived threats of modernization and secularization in western Europe and North America. Both accounts, and many others, have their supporters. An equally fruitful but perhaps less heated approach to evaluating the "wars over the Mass" unleashed on Advent Sunday 1964 would be to consider the liturgical changes of 1964 from the standpoint of the sociological theory classically embodied in Emile Durkheim's *Elementary Forms of the Religious Life*. For while Durkheim's foundational work in sociology has been challenged and nuanced by social scientists of both the "left" and the "right," it nonetheless offers a lucid and accessible starting point for accounting for *both* the supporters and detractors of Vatican II's reformed liturgy.[17]

Lex Orandi Lex Credendi

Durkheim noted in the conclusion of his seminal work on the role of religion in human societies that many "theorists" account for religion in explicitly *rational* terms; that is, for many students of the phenomenon, religion is

> above all else a *system of ideas*, corresponding to a determined object. This object has been conceived in a multitude of ways: nature, the infinite, the unknowable, the ideal, etc.; but these differences matter but little. In any case, it was the *conceptions* and *beliefs* which were considered as the essential elements of religion. As for the rites, from this point of view they appear to be only an external translation, contingent and material, of these internal states which alone pass as having any intrinsic value.[18]

But Durkheim goes on to observe that such an essentially "cerebral" definition of religion rarely rings true for most "believers," for those who actually live the religious life and have a direct sensation of what it *really* is. For such as these, Durkheim notes, the real function (and definition) of religion has little to do with making us *think* or enriching our knowledge of the epistemic structures of the world. Rather, for most believers, religion's purpose and true definition is to make human beings *act,* to aid them in living. An idea, Durkheim reminds his readers, is really only *part* of ourselves. However creative and rich any idea might be, it can "add nothing to our natural vitality." The believer who has encountered the holy is thus not merely one who "sees new truths of which the unbeliever is ignorant; he is a man who is stronger. He is saved from evil." As he then dryly observes, "it is hard to see how a mere idea could have this efficacy." Indeed,

> from the mere fact that we consider an object worthy of being loved and sought after, it does not follow that we feel ourselves stronger afterwards. For that, it is not enough that we think of them; it is also indispensable that we place ourselves within their sphere of action. In a word, it is necessary that we *act*, and that we repeat the acts thus necessary every time we feel the need of renewing their effects. From this point of view, it is readily seen how that group of regularly repeated acts which form the cult get their importance.[19]

Durkheim then offers what remains one of the most brilliant social scientific rationales for understanding the role of liturgy and ritual in religious systems: as every believer well knows, he asserts, it is the *cult* — the act and ritual of worship — that offers the locus for religious experience. It is the act of worship itself which offers the believer the "experiential proof of his beliefs" — the impressions of joy and ecstasy, of serenity and enthusiasm. Indeed, the "cult," he announces, is not merely, or even primarily

> a system of signs by which the faith is outwardly translated; it is a *collection of the means by which this is created and recreated periodically....* We admit that these religious beliefs rest upon a *specific experience* whose demonstrative value is, in one sense, not one bit inferior to that of scientific experiments, although different from them. Thus is explained the preponderating role of the cult in all religions, whichever they may be. This is because society cannot make its influence felt unless it is in action, and it is not in action unless the individuals who compose it are assembled together and act in common. It is by common action that it takes consciousness of itself and realizes its position; it is before all else an active cooperation. *The collective ideas and sentiments are even possible only owing to these exterior movements which symbolize them.* Then it is action which dominates the religious life, because of the mere fact that it is society which is its source.[20]

Durkheim's understanding of the relationship of religious beliefs to ritual, then, involves considerably more than simply asserting that "rituals" embody "beliefs," or that worship is merely or even partially a public expression of preexisting or philosophical ideas about the Holy. On the contrary, it is the precise opposite that really defines the relationship of belief to worship: it is the experience of the Holy in worship and prayer that gives rise to, and interprets, beliefs about the Holy. Such a (Durkheimian) understanding of religious systems thus rests — and, to a large extent, derives — religious "belief" from religious "experience," especially from the communal experience of liturgy and ritual that Durkheim calls "cult."

Durkheim here might very well be read as offering a social scientific version of one of the most ancient and revered Christian dictums about the origin and role of theology offered by the fifth-century theologian and papal secretary Prosper of Aquitaine: *lex orandi lex credendi,* literally, "the law of praying founds the law of believing." More colloquially put, this patristic dictum states that the dynamics of *worship (lex orandi)* form the true heart and locus of all Christian theology, and that the beliefs or ideas of the Holy — expressed in even the most abstruse and "disembodied" *lex credendi* (literally, "law of belief") such as doctrines about the Trinity of the Godhead, the dual natures of Christ, and the mode of Christ's presence in the eucharistic elements of bread and wine — are really the attempts to account for the concrete *experience of worship.* Prosper of Aquitaine's famous phrase about the "laws" of worship and believing thus asserts that experience precedes theologizing, that doctrine must be tested by communal worship, and that the manner of praying shapes the manner of believing. Important — and ancient — stuff, this.[21]

The implications of both Durkheim's and Prosper's insight for understanding the First Sunday of Advent 1964, quite obviously, are rather interesting: if worship shapes belief, and experience forms doctrine, then the "changes" mandated in worship by the Second Vatican Council represented something considerably more dramatic and profound than simply "updating" the liturgy by changing some words and gestures during the celebration of Mass. If the church's own self-understanding — its "ecclesial identity," in the language of formal theology — ultimately derives from, and is centered on, its communal worship (as both Durkheim and Prosper of Aquitaine insisted it did), then *changing* that worship would ineluctably and irresistibly sponsor a theological *rethinking* of ecclesial identity, a rethinking that was further supported by the council's privileged definition of the church: the "people of God." Thus, while good Pope John and the vast majority of bishops conceived of the first document to issue from their ecumenical council, *Sacrosanctum Concilium,* as being more pastoral and "gradualist" than dogmatic and radical, they were soon to discover the error of their beliefs.

Viewed from such a patristic/Durkheimian perspective, perhaps both the "conservatives" who opposed the new Mass and the "liberals" who assiduously welcomed it more clearly intuited the "stakes" involved in the liturgical changes than the church leaders who mandated the reforms while asserting that nothing had changed, that the church was still the church, and that a mere updating in public worship represented a "no tears" *aggiornamento,* a mere "opening of the windows." For those who cherished the fortress-like peace provided by Catholicism on the battle-scarred plains of modernity, the "new Mass" was perceived as the Trojan horse through which the secure, medieval walls of Holy Mother Church would be breached; for those who sought a closer engagement of the church with the intellectual and social problems of contemporary civilization, the new liturgy represented the best opportunity in four hundred years to "modernize" the church by providing (almost literally) a "new experience of God." In the event, both groups were arguably more prescient than liturgists and bishops who believed that worship could be "updated" while retaining the older theology and ecclesial self-identity largely unchanged. As Yves Congar noted with the authority of a prophet at the time that the Constitution on the Sacred Liturgy was overwhelmingly passed by the bishops of the council, "something irreversible has happened in the Church."

"Coming Home" in Advent 1964

The Vatican Instruction of September 26, 1964 — the canonical "instrument" that concretely implemented the liturgical changes implied in *Sacrosanctum Concilium* — sought a gradual, well-explained process "restoring" the Mass. In his *motu proprio* of January 25, 1964, Pope John XXIII's successor in the Chair of Peter, Paul VI, had announced that the Vatican Council's first document to be promulgated would become the universal law of the church on February 16, 1964; Paul further set September of 1964 as the date by which the official committee (*concilium* in canon, or church, law) deputed to oversee the liturgical changes would issue its formal directive setting out the timetable and nature of the changes. This *Concilium,* an international body made up of scholars and bishops from around the Catholic world and ranking in authority above even the official Roman Congregations, thus issued its formal directive, or "instruction," on implementing the changes on September 26 with the authority of the pope himself, as well as with the approbation of Cardinal Larraona, prefect of the Vatican Congregation of Rites.[22]

The Instruction itself sought to be strongly pastoral in tone and aims, stating in its opening paragraph that both clergy and laity would profit fully from the renewal only if they were offered a "deep understanding of what the Church requires and a genuine willingness to put its directives into practice." Moreover, the "restoration" of the liturgy that it took as its aim was to be carried on "gradually, in stages," a policy strongly endorsed by the bishops of the United States. The first "stage" of this restoration was to involve the introduction of some vernacular (English in the U.S.) into the first part of the Mass, as well as certain other "innovations" that would have the force of universal church law by March 7, 1965. But the First Sunday of Advent — the day that began the church's liturgical year — was set as the date by which parishes were to begin implementation of the Instruction's "restoration." Other changes would occur as the liturgical year unfolded toward Advent Sunday 1965.[23]

Both the pastoral tone and gradualist timetable of the Instruction notwithstanding, however, the nature of the changes mandated held the seeds for both a liturgical and an ecclesial revolution. Over against the rigid and quite precise rubrical directions of the Tridentine Mass celebrated by Catholics of the Roman Rite since 1570, the "new rite" outlined in the September Instruction opened up a number of choices, alternatives, and variations, especially in the first part of the Mass, the "Liturgy of the Word." Concretely, this meant that more of the details shaping what would actually go on at the front of the church were left to the judgment and responsibility of the individual pastor and celebrant and would not be "set" for every celebration. Perhaps most dramatically and certainly first in the order of "new things noticed" on just entering the church building, the altar which formed the locus of attention of all present for the celebration was now to be "pulled away" from the wall, so that the priest would face the congregation rather than stand with his back to the people — a simple logistical move that, while restoring liturgical practice of the twentieth century to the tradition of the early church, overturned the style of worship that had obtained for over a thousand years. Who, many Catholics would soon ask, was being "addressed" in the rite? And on "whose side" was the priest: representing the congregation before God, or standing *in persona Christi* (and thus on the "side" of God) before the gathered people? Moreover, the logistical rearrangement also meant that the priest-celebrant had to "clean up his act," as now the entire congregation (and not only the altar boys and, presumably, God) could detect "goof-ups" in the choreography of the celebration. Among other things, this dealt a death blow to generations of altar boy stories about liturgical snafus.[24]

The second, equally dramatic change that immediately struck worshipers once the celebration of the liturgy commenced on Advent Sunday 1964 was that significant sections of the rite were now conducted in the vernacular rather than in the ancient argot of "Church Latin" — a change that rivaled only the "turning of the altars" in its long-term significance. Rather than carrying on private devotions against the often barely audible mumble of Latin by the priest or the music sung by a choir, worshipers were now to be engaged in their own language and asked to do quite specific acts ("Let us pray") that demanded attention on their part.[25]

But other, equally significant if less dramatic, changes would greet worshipers during the course of the rite: in contrast to the quiet organ "background music" marking preconciliar celebrations of the Eucharist, most parish masses would now be punctuated by regular (if sometimes faint) congregational hymns. Indeed, within twenty years of the "changes," over 90 percent of all Sunday masses in the United States, and 70 percent of Saturday evening celebrations, had at least some congregational singing. While such an innovation might appear minor or insignificant to non-Catholics, hymn-singing itself — and the nature of the hymns sung — would emerge in the decade after the liturgical renewal as one of the most neuralgic points of parochial battles over communal worship. To the devout accustomed to the familiar and comforting world of Catholic popular devotions to the Virgin Mary and one's "household saints" — devotions widely performed on Sunday morning during Mass against the "background noise" of murmured Latin at the altar — the sudden "intrusion" of congregational singing appeared foreign, even suspiciously Protestant. No longer the familiar round of inaudible petitions and thank-yous offered to holy ones for favors sought and received against the solemn if unaccessible background of Holy Mother Church's "Great Prayer," of which the priest was often the only person present paying full attention; now everyone was asked (and expected) to participate "fully and prayerfully."[26]

Moreover, familiar parts of the Mass were dropped or changed on that First Sunday of Advent: the long psalm that constituted the heart of the "Prayers at the Foot of the Altar" — said by the priest cele-

brating the Mass in a low, inaudible voice while facing the altar —
was dropped entirely, thus emphasizing at the very opening of the liturgy the *public,* communal nature of the celebration, as opposed to
an essentially private understanding of the Mass held by many Catholics (including priests); the biblical readings that constituted the heart
of the first part of the celebration, the Liturgy of the Word, were to
be now permitted to be read by a lay "lector" (as opposed to being read by the priest himself), and read in the vernacular (English),
instead of in Latin, thus foregrounding the biblically based nature
of the worship; the readings assigned for the day, and especially the
gospel, were to provide the basis for the homily preached by the celebrant, thus sponsoring a more scriptural (as opposed to doctrinal,
"disciplinary," or financial) weekly application of the Tradition to the
lives of the faithful. The ancient "secret prayers" that punctuated the
Mass, which had always been whispered by the celebrant, were now
to be either "chanted or recited in a loud voice," signaling an end to
an understanding of the rite as a "duet" between the celebrant and
God which the congregation was allowed to witness as a silent and
awe-filled audience; the "propers" of the Mass that had always been
sung by the choir or recited by the celebrant alone — the Gloria, the
Creed, the Agnus Dei — were now mandated to be recited or sung by
the entire congregation, who were no longer signaled to sit while the
choir sang glorious Mozart or Byrd renditions of "Glory to God in
the Highest."[27]

The immediate response to the changes in many (if not most)
parishes in the United States at the end of 1964 and in the early
months of the new year appears to have been dutiful compliance
with singularly few episodes of outraged sensibilities: Catholics, whatever else they might have in common, were accustomed to obeying
church authorities dutifully, and the initial reaction was shaped by
that dutifulness. As the author of a perceptive article published in
The Critic magazine in early 1965 noted, most polls taken by diocesan newspapers to measure the initial response to the changes in the
Mass revealed that most Catholics were neutral or approved of the
"new liturgy." But the joy inspired by such polls among promoters of
the changes, he averred, was somewhat premature, evincing perhaps
that liturgists and church leaders had lost touch with the "ordinary
people," or at least misunderstood them:

> The people approve of the liturgical changes because they are the
> result of the decisions of the Council Fathers — and for the ordi-

nary Catholic in the U.S., this is enough. What the Church wants, they want. Some are happier than others about the changes, but all share in what I believe to be the prevalent mood in the laity in the Church in the United States today — they are a little bewildered, frustrated, and, if not dissatisfied, *unsatisfied* by all that has happened.[28]

Such a construal of lay reaction to the changes in the Mass would appear to be borne out in at least some American parishes, as evinced in the "preparation" for the new Mass announced by the pastor of a suburban New Jersey parish the week before the new rite would be introduced: this took the form of a simple announcement that, "as some of you are probably aware, there will begin next Sunday the implementation of a series of changes in the Mass issued by the Holy See." After outlining with breathtaking brevity the most dramatic of those changes — the Mass said in English, the singing of hymns in the vernacular, responses expected from the pews — the pastor ended his "preparation of the People of God" by simply announcing that "we realize that this will be difficult for many of you, but realize that this is the will of the Holy Father, the Vatican Council and his Excellency [the local bishop], and we know we can count on your fine cooperation just as we have so many times in the past."[29]

Not every parish, however, experienced the same level of bewilderment and frustration, or at the same time. Some parishes under liturgically progressive pastors — like Sacred Heart, a self-described "hootenanny" parish in Warrensburg, Missouri — had begun to implement the changes well before the mandated date of Advent Sunday, so that changes had become fairly familiar by the end of 1964, at least to its regular parishioners. For visiting Catholics, however, or those "on the road" popping in to fulfill their "Sunday obligation," this often led to genuine confusion and humor. As a reporter featuring the parish in the October 28, 1964, issue of the *National Catholic Reporter* noted at the opening of his article, "hardly a Sunday goes by, say the ushers, but a stranger will nervously edge up to one of them during Mass and whisper, 'Pardon me, but is this a Catholic church?'" Likewise, the friends of the pastor of Sacred Heart, Msgr. Ernest Fiedler, jokingly congratulated him for the fact that their parish was "getting more Protestant every day."[30]

The journalist reporting on this progressive Midwestern parish in the *NCR* a little over a month before every parish in the U.S. was to initiate similar changes offered an optative portrait of the place in the midst of change: randomly questioning parishioners after the Sunday masses, he found that most offered surprisingly reflective positive responses. Thus Pearl DeBacker, the wife of the town florist and a parishioner for twenty-five years, said: "I like it. Some people didn't like it at first, but it's been gradually building up like this. Now I can't think of anybody that doesn't like it." Her son accompanying her to Mass that morning opined, however, "You should have talked to her six months ago. She'd have given you an earful. She hated it." And the reporter confessed at the end of his "report from the front lines" that, to the parishioners "the changes may or may not have seemed gradual. To a newcomer they're almost head-reeling."[31]

Other Catholics, sympathetic to certain aspects of De Pauw's plaints but too well-schooled in parochial docility to carry placards outside churches, lamented the speed, manner, and style of the changes in print and in parish meetings. Thus one rather muted but prescient critic observed in May of 1965 that it was "practically heresy to say so, but a case can be made that the victory of the 'litniks' at the first session of the council came too quickly and was achieved by the wrong means. It was largely a victory of intellect." But such an intellectual victory in no way guaranteed that the changes would be effective in "updating" the worship of the church. The critic admitted that "worship needs theory," but also noted that, finally, worship itself is not theory, but an art. The priest at the altar is of necessity an artist — whether a good artist or a bad one. "It's not a matter of being graceful or clumsy, or of merely looking pious, but of engaging all one's powers in an act of great consequence. . . . Needless to say, this has not been the standard approach to worship in the recent past in the Catholic Church."[32]

Further, the anonymous critic offered a rather profound observation on the practical implications of all the changes: "passage of the Constitution [on the Liturgy] meant *acceptance of a radical change in Catholic piety.*" Thus, from the First Sunday of Advent 1964 on, there appeared to be a small but growing minority of Catholics who recognized the larger implications of the mandated changes: that changed worship sponsored changed piety, and possibly something even more profound. Even those sympathetic to such a change of piety (as many of the critics of the mandated changes were) realized that such a seismic change couldn't be rushed and entailed traumatic changes in spirituality and belief for the faithful. It would be in the decade *after* 1964 that the genuinely acrimonious "battles over the Mass" would emerge, between Catholic "traditionalists," centrists, and a newly defined "left wing" of liturgical experimenters in places like St. Paul's Chapel at Columbia University and the Newman Center at the University of California at Berkeley.[33]

Even Thomas Merton — arguably the major figure in making the postwar "Religious Revival" accessible to American Catholics and himself drawn to the Trappist order by (among other things) the austerely beautiful, centuries-old chant of the Divine Office — called for a "gentle touch" in enforcing the new liturgical changes. Merton argued in the November 1964 issue of *The Critic* that "liturgical reform merely from the top down, renewal by juridical fiat alone, is not likely to work." Merton, soon to emerge as one of the most vocal "progressives" in matters of theology and spirituality, opined that the liturgical renewal sought by the church really meant the replacement of constraint with the "openness of simple and joyous participation," rather than by a new "legalism of the left," which he cannily recognized to be waiting in the wings:

> The new liturgy, like the old, can become static unless Catholics respond openly and spontaneously. Whatever continues to foster rigidity, suspiciousness, timidity, coldness and resentment is going to threaten the liturgical reform with sterility. The great enemy is constraint, which brings all these other devils with it.[34]

As in so much else, Merton's concerns proved to be quite prescient: the spirit of the old legalism, which viewed most of the church's great questions to be already answered in static terms, hardly died a sudden death in Rome at the council. Further, and far more to the point, the "victory of the intellect" achieved by the solid scholarship of liturgical scholars and theologians and blessed by the universal episcopate at Vatican II, would not be implemented into a "victory of renewed piety" by a simple juridical fiat from the top down — even a fiat issued from a *concilium* constituted by the pope himself. For the changes contained within them much else besides the mere "renewal" of a Catholic identity and theology believed to be essentially unchanged and unchangeable by most of the bishops who so overwhelmingly voted for them in December 1962. For this very reason, many of those same bishops who so fulsomely supported the promise of renewal at the first session of the council would emerge as its sharpest critics within a few decades of its close.

Council "progressives" like Joseph Ratzinger (within twenty years to be appointed cardinal prefect of the Holy Office, the Vatican's "second-in-command" figure) and Bishop Karol Wojtyla (elected Pope John Paul II fourteen years after the council) would, within a short time, become sharp critics of the "excesses" — liturgical and other — that seemed to proceed from Vatican II's "reforms." The "Restorationist" movement that would emerge in the two decades after the council as the rallying center for "conservative" interpreters of Vatican II's purposes and aims would be led by many former progressive figures hailed during the council's sessions between 1962 and 1965 as voices spearheading reform. This new Restorationist loyalty on the part of so many former supporters of Vatican II, in fact, did not necessarily represent either a "move to the right" theologically (as some ecclesiastical pundits claimed) or a loss of faith in the council's purposes of renewal and reform (as others averred). In part, at least, the new loyalties of these conciliar "progressives" can be fruitfully read as a belated but quite vivid realization that *lex orandi* does indeed shape and determine *lex credendi* in ways that the council fathers never dreamed.[35]

Like Miss Haversham's House

As Garry Wills (himself not an unbiased commentator on the post-conciliar Catholic world) noted in his memoir-cum-critique published in 1971, all of the seemingly historically researched and pastorally inspired liturgical changes mandated by the September 1964 Vatican Instruction carried with them profound epistemological and psychological implications that would help to sponsor an ecclesial revolution in the decades after the council. The "updating" of the Roman Rite that motivated the thousand-plus bishops and cardinals who endorsed the promulgation of *Sacrosanctum Concilium* in December 1962 carried within itself the seeds of significant changes in piety, discourse, and attitudes toward church authority that were unforeseen and unwelcome by most of the council's strongest supporters. Perhaps most disturbingly for the average Catholic in the pews, the liturgical "updating" introduced to most U.S. parishes on the First Sunday of Advent 1964

> let out the dirty little secret, in the most startling symbolic way, the fact that *the church changes.* No more neat ahistorical belief that what one did on Sunday morning looked (with minor adjustments) like what the church had always done, from the time of the catacombs. All that lying eternity and arranged air of timelessness (as in Mae West's vestmented and massive pose) was shattered. The house with arrested clocks, like Miss Haversham's

Satis House, collapsed, by reverse dilapidation, out of death's security into uncertain life.[36]

And the trajectory of the "uncertain life" born on that Sunday morning in 1964, as the next decade would reveal with unnerving clarity, proved to be difficult to contain or control. Quite by accident — or providentially, for those inclined to an Augustinian view of the world — the implementation of the "changes" mandated by the Second Vatican Council coincided with the emergence of cultural and political movements in the United States (the civil rights movement, the feminist awakening, the "Free Speech" movement on university campuses) that helped to sponsor a feeling among Catholics (and among many other Americans as well) that the "center was not holding," that the "givens" in an uncertain world were themselves collapsing. The resulting uncertain life was, for many if not most American Catholics, both exhilarating and unnerving at the same time.[37]

It is now almost something of a truism to assert that the Second Vatican Council, in its plethora of metaphors describing the Christian community in its most significant theological statement, the Dogmatic Constitution on the Church (*Lumen Gentium*), "privileged" a new and biblically based metaphor in describing Christ's Church: that of the "People of God." Certainly older and revered descriptions of Holy Mother Church — sheepfold, Body of Christ, bride, institution, etc. — appeared in the document, but "People of God" stood out as a new and important metaphor in the document. Indeed, this new metaphor — at least this metaphor as understood by some of the council's supporters — appeared to challenge Cardinal Bellarmine's classic Counter-Reformation definition of the church as a "perfect society."

Cardinal Robert Bellarmine — arguably the greatest and certainly the most influential ecclesiologist in the Catholic firmament between the sixteenth-century Council of Trent and the Second Vatican Council — had adumbrated a resolutely visible and ahistorical definition of Christ's "True Church" that had defined Catholic discussions for close to four centuries. Protestant theologians, starting with Luther, had offered essentially "mystical" definitions of the church — as "the faithful company of all true believers" — to account for the true church's troubling "invisibility" during the long centuries of papal autocracy: not for Bellarmine (or for Counter-Reformation Roman Catholicism) so amorphous and disembodied an identity. Taking its cue and its phrases from one of Bellarmine's most famous essays, Roman Catholicism for nearly four centuries had defined itself theologically as a *societas perfecta* — a "perfect society" — embodied institutionally and historically in the person of the pope, and those clergy and laity in union with him. By definition, such a society (as "perfect") stood above the vicissitudes of historical change and accident: the church was alarmingly visible, specific, and unchanging, known by its structure and government, and possessed the fulness of authority to judge ideas and nations. Holy Mother Church, as the *Baltimore Catechism* assured generations of Catholic school children, could "neither deceive nor be deceived." The Church was a hierarchical *institution* with laws and power structures that governed with the authority of Christ himself: *Tu es Petrus* — "You are Peter" — the Sistine Choir sang as the pope was carried into St. Peter's Basilica on great feasts. The ambiguity was almost nonexistent here.[38]

Vatican II appeared to privilege a very different, significantly more ambiguous, metaphor for understanding the mystery of the Christian community in history. Eschewing both the rigid, essentialist definitions and the juridical, scholastic categories of the post-Reformation era, Vatican II showed a marked preference for biblical metaphors and historically contextualized language. Instead of beginning with a discussion of the structures and government of the church's centralized hierarchy, as both Bellarmine and Vatican Council I had done, it began with the notion of the church as a "people on pilgrimage" with whom God communicates, in love and in judgment. Indeed, before its consideration of the hierarchical structure of the church's government in Chapter III of *Lumen Gentium,* it offered a quite remarkable discussion of Christ's holy church in Chapter II as the "People of God":

> Among all the nations there is but one People of God, which takes its citizens from every race, making them citizens of a kingdom which is of a heavenly and not an earthly nature. For all the faithful scattered throughout the world are in communion with each other in the Holy Spirit.... In virtue of this catholicity each individual part of the Church contributes through its special gifts to the good of the other parts and of the whole Church.[39]

In the view of some historians of the postconciliar Roman Church, both the nature and the trajectory of the language of this constitution, in synergy with massive culture-wide movements in the West for racial and gender rights, helped to sponsor a revolution in Catholic identity throughout the 1960s and well into the next decade. The council's dogmatic constitution, in such a reading of the Catholic redaction of the "1960s," provides the "smoking gun" for understanding the unrest and debates of the decades after the council. "The People of God," in such an interpretation, came to embody the egalitarian promise of the council's theological *aggiornamento,* with disastrous results for Cardinal Bellarmine's definition of "church."

The problem with this interpretation of the council and its products (like *Lumen Gentium*) is that it presumes that ordinary Catholics, even well-educated ones, read and understood the theology of Roman-promulgated documents and organized their lives accordingly. Such an interpretation of the "effects of the council" rests on a rather simplistic appropriation of intellectual history, which presumes that ideas by themselves change history, that dominant intellectual constructs reshape historical actors and institutions more than other factors, and that one can understand cultural change simply by reading official documents promulgated by "hierarchies." Ideas, as any historian of culture or religion will readily admit, have profound historical ramifications; but ideas alone, as most historians will also admit, cannot "explain" history to the exclusion of other factors. Indeed, in the realm of religion, as both Durkheim and Prosper of Aquitaine argue, "ideas" might very well rank somewhat lower than "ritual experience" in explaining significant changes in religious belief and self-understanding.

The potentially revolutionary nature of the council's formulation of the church as "People of God" was most probably unclearly grasped by most of the council fathers in 1962 — a safe bet, given the essentially conservative understanding most of them had of "ecclesial reform" at the time. An even safer bet is the assertion that the implications of this new ecclesiological model remained opaque and ignored by the vast majority of Catholics unschooled in the niceties of church definitions. If one wants to bet at all, the safest (and most ironic) bet is to see the "revolution" unleashed by the council — at least on the parish level of Catholicism, where the majority of the church's faithful lived and understood their faith — as most likely set off by the council's document on the liturgy, which offered a new experience of "what they were about" for many, if not most, Catholics.

The September Instruction of 1964, implementing on the parish level "reforms" in worship, quite literally offered new experiences of the Holy, of the religious community, and of themselves. Gone was the sense of timeless ritual — of stepping into eternity or at least into the bygone era of *in illo tempore* ("at that time [of Jesus]"); gone was the awe-filled distance between the laity, lost in their private prayers, with the priest facing alone the living God on the "other side" of the altar rail; gone was mysterious "official" language of prayer with its unseen and unseeable rituals tended by "professionals." Like the opening of the windows to let the streaming sunlight into Miss Haversham's house, which instantaneously destroyed the timeless, death-defying world of her jilted wedding day decades before, all of that former world was now gone. Out of death's security, an uncertain life rushed in with the sunlight.

As Durkheim so brilliantly recognized in studying the religious life, it was not the "ideas" unleashed by Vatican II so much as the actual *experience* it offered to the previously docile faithful in worship that shaped a new religious self-understanding of themselves as the People of God. As he observed so well in talking of the seminal role of "ritual" in the religious life,

> Society cannot make its influence felt unless it is in action, and it is not in action unless the individuals who compose it are assembled together and act in common. It is by common action that [the community] takes consciousness of itself and realizes its position; it is before all else an active cooperation. The collective ideas and sentiments are even possible only owing to these exterior movements which symbolize them. Then it is action which dominates the religious life.[40]

The "specific experience" of the Holy implemented by the September 1964 Instruction, the "common action" that defined the Catholic community's consciousness of itself, was different from that of the 1570 Missal of Pius V, with profound implications for the stability of that older static theology: all the baptized faithful, now facing each other at liturgy, were, in the deepest sense, "priests" and ministers; all the faithful, as members of one body, stood under Christ's command to preach the gospel to every creature; all of the faithful recognized that the "mystery of faith" referred to something more profound than an unknown, foreign tongue in addressing the Holy One. The *lex credendi* — the "law of belief" about the nature of the church, a law that Prosper of Aquitaine recognized as being so profoundly shaped by ritual experience — was now powerfully reshaped by a new *lex orandi*. The older, static, juridical identity of "church" described by Cardinal Bellarmine that had served the Roman Catholicism so well (and ill) in the centuries after the Reformation was now reexperienced as, in some sense, untrue to experience.

As in so much else defining American Catholic history in the decades after 1945, there is much of the ironic in this unlooked-for and unwelcome effect of good Pope John's "opening of the windows": the Spirit, blowing where It willed, appeared to have blown down the supporting walls of the Counter-Reformation church, much to the surprise of everyone, including (and perhaps especially) of those church leaders who had warmly supported the reforms of *Sacrosanctum Concilium*. One can almost hear the psalmist in historical retrospect, looking back toward 1964, "the One who sits in the heavens shall laugh. . . . "

Chapter 8

"To Be Beautiful, Human, and Christian"

The IHM Nuns and the Routinization of Charisma

> "[Sisters] make new wineskins. And if our business is to put the always-new truth into new wineskins, we need to know the very latest about wineskin making. This means we should be listening to the most experimental music, seeing the newest plays and films, reading the latest poems and novels. . . . We need to be hungry for new insights." — SR. MARY CORITA KENT, IHM[1]

The Cardinal and the Good Sisters

On October 16, 1967, the Los Angeles congregation of the Immaculate Heart of Mary — a 119-year-old teaching order of 560 religious women famous for the academic excellence of their schools in California and the Northwest, and perhaps equally famous in the mid-1960s for the presence among their number of Corita Kent, a nun-artist whom theologian Harvey Cox termed "an important contribution to the whole church and to the whole of life" — announced that it would begin a several-years-long process of "liberal changes" in their rule and lifestyle. Reported Mother Mary Humiliata Caspary, the order's superior, to the *Los Angeles Times,* the "reforms" approved by the IHM's Ninth General Chapter were undertaken so that the order could become "more open to the world, reaching out into fresh fields, more a part of the world, and more responsive to it and involved in it."[2]

Among the goals sketched out in this "experimental and gradual" process of change approved by the order's forty-three-member General Chapter were several that struck instant fear in the heart of pastors whose parish schools were staffed by the order. IHM sisters "who feel called to another kind of work" were now to be allowed to choose that work; likewise, concern for the quality of the education they were offering Catholic schoolchildren led to the demand that maximum classroom size in the schools they staffed be lowered from forty to thirty-five students. Other changes were more symbolic, but proved in the long run to be more neuralgic: members would have a great number of options to choose from in the clothes they wear (meaning that distinctive habits would soon be a thing of the past in most of the institutions staffed by the order). Likewise, in terms of "lifestyle" — a new word in the vocabulary of religious women — autonomy would now be (literally) the order of the day. Over against a regimented past in which "each convent had a superior who was in charge and community prayers were set out in detail by the order's constitution, members of each local convent will decide what kind of government they want and then set it up, and when and how they will say their community prayers."[3]

Dan Thrapp, the *Los Angeles Times* reporter covering the story two days after the General Chapter meeting, quoted one of the nuns pressing for the "renovation" undertaken by the Los Angeles group as a "major breakthrough for Roman Catholic nuns in America." Indeed, Thrapp quoted Mother Caspary herself as announcing that the reforms were "more profound than any thus far announced by any American religious society of Catholic women." But he likewise quoted Mother Caspary's observation that this entire process of "experimental and gradual" change was rooted in the mandate of Holy Church herself; specifically, the reforms undertaken by the IHMs were rooted in the call of the bishops of the Second Vatican Council to the religious of the Roman Catholic Church, in the council's Decree on Renewal of Religious Life, to listen to the "signs of the times" in order to serve the "present age" more effectively. Even more specifically, such reforms were an obedient response to the August 6, 1966, *motu proprio* of Pope Paul VI, *Ecclesiae Sanctae,* which urged religious men and women to undertake a long-overdue process of "adaptation to the modern world." Holy hell was about to break out in the archdiocese of Francis Cardinal McIntyre — prince of the church, head of the Los Angeles Catholic archdiocese, and foe of "modern nuns" — thanks to a decree of a universal council promulgated at the hands of the pope himself.[4]

While remaining publicly silent regarding the reforms proposed by the order, Francis McIntyre was privately not amused. While the sisters were a pontifical and not a diocesan order — and thus ultimately responsible to the Sacred Congregation of Religious in Rome and not directly to him — they *were* nonetheless Catholics in his diocese and

had staffed his diocesan schools; further, the cardinal had personally
been generous and supportive of the order, offering a *laissez-faire* public response to charges of diocesan conservatives that things had come
close to being out of hand after Sister Mary Corita Kent — the "star"
of the order — had reenvisioned Immaculate Heart College's annual
"Mary Day" into a hippies-type "happening." Both the discussion and
the announcement of the order's proposed reforms and, more to the
point, their demand for classroom reform had taken place without his
knowledge, counsel, or permission. And as "ordinary" (bishop) of the
Los Angeles diocese, McInytre was a figure to be reckoned with. As
John Gregory Dunne has noted,

> In his own diocese a bishop (or ordinary as he is called in canon
> law) has virtual Caligulan powers; his word is law, and if, unlike
> Caligula, he cannot ordain a horse, there is little else not within
> his power and the reach of his discipline.[5]

Thus, while the sisters very well *may* have been within their "rights"
from the standpoint of canon law to have undertaken a reform of their
order without his blessing (a debatable and debated question quickly
appealed to Rome), it was both impolitic and (in his eyes) ungenerous
to have done so. On October 24, 1967, the chancery of the Los Angeles archdiocese asked the order, undoubtedly at the cardinal's bidding,
for an official response regarding how many of the sisters — given
their newfound freedom to choose their apostolic work — would return to their teaching posts the following year. That formal request,
while *perhaps* neutral in both tone and content, unleashed a firestorm
of controversy between the Angeleno Catholic "left" and "right," so
that unseemly headlines reading "Told to Quit Schools, L.A. Nuns
Say" soon appeared in the local and national press. Likewise, Catholic lay people in Los Angeles now took "sides" on the proposed IHM
reforms: "sides" — a shocking word, and an even more shocking concept, defining the relationship of Roman Catholics to a bishop of the
church. Something radically new, and profoundly unsettling, had appeared in the Los Angeles diocese in the efforts of dedicated Catholics
to implement the "reforms" of the Second Vatican Council.[6]

   While the entire scenario between the nuns and their archbishop
that would unfold in the next eighteen months might appear ludi-
crous and/or melodramatic to "outsiders" to the Catholic subculture
in the United States, the battle between the Los Angeles IHMs and
Cardinal McIntyre was, symbolically, quite important. In 1967, there
were 180,000 religious women in the United States, that is, approx-

imately three times the number of priests. Even allowing for the significant number of religious women living the contemplative life inside cloisters, then, religious women were far more visible as "official representatives" of the Roman Church than ordained clergy. If one factored in primary and secondary schools, hospitals, and orphanages as the locus of the encounter, then nuns increased exponentially as the most likely icon of "things Catholic" in the eyes of millions of schoolchildren, hospital patients, and shut-ins. For many Americans untouched by parochial concerns, the good sisters *were,* in a uniquely Catholic, "embodied" sense, Holy Mother Church. What the sisters said, how they acted, even (or perhaps, especially) the clothes they wore — these were the "visible signs" of the true church in the United States. Almost instinctually, both the IHMs and Cardinal McIntyre recognized the iconic stakes involved in the question of "reform" in nuns' lifestyles — including the question of the length of the hemlines of their habits.[7]

And the IHMs cut a broad swathe in McIntyre's archdiocese: with two hundred sisters teaching seventy-five hundred students in twenty-eight elementary and eight high schools in greater Los Angeles, the order had a reputation among satisfied parents for producing well-trained, devout, and devoted students. Many a pastor had thus fought, without success, to get the IHMs to staff his parish school. The order also ran the respected Immaculate Heart College, whose Art Department was presided over by the talented and much sought-after Sister Corita Kent, a darling of the secular media and of public intellectuals writing about art and communication in the just-then emerging "Sixties Consciousness."

"Corita" (as she became known to millions of fans in the mid-1960s) was known nationwide for her whimsical and often provocative art work — creative pastiches of biblical quotes, boldly juxtaposed colors, and commercial images. In 1964 she had transformed Immaculate Heart College's annual religious festival, "Mary Day," into what was, arguably, the first college-based "happening" in the U.S., grabbing national headlines: with black-robed nuns parading in flowered necklaces, poets declaiming from raised platforms all over campus, and painted students parading in the grass, Mary's Day became a prototype for the hippies' 1967 "be-in" in San Francisco. The next year, at the 1965 World's Fair in New York, Corita designed a fifty-foot-high mural inside the Vatican pavilion, the first piece of "modern art" that hundreds of thousands of visitors to the pavilion both understood and liked. At a 1966 convention of broadcasters in Philadelphia, she had cajoled hundreds of usually sober media journalists to put on paper hats, float balloons, and recite poetry to the person sitting in the next seat. Said one New York–based artist and admirer, "she is the most extraordinary person I know. She has life in a highly concentrated form, and when she laughs — which she does easily — the effect lasts a long time." The *Los Angeles Times* had named her one of the "Top Nine Women of the Year," while *Harper's Bazaar* had featured her as one of its "American Women of Accomplishment." Her widely acclaimed book of serigraphs and poetry, *Damn Everything but the Circus,* would become one of the best-sellers of 1970. Here was a nun — and a group of nuns — to be reckoned with.[8]

Thus, the reforms proposed by the Los Angeles IHMs in the fall of 1967, beginning as an issue no larger than a nun's hand, quickly mushroomed into something considerably more distracting on the Los Angeles horizon: in January 1968, the order sent out a letter to the parents of students in thirty-five parochial schools warning of the possible closing of their schools the following fall, to which the archdiocese responded that, the outcome notwithstanding, the schools would remain open. By early March it was revealed that a secret four-point ruling had been delivered to Cardinal McIntyre a month before from the Sacred Congregation of Religious in Rome, ruling against the order, and demanding their compliance with the directives of their local bishop. On March 8, 1968, the IHMs announced that a "straw vote" within the order had revealed that a significant number of their sisters would rather resign from the congregation than comply with what they perceived to be extrinsic meddling in the cause of legitimate renewal undertaken in good faith and in response to the directive from an ecumenical council promulgated by the pope. On March 10, an "emergency meeting" of the order was called, leading to the announcement the next day in the *New York Times* that the nuns were appealing the entire case to Rome. By March 27, three thousand women religious in the United States had signed a public petition supporting the IHMs in their "battle" against Cardinal McIntyre; by April 17, 1968, 194 prominent educators, artists, writers, and clergymen had signed a letter to Pope Paul VI, urging freedom for the nuns to "experiment." The list of names on that list was, both at the time and in retrospect, extraordinary: the retired presiding bishop of the Episcopal Church, Arthur Lichtenberger, and Paul Moore, Episcopal suffragan bishop of Washington; John Bennett, president of New York's Union Theological Seminary; theologians Reinhold Niebuhr, Krister Stendahl, George Lindbeck, Rosemary Ruether, and Harvey

Cox; architect Buckminster Fuller; journalists Justus George Lawler, James O'Gara, and Daniel Callahan; W. M. Linz, vice president of Herder and Herder Publishing Company; William Morris Hunt, director of the Cambridge (Massachusetts) Drama Festival, and designer Norman Laliberte. By the beginning of May in that spring of 1968, 25,556 persons had signed a petition, organized in four weeks by volunteers in Southern California, urging the pope "to allow the Sisters of the Immaculate Heart of Mary additional time to evaluate the program of renewal adopted by them." Public intellectuals — Catholic, Protestant, Jewish, and indifferent — lined up to support a group of nuns: nothing like it had ever been seen before in the history of the Catholic Church in the United States.[9]

Rome had never responded well to public discussion of matters of "ecclesiastical discipline," especially in the fractious American context: on April 4, 1968, the Congregation of Religious announced that "it is surprising that such a wave of has been stirred up around points which are not open to questions, and that radio, press, and television have been enlisted to publicize arguments which are devoid of objective foundation and can only cause trouble." Despite the old truism of *Roma locuta causa finita* ("Rome has spoken, the case is closed"), the "case" was far from finished, and 1968 would witness the singular event of the Los Angeles IHMs voting 10 to 1 to leave their order to found a new, "reformed" group.[10]

What might one make of this "comic opera" schism so analogous in name and impulse to that of Leonard Feeney and his "Slaves of the Immaculate Heart of Mary"? How to interpret this ironic "shift to the left" of Catholic reformist, prophetic impulses in the late 1960s to balance the earlier Boston "IHM" case in the years immediately following World War II? Why the remarkably *public* nature of Rome's participation in the case as opposed to the indirect, discreet part Rome played in Feeney's condemnation?

Clearly the place, the time, and the ecclesiastical "circumstance" of the Los Angeles nuns had changed dramatically from that of Feeney; gender undoubtedly played a not-insignificant part in the event as well. The historical factors — and the historical irony — in the story of the Sisters of the Immaculate Heart of Mary and Cardinal McIntyre are multileveled and complex, and no single historical interpretation can hope to do justice to the event. Clearly the locus of the dispute, Los Angeles and not Boston, played a role, as did the time: the "Sixties" and the Second Vatican Council had dramatically reshaped both the culture and the church in ways the postwar, still-Tridentine church of 1945 could not have foreseen. The public spectacle of religious *women* — vowed to stay, pray, and obey — as opposed to a fractious, schismatic group led by a male religious, likewise clearly engendered a somewhat different set of responses. All of these social, historical, and ecclesiastical factors (and more) powerfully shaped the "IHM Story" of 1967–68. But social theory can also help to shed some light on this singular "schism" in the City of the Angels, especially the insights of the great German sociologist Max Weber.

Max Weber and Charisma

Max Weber, in writing about the synergistic relationship of "charisma" and "routinization," noted at the beginning of the twentieth century that the history of the world's great religious traditions seems to be bipolar; that is, all such traditions appear to operate between two dialectical impulses. On the one hand, all religious traditions rest on the insights of "charismatic prophets" whose authority and *dynamis* transcend history and its structures. Such prophetic "charisma" in the Weberian sense is a

> certain quality of an individual personality by virtue of which he is set apart from ordinary men and treated as endowed with supernatural, superhuman, or at least specifically exceptional powers or qualities. These are such as are not accessible to the ordinary person, but are regarded as of divine origin.[11]

"Charisma" in its pure form represents a quality of knowledge and power "contrary to all patriarchal domination." In contrast to any kind of bureaucratic organization in which duly received "offices" legitimate the exercise of power, charisma "knows nothing of form or of an ordered procedure of appointment or dismissal"; indeed, such charisma is the epistemological insight opposed to "ordered reality." By its very nature such charisma undertakes a frontal attack on institutional and permanent structure, as it embodies the very opposite of the institutionally permanent. According to Weber, all the great religious "prophets" in human history — Siddhartha Gautama, Moses, Jesus, Mohammed — embodied such charismatic power and authority. All such prophets spoke with the authority of "But I say unto you" that undercut the "rules" of their religious context. Thus Moses could denounce the ancient superstitions of a Semitic tribe in the name of a higher authority, while Jesus could chide the scribes and the Pharisees, the "official" religious teachers of first-century Palestine, with the confident assurance that "one greater than Moses is with you." From Weber's point of view, both Moses and Jesus possessed "charisma" in almost classic religious form.[12]

But by its very nature such charismatic authority is unstable: charisma inheres in "magical" and "divine" prophets who are themselves the guarantors of their revelations, but it is, for that very reason, short-lived. The question inevitably arises in all religious traditions founded by such prophets: "how shall we pass on the truth revealed, the authority uncovered?" How shall the memory of the charismatic moment of ecstasy and revelation, unveiled by the "prophet," survive the disappearance and/or death of that moment's bearer? Weber brilliantly observed that the (almost inevitable) transformation of the great charismatic vision into some more continuous social organization and institutional framework represents a "routinization of charisma" that allows followers to pass on the gospel. The charismatic message of truth, redemption, and unity — delivered as a word against all mere human authority and power — is inevitably transformed into the ordered and structured religious artifacts of Scripture, ritual, and hierarchy. Charisma as a creative, nonhierarchical source of legitimacy *hardens* in such routinization into lasting institutions that themselves "formally" legitimate the hierarchical power structures of society: In its pure form charismatic authority has a character foreign to everyday routine structures. If this is not to remain a purely transitory phenomenon, but to take on the character of a lasting relationship forming a stable community of disciples, it is necessary for the character of charismatic authority to become radically changed. It cannot remain stable, but becomes either traditionalized or rationalized, or a combination of both.[13]

Monasticism — living the "vowed life" of poverty, chastity, and obedience in the context of organized community life — represented for Weber the classic Western Christian example of such routinization of charisma. Inspired by the charismatic example of the likes of St. Benedict or Francis of Assisi, disciples *routinized* the original antistructural message of living a "life against the world" offered by such prophets into an organized, structured lifestyle open to others: the very "routine" of a convent or monastery represented the institutional price for the continued life of the original anti-structural charism. In time, of course, such routinization of the monastic charismatic impulse always risks becoming too stable, too "safe" — a fate inherent in all institution building but inimical to the original prophetic impulse itself. Thus, as Weber himself observed, the history of Catholicism was replete with religious reform movements whose mission was to call overly rigid, structured communities *ad fontes* — that is, back to the authentic, anti-structural "fountains," or sources, that founded those communities. Viewed from Weber's perspective, the call of the Second Vatican Council to men and women religious, voiced in *Perfectae Caritatis* to return to the fresh insights of their founders in order to appropriately adapt to the modern world, represented just such a reform movement. The famous introduction to that document announced that

> the appropriate renewal of religious life involves two simultaneous processes: (1) a continuous return to the sources [*ad fontes*] of all Christian life and the original inspiration behind a given community and (2) an adjustment of the community to the changed conditions of the times.[14]

The women religious of the Immaculate Heart of Mary thus undertook both a return to the radical "sources" of their lifestyle and an adjustment of their order to the "changed condition of the times" as they found them in Los Angeles in 1967 at the behest of the highest authorities in their religious tradition: the decree of an ecumenical council propagated by the Supreme Pontiff himself. Such authority they — like all devout Roman Catholics — believed originated with the Holy Spirit and guaranteed the legitimacy of their reform efforts. The charismatic (or perhaps better, pneumatic) power unleashed by that "reform," however, threatened the routinized stability of the very institution that had called for it — at least the Los Angeles manifestation of that institution. "Knowing the very latest about wineskin-making" turned out to be far more dangerous than anyone expected.

Vatican II in Los Angeles

At least since 1727, when the Ursulines opened their first school for girls in New Orleans (then a colony of France), women religious in North America were compelled to balance two competing impulses in their religious lives: on the one hand, the ancient tradition of the "cloistered life" as normative for women living as vowed religious, and on the other hand the immediate and incessant apostolic demands of a young church in desperate need of schools, hospitals, and orphanages. From the standpoint of official church law, Roman Catholicism formally recognized only one form of vowed life for women: the term "nun" in canon law referred only to women with solemn vows living in cloistered community, whose apostolic work was prayer and the chanting of the Divine Office. The very idea of nuns living a vowed life focused on service "in the world" was, technically speaking, not only discouraged but forbidden. As the "weaker sex," women wishing to live in the state of perfection were compelled to congregate in contemplative, cloistered community with at most indirect contact with "externs."[15]

Thus, orders of religious women founded in the United States — groups like the Daughters of Charity founded by Elizabeth Ann Seton in 1809 in Emmitsburg, Maryland, and the Dominican sisterhood founded in Kentucky in 1822 by the Dominican priest Samuel Wilson — were not even (technically speaking) "nuns" at all in the eyes of the church, by which canon law meant only "second orders" of contemplative, cloistered women. Groups of women active in the "works of mercy" and bound together by simple vows of poverty, chastity, and obedience — that is, precisely groups like the Daughters of Charity — came to mark the majority of Catholic "sisters" only after the French Revolution, and from the standpoint of church law constituted "third orders" of pious lay people living a common life for edification and good works; but they were *not* "nuns." It was only in 1900 that Rome recognized "active" communities that taught, nursed, and helped the needy as "authentic" women religious in the papal bull *Conditae a Christo.*[16]

But in the American context such groups of "third order" women flourished and became pillars of the young church. Twelve different groups of nuns attempted to establish religious communities in the United States between 1790 and 1830: six were founded along distinctly American, "activist" lines, and six were modeled on the cloistered, European understanding of women religious. By the late twentieth century, all six "American" groups still existed, but only one of the "European," cloistered groups was still in existence.[17]

It was the period from 1830 to 1900 that saw the most impressive growth of women religious in the United States: the sheer number of "sisters" increased from 1,344 in 1850 to 30,340 by 1900. Likewise, 106 new communities of nuns were founded during those seventy years: 23 by Americans, 8 by Canadian motherhouses, and 75 by European foundations. By 1900 the papal bull *Conditae a Christo* extended the term "nun" to all groups of women willing to accept the conditions of "partial cloister," including those American groups with no intention of living a contemplative life. Among those conditions were some control of contact with the "outside world," the pairing of nuns leaving the convent, regular hours of common prayer and Divine Office, etc. But even with their newfound canonical status as "nuns," however, American women religious found their lives increasingly circumscribed by "cloistered" concerns. The promulgation of the New Code of Canon Law in 1917 made the cloister mentality even more pronounced, and by the 1920s all American sisters were being warned by both Roman officials and by local bishops to restrict their contact with the outside world as much as possible.[18]

Thus the trajectory of religious life for women in the opening decades of the twentieth century — at least as such religious life was understood by Roman and episcopal authorities — appeared to be shifting away from "activist" impulses and moving inexorably toward a more traditional, cloistered understanding of nuns. But two countervailing impulses emerged in the United States in the decade before the convening of the Second Vatican Council, impulses that changed the direction of nuns' lives: in 1949 Sister Mary Madeleva, president of St. Mary's College at Notre Dame, Indiana, presented an epochal paper at the National Catholic Educational Association (NCEA) questioning the style and depth of the education given to American women religious by their own orders. The formation program of most orders of American nuns in the first half of the twentieth century might be accurately described as tending, at best, toward the "minimalist": sisters in formation took classes in the evenings, on Saturdays, and during the summer, actually earning academic degrees years after they had begun teaching schoolchildren. Parochial schools were booming in the first five decades of the century, often with average class sizes of fifty or sixty students, and every available body in a veil was needed to staff them. Most orders of religious women placed young sisters in the classroom *first*, and *then* sent them off for degrees "on the fly." Madeleva's paper, published as *The Education of Sister Lucy*, questioned this entire process of placing the institutional needs of pastors before the needs of intellectual and spiritual growth of young nuns, sparking a lively (and at rectory tables across the country, heated) discussion.[19]

But it was the creation of the Sisters Formation Conference in 1954, which grew partly out of the discussions set off by Madeleva's paper, that would have the most lasting (and radical) influence on American nuns. The year after Sister Madeleva had presented her paper, Pope Pius XII had called the major superiors of religious women to Rome for the first of two international conferences on sisters' formation, the second being convened in 1952. At both of these Roman meetings

Pius urged the women superiors to offer programs of thorough professional education and spiritual formation *before* sending young sisters to apostolic assignments. In 1952 the Conference of Major Superiors of Women was established in the United States to discuss the problem of formation and other issues. Both of these streams — that of Madeleva's book and of Pius XII's Roman meetings — eventuated in the creation of the Sisters Formation Conference (SFC) under the aegis of the NCEA, and with the able direction of Sister Mary Emil Penet (herself a Monroe, Michigan, "IHM" sister).[20]

The SFC thus undertook a national collaborative renewal of sisters' formation and spirituality fully a decade before the first documents on religious life were promulgated by the Second Vatican Council: the newsletters and annual conferences of the SFC throughout the 1950s and early 1960s addressed issues of psychological maturity and personal accountability for apostolic work, more responsive community governance, and better professional preparation. And largely because of the tireless efforts of Penet and others associated with her, few other Catholic groups in the U.S. responded to the decrees of Vatican II with the alacrity, openness, and creativity as American nuns. Groups like the Los Angeles IHMs had been well-trained from a decade of reform documents proceeding from the Sisters Formation Conference to study documents and pick up the theological and biblical nuances shaping issues of personal and communal "renovation." Cardinal McIntyre, himself a Roman participant in the Vatican Council, had met his match in the good sisters in "reading" church documents calling for communal reform and apostolic creativity.[21]

The call issued by bishops at the Second Vatican Council in 1965 for an evangelical renovation of the religious life lived by both men and women throughout the Catholic world thus fell on ready and open ears among American nuns. For orders whose histories had been almost forcibly channeled by personnel-strapped American bishops into institutionally defined, cloister-centered streams that had little to do with the vision of the original members, the command to uncover the original (often quite radical) charism of "founding mothers" appeared like the inspired directive of the Holy Spirit herself. Women's communities founded by eighteenth- and nineteenth-century free-spirited foundresses inspired by egalitarian impulses but governed by the mid-twentieth century in authoritarian ways often found the "opening of the windows" envisioned by good Pope John to eventuate in something much closer to a cyclone than the "gentle breeze" of Scripture. "Renewal along the lines envisioned by founders" often resulted in the replacement of unquestioning obedience with the idea of corporate responsibility in defining and implementing a community's mission. As Rosemary Rader has so keenly observed, the "Catholic feminist movement" was flourishing well before the 1970s, a movement formally recognized and lionized by the (largely conservative) "fathers" of the Second Vatican Council.[22]

Council documents calling for a "reform" that had appeared both moderate and salutary in Rome took on a life of their own in the context of American discussions that had been underway for a decade. Thus, paragraph 17 of the council's Decree on the Appropriate Renewal of Religious Life — a soon-to-be much-controverted conciliar statement about clothing — had appeared to be unexceptional when passed almost unanimously by the bishops:

> Since they are signs of a consecrated life, religious habits should be simple and modest, at once poor and becoming. They should meet the requirements of health and be suited to the circumstances of time and place as well as to the services required by those who wear them. *Habits of men and women which do not correspond to those norms are to be changed.*[23]

Likewise, paragraph 20 of that same document — on the "adjustments" in lifestyle and apostolic work that missionary communities should undertake in fulfilling the directive for reform — had urged religious men and women to "resort to suitable techniques, including modern ones" in preaching the gospel to the contemporary world, adding that they should "abandon whatever activities [that] are today less in keeping with the spirit of the community and its *authentic* character."[24]

For good religious women like the Los Angeles sisters of the Immaculate Heart of Mary, the "call" of the council to abandon "activities less in keeping with the spirit of the community and its authentic character" was acted on with alacrity: meeting at the IHMs' vacation house in Santa Barbara on October 14, 1967, the first session of the Ninth General Chapter of the order called for a "period of experimentation" with dress, lifestyle, and apostolic works, which would continue until the next General Chapter of the order, in 1975. While the experimental period was announced as being "effective immediately," specific changes would be annually evaluated by annual interim sessions of the Ninth General Chapter. Sisters were now given the option of retaining their "names in religion" or returning to their "given names"; they could retain the traditional habit, a "modified habit," or — following the directives of Vatican II — adapt any style of dress that was "simple and modest, [and] at once poor and becoming." And while the General Chapter had no intention of abandoning its "traditional works" — which in the Los Angeles archdiocese meant a heavy commitment of sisters to the parochial school system — they allowed the possibility for a "change of apostolic venue" for sisters attracted to other forms of service. As the *Los Angeles Times* reported this decision,

> "we won't abandon our traditional works," said the reverend mother [Caspary], "but we also say that diversity in works is not to be discouraged, but encouraged. Thus we may assume social service, or work with economic opportunity projects, or such specialized tasks as with the mentally retarded, or with young people. If one of our sisters has a special talent or interest, we will encourage her to pursue it. She might be a commercial artist, or a newspaper woman, or a musician, or almost anything else."[25]

The Catholic archdiocese of Los Angeles, whatever its commitment to the reforms mandated by the Vatican Council — and Catholic pundits at the time and since have observed that it would be understating the situation by half to note that the spiritual head of the Los Angeles church, Francis McIntyre, was less than enamored with the vision of a "modernized Catholicism" — immediately recognized the institutional threat posed by the IHM General Chapter. The network of Catholic grade and high schools was one of the jewels in the crown of L.A.'s Catholic empire, and the IHM sisters ranked near the very top of the list of superb parochial school teachers. What looked like "diversity of works" to Mother Caspary resembled institutional chaos to the cardinal and the chancellor of the archdiocesan school system. A "return to the founding charisms" looked fine as a phrase in Roman documents; it was quite another matter for such phrases to interfere with the immense school system that the Los Angeles archdiocese had to oversee.

Less than a week after the IHMs' General Chapter meeting, on October 24, Monsignor Donald Montrose, superintendent of the archdiocesan school system, forwarded a letter to the sisters from the cardinal, asking them "to determine promptly how many of the sisters will wish to retain their teaching capacity in our schools as religious." But it was the Ninth Chapter's decision "arbitrarily" to limit class size in diocesan schools that appeared to most raise McIntyre's ire and led him to fling down a gauntlet of his own:

> it would appear that the action of the chapter presents to the archdiocese of Los Angeles an ultimatum that does not even admit of discussion or negotiation. This ultimatum, with its elements, is not acceptable to the archdiocese of Los Angeles and its ordinary. Consequently, there is no other alternative than to accept the threat of the community that they withdraw from the teaching staffs of our parochial schools in the archdiocese.[26]

The IHMs, seemingly with the backing of both Vatican II and the pope, responded "in kind" with two actions that contributed immediately to the animosity and newsworthiness of the interchange. First, the order announced that it had no comment to the press because the entire matter had been handed over to the pope's representative in the United States, the apostolic delegate Archbishop Luigi Raimondi — thus escalating the interchange to a new and potentially acrimonious "canonical" level; and secondly, the order sent out a letter to the parents of the seventy-five hundred students taught by the order, stating that nuns "are being asked to stop teaching your children in the parochial schools of the archdiocese." Noted Sister Anita Caspary to the press, "We would like to make clear that we have tried, by every means possible, to avoid such an eventuality." But the eighty-one-year-old cardinal immediately denied that the sisters had been "ousted" or pressured to consider such a move: the archdiocese had *not* dismissed the sisters of the Immaculate Heart of Mary. Rather, "the community has simply been asked to determine promptly how many of the sisters will wish to retain their teaching capacity in our schools as religious."[27]

A week later the archdiocese announced that the thirty-five schools staffed by the order would remain open regardless of the sisters' decision. But the "magnanimous" decision of the archdiocese, whatever the hopes of church officials, failed to quell a controversy that had begun to garner national attention. A new Catholic organization formed in January of 1968, the "Los Angeles Association of Laymen," assiduously jumped into the middle of the dispute between the cardinal and the sisters by issuing a statement strongly endorsing the nuns, and (implicitly, at least) calling on the cardinal to "back off":

> For the Immaculate Heart Sisters, the leaders of all the religious in this country, to be refused the right to experiment and make

their own rules leads to the decline of not only the religious orders, but to the quality of Catholic education.[28]

And support for the "leaders of all the religious in this country" spread to an order previously famous for unquestioning obedience to the church hierarchy. The February 3, 1968, issue of *Ave Maria* — a popular Catholic magazine published at the University of Notre Dame — carried a letter signed by thirteen Jesuit seminary professors praising the reform efforts of the IHMs. The Jesuits, all professors at Alma College in Los Gatos, California, called the experimentation undertaken by the nuns "a splendid response to the call for renewal and adaptation of religious life" and added that the sisters' stand, even in the face of episcopal disapproval, "made a notable contribution to a restored understanding of authority in religious life":

> You have taken seriously the principle of subsidiarity commended by both the council and the Pope, according to which no task or problem should be referred to a larger group or to a more general authority if it can be handled by the smaller subsidiary group.[29]

By March 8, 1968, the fracas between the California nuns and their ordinary had reached a disturbing level of unpleasantness: Station KNBC-TV in Los Angeles reported on its evening news that the nuns were prepared to resign from the order rather than comply with the demands of Cardinal McIntyre; four days later it was reported in the *New York Times* that the order would appeal its case to Pope Paul VI himself. On April 16 the Vatican's Sacred Congregation of Religious and Secular Institutes, the Roman body assigned to deal with issues relating to religious women, appointed a four-bishop committee to investigate the affair and make recommendations back to Rome as to its resolution. Presided over by James Casey, the archbishop of Denver, the committee included Joseph Breitenbeck, auxiliary bishop of Detroit, Thomas Donnellan, bishop of Ogdensburg, New York, and Msgr. Thomas Gallagher, who represented the apostolic delegate in Washington. The *New York Times* noted that the "naming of the committee would appear to be an answer to the petition filed by the nuns with Pope Paul."[30]

What would only be revealed later, however, was that well before the naming of the "investigative committee" on April 16 the sisters had already received a four-point ruling from the Sacred Congregation of Religious in mid-February that they only made public a month later. The *National Catholic Reporter* described the four-point ruling from Rome as a response to McIntyre's own appeal to Rome on the controversy, calling its contents a "crushing defeat for the sisters": the Roman congregation ruled that the order must adopt some kind of uniform habit; that the sisters must retain their original "apostolic commitment" to teaching rather than "branch out into a variety of work"; that they must retain at least some daily prayer in common, including Mass; and that, even though they were subject to the Roman Congregation for Religious, they were still "subject to the local bishop." What made Catholic headlines across the country, however, was not the Roman "ruling" that appeared to favor the cardinal, but that the "IHM Nuns put off compliance" with the Roman directive — an announcement that was greeted by petitionary "write-ins" of support by thousands of American nuns and priests, Protestant denominational leaders, and public intellectuals who heretofore had little to do with the Roman Church, much less with nuns. The last state, it appeared, was considerably worse than the first.[31]

The resolution to the now tripartite "stand-off" between the sisters, McIntyre, and the Roman Congregation of Religious was announced by Archbishop James Casey, head of the four-man committee appointed by the Congregation of Religious. In the estimation of the investigating committee, the 540-member order of the Immaculate Heart of Mary *already* constituted, in fact, two separate religious communities — a progressive faction that claimed the loyalty of the vast majority of sisters in the order, a faction that would follow the lead of Caspary and Corita Kent, and a much smaller (and generationally older) faction, hoping to hold on to the old habit, lifestyle, and apostolic commitments. Why not, the investigating committee announced, let the IHMs themselves choose their future, thus offering a Solomonic conclusion to the entire affair: Cardinal McIntyre and his schools would thus inherit the "no-nos," and Rome would be free of the ruckus created by the "go-gos" while affirming its right to decide in the matter. Roman authority, diocesan institutional needs, and American democratic ideals would thus all be (more or less) affirmed and placated. Announced Casey to the press, "for practical purposes, while a final decision by the Holy See is pending, two groups are recognized, and each is authorized to act separately."[32]

In the event, about fifty nuns voted against the "reforms" advanced by the progressives and found a peaceful solution to the affair under the leadership of Sister Eileen MacDonald. These nuns — the "California Institute of the Sisters of the Most Holy and Immaculate Heart of

Mary" — retained modified habits, common prayer, and a commitment to teaching in nine parochial schools of the archdiocese. The great majority of women in the order, however, "decided rather to switch than fight." Close to 150 of the former sisters chose to leave religious life altogether, while 285 of them organized themselves into the "Immaculate Heart Community," under the leadership of "Miss" Anita Caspary, the president of what might be termed an "intentional community" of laywomen committed to living out the Christian life "in the world." In 1970 they became the single largest group of religious women in the history of the American Catholic Church to become "laicized" — that is, formally released from their vows by the Congregation of Religious, having found the church's regulations for religious women, even after Vatican II, "still too restricting for their objectives." Each group — the Institute and the lay community — received an undisclosed financial settlement, but the larger community retained the right to administer Immaculate Heart College, one of their premier high schools, Queen of the Valley Hospital, and their retreat center overlooking the Pacific near Santa Barbara.[33]

By April of 1970, more than half of the women (187) in the newly founded lay "community" were still in the teaching profession: more than thirty taught in public schools in the Los Angeles area, while a half dozen committed themselves to a bilingual program for Mexican-Americans run by the archdiocese. Bishops in seven West Coast dioceses welcomed some of these "laicized" women, while some, like Corita Kent, retained their previous positions at Immaculate Heart College. The decision of these "progressives" to allow "affiliate members" (including married couples) led to over a hundred applications for affiliate status in the first year of experimenting with this new form of community life.[34]

Arguably one of the more palpable impulses among the 285 "progressives" in the early 1970s was the confident sense, mixed in with a former nun's humility, that they were changing both the church and the world for the better, living in a sort of ecclesial vanguard of history. Said one of the members of this group,

> Many of the sisters, personality-wise, are not going to be in the forefront of social change. But there are still many who are very much concerned about bringing change — they might express it in a quieter way.[35]

Viewed with the benefit of the 20/20 vision of hindsight, of course, the effusive and generous plans of the "progressives" to join in the culture-wide effort of the 1960s to effect social change appears a tad optimistic, if not naive. Sister Corita Kent, herself on a personal trajectory of artistic exploration and self-discovery that would lead her out of the convent within a decade, manifested many of the dreams that would lead thousands of sisters beyond the convent walls into secular lives. With a buoyancy and optimism that would mark much of American culture during "The Sixties," she advised her sisters that

> to live constructively in such a time the sister needs to be an artist — to be a maker, which is simply to say that she must be beautiful and human and Christian....A sister is only different in the job she chooses to do. And to do this job she has promised to enjoy things fully and not to possess them for herself, to love people greatly and not to possess them. To the extent that her community prevents her from being beautiful and human and Christian, that community must be remade over and over again.[36]

To be "beautiful and human and Christian," in the event, led to the most massive disruption of religious life in the Roman Church in four centuries. The Los Angeles IHMs, like religious women nationally, entered a troubling season of membership declension, institutional self-doubt, and identity crisis in the late 1960s from which most groups had not fully recovered by the closing years of the century. The conciliar "reforms" mandated by the Second Vatican Council — reforms that sought to breathe new life into religious through a "return to the founding charisms" of orders — in fact set off several decades of personal and institutional chaos for many religious women in the United States. The numbers don't tell the entire story, but they nonetheless portray a troubling picture: in 1966, there were 7257 novices in women's religious communities nationally; by 1981, that number had plummeted to 780. In 1966, 3406 women had applied for entry into convents; in 1981, only 569 made such application. The year after the end of Vatican II, 13,588 women were in "first vows" in American convents; fifteen years later, only 1932 lived in such a commitment. In 1950, 381 women left convents in the United States; in 1970, 4337 novices and sisters left. And the institutional commitments of those who stayed in community changed almost as dramatically as the demographics: in 1966, 58 percent of American religious women taught in the vast network of parochial education in the U.S.; by 1982, only 23 percent of American nuns defined their apostolic work as teachers. Cardinal McIntyre's intuitive fears about the jewel in the crown of the archdiocese of Los Angeles — its parochial school system — would appear to have been very well-placed.[37]

Many observers both in the church and out felt that the charismatic "reforms" unleashed by the council — reforms that were understood by some nuns as abetting their efforts to be more "beautiful, human, and Christian" — in fact sponsored the near-eclipse of religious life in the post–Vatican II Catholic world. The new wineskins burst asunder, spilling their contents all over the floors of diocesan offices from coast to coast, perhaps most dramatically on that of Francis Cardinal McIntyre of Los Angeles. The neat channels of institutional "routinization," by which the Catholic Church staffed its myriad schools and hospitals in the centuries after the Reformation, were weakened and recrafted by the charismatic enthusiasm that the highest body of that institution, an ecumenical council, had itself authorized and mandated. To unleash the Spirit, as Jesus himself had warned, led in directions that the institution could not foresee or control.

The Ecclesial Shattering of Charisma's "Routine"

As Weber himself elucidated long before "Good Pope John" announced plans for an ecumenical council, all human institutions founded on the charismatic revelations of prophets and then routinized into the "safe" channels of law, hierarchy, and institution-building must undergo periodic reform if they are to adapt to changed cultural conditions — reform that brings them back into contact with their founding "charism." But such reform is fraught with challenges, for "pure" charisma represents the "very opposite of the institutionally permanent." Such charisma — by its very nature — is short-lived and temporary, and must give way to yet another "routine" of hierarchy and institution building:

> Charisma, as a creative power, recedes in the face of domination, which hardens into lasting institutions and becomes efficacious only in short-lived mass emotions of incalculable effects. Nevertheless charisma remains a highly important element of the social structure, although of course in a greatly changed sense.[38]

Charisma as a "highly important element of the social structure" was indeed routinized in the complex history of Western Christianity into religious communities of men and women, communities in which an uneasy "truce" was struck with hierarchy and authority derived from inherited office. This "truce" was both uneasy and volatile because

two traditions of power and authority were set up in fragile relationship within the bosom of Holy Mother Church: one source of
authority, like that of Francis McIntyre, derived from office — an *ex
officio* authority claimed by every bishop in the Roman Church as
successors of the apostles. But the other tradition of authority and legitimate power recognized by the church, evinced in groups like the
sisters of the Immaculate Heart of Mary, derived not *from* office, but
rather brought power and legitimacy *to* it. This authority came from
living a life "against the world" in community and sharing in charismatic witness to a realm of values beyond structured historical reality.
While the church (in one sense) "co-opted" such charisma by *officially* sanctioning celibate religious life as an honorable state within
the church, total control of such power always eluded its reach. For,
as Weber himself recognized,

> a charismatic principle which originally was primarily directed
> to the *legitimization* of authority may be subject to interpreta-
> tion or development *in an anti-authoritarian direction*. This is
> true because the validity of charismatic authority rests entirely
> on recognition by those subject to it, conditioned as this is by
> "proof" of its genuineness. This is true in spite of the fact that
> this recognition of a charismatically qualified, and hence legit-
> imate, person is treated as a *duty*. When the organization of
> the corporate group undergoes a process of progressive rational-
> ization, it is readily possible that, instead of recognition being
> treated as a consequence of legitimacy, it is treated as the basis of
> legitimacy.[39]

For Misses Anita Caspary, Corita Kent, and several hundred other
women who formally left religious life for deeply held principles,
the "legitimacy" of the reform they had undertaken in 1967 *at least*
rivaled the legitimacy of the concerns of the archbishop of Los Angeles. The very public and emotionally charged debate unleashed by the
reform agenda announced by the General Chapter of the IHMs in fact
revealed a deep truth to both the nuns and the archbishop: no "charismatic" group — however "routinized" into structured form — is ever
completely coopted, and thus completely "safe" from the point of view
of hierarchy. The potentially "wild" impulses of charismatic power
are always lurking just below the surface of normalcy and routine.
The "flattened out" communal lifestyle of women's religious life —
the seemingly unemotional singing of plainchant and the wearing of
anonymous habits and veils — was built on and actually passed on

profoundly *anti-structural,* prophetic impulses, impulses always potentially destructive of order and of inherited power and authority. For the "call" to such a life, by its very nature, could not be legislated or inherited by any routinized authority, but only immediately felt and individually discerned. Its deepest and most profound "legitimacy" could not be bestowed by any hierarchical authority, however august or ancient.

As Weber recognized so clearly, the legitimacy bestowed on charismatic prophets and their epigoni by hierarchy is always (at best) fragile and uneasy, and thus liable to disturbance. It is a legitimacy that acts to protect the routinized hierarchy granting it as much as the charismatic community receiving it, for the routinized hierarchy itself (if it is effective in ordering chaotic reality) recognizes in the charisma of the prophets the potential for its own undoing. The disturbance, in other words, is *always* potentially there, liable to "outbreak." Indeed, one might structure an illuminating history of Christianity around just such charismatic disturbances. The irony of the IHM story is that the "disturbance" was initiated *not* from the charismatic side, as might have been expected, but rather by the *very* routinized company of bishops of the Roman Church.

The "adaptation to the times" that Vatican II mandated for religious men and women most assuredly gave canonical legitimacy to the reform goals of nuns like the IHMs; but one may reasonably doubt that the sisters recognized in such "legitimacy" the complete reason for their renewal, or the only "authority" from which their lives derived sanction. Indeed, one might reasonably argue that such conciliar legitimacy was, in the perception of groups like the Immaculate Heart sisters of Los Angeles, a happy (or unhappy, depending on one's view of the result) confirmation of charismatic impulses that had never been totally curbed by the "routinization" of institutional needs and hierarchical guidelines. These charismatic impulses had seen expression well before the decrees of Vatican II — in the publication of Sister Mary Madeleva's *Education of Sister Lucy* and in the creation of the Sisters Formation Conference — and derived authority (or "legitimacy," in Weber's words) from springs other than just episcopal approval.

In sanctioning, commending, and even legislating a charismatic return *ad fontes* for the religious men and women of the Western church by issuing a call to break the "dead" habits of routinization and return to the fresh springs of their founding, the fathers of the Second Vatican Council issued an *imprimatur* for experimentation that many of them would come to despise and oppose. Francis Cardinal McIntyre of Los

Angeles was, arguably, no more conservative than many or even most of the bishops who had attended the council and who had approved the Decree on the Appropriate Renewal of Religious Life. He was, perhaps, more prescient in recognizing the potentially chaotic effects of that decree on the routinized structures of Catholic culture like schools or hospitals, and more public in opposing the institutional disruption such charismatic renewal portended. In such a reading of the events of 1967 and 1968 in his diocese, neither McIntyre nor the IHM nuns he opposed constituted the "villains" of the story. Both were, from the standpoint of Max Weber and the "history of salvation," ironic pawns of that same Holy Spirit who had inspired conservative Pope John to call Vatican II in the first place, with results that no one could have foreseen, predicted, or approved. As it turned out, the pneumatological call "to be beautiful, human, and Christian" issued by the council *fathers* to *sisters* around the globe found a ready reception in Los Angeles, where its potential for recovering "charisma" was realized to the full. Perhaps someone in Rome, on the day that decree was passed in the nave of St. Peter's, should have read the sobering words of Jesus applicable to the matter to the men who so overwhelmingly supported that conciliar document in the hopes of *institutional* renewal: "But the Spirit listeth where it will, and no one knoweth from whence it came, and to whence it shall go."

Chapter 9

Thomism and
the T-Formation in 1966

*Ethnicity, American Catholic Higher Education,
and the Notre Dame Football Team*

"Working people saw in the Notre Dame players their own sons
[and] saw in Notre Dame a place that celebrated ethnicity and the
religion that the immigrants brought with them."

— MIKE CELIZIC, *The Biggest Game of Them All*[1]

The "Game of the Century"

American college football's "Game of the Century" (at least so the
common wisdom goes) was played in East Lansing, Michigan, on a
leaden-skied Saturday afternoon in 1966. On that November afternoon, and on many fall Saturday afternoons since, college football
fans, media sports commentators, and collectors of football lore have
rehashed The Game and debated the coaches' strategies — almost
minute by minute.

On that day in 1966, Roman Catholic nuns throughout the Midwest had offered their Mass intentions and tolled their beads for the
success of Our Lady's Team, the "Fighting Irish" of the University of
Notre Dame, in their great battle against the forces of darkness, the
Spartans of Michigan State University. As Mary Jo Weaver, now a professor of religion at the University of Indiana and herself the product
of Midwestern parochial schools, has recalled, it had become something of an established rite in Roman Catholic primary and secondary
schools on the Fridays of the fall football season during the 1950s for
nuns to lead their classes in prayers for a Notre Dame victory the following day: "It was an important part of our 'Holy War' against the
Protestant majority in the United States."[2]

As events would unfold a decade later, perhaps more Hail Marys (and Hail Mary passes) were needed that fateful afternoon in 1966. With one minute and twenty-four seconds showing on the stadium clock, the Notre Dame faithful across the land (numbering in the tens of millions) pleaded with their TV sets while attempting to recover from collective heart failure after Michigan State's last drive: with the score tied 10–10, the Fighting Irish coach, Ara Parseghian, a consummate competitor who would win more victories for the Fighting Irish than any other coach save for Knute Rockne, was (almost visibly) weighing his options. While famous for his "fire on the sidelines," Parseghian was a cool customer in terms of strategy, not given to operating on impulse. Having himself played under football greats Woody Hayes and Paul Brown, Parseghian had not risen to the pinnacle of college coaching (his job that very afternoon) through impulsive decisions. As the chronicler of that afternoon's game put it, "it was nearly impossible to find another football coach as organized and with as fine an eye for details" as Parseghian, under whom Notre Dame would appear in five major bowl contests and produce forty-four "All American" athletes. While to almost all of the millions of "Domer" fans glued to their sets he had only one option, Parseghian weighed possibilities: go for a score and put the ball in the air, risking an interception that could hand the game over to Michigan State or — an option that no one dared even whisper to the Fighting Irish faithful — go for a tie.[3]

Notre Dame and Michigan State (respectively the Number 1 and Number 2 ranked college teams in the nation) ended the game with a 10–10 tie that afternoon — November 19, 1966. This "first megagame of the modern television era, the first monster game seen in color, with instant slow-motion play" made headlines the next day across the country: the *New York Times,* like many other papers all over the U.S., offered a play-by-play reconstruction of the "long-awaited clash of unbeaten and untied titans" on page 1 of its sports section. Arthur Daley, in his column "Sports of the Times," announced on the day after the game that "there is not a No. 2 in the National Collegiate rankings. In a savage display of football at its primitive best [sic], the two strongest campus teams in the land battled furiously to a 10–10 tie under skies laden with snow." That result, he dryly noted, was about "as satisfactory as kissing your sister."[4]

But the "agenda for the ages" (as The Game's most recent chronicler has phrased it) was delivered by two sportswriters, Dan Jenkins of *Sports Illustrated* and Jim Murray of the *Los Angeles Times,* both of whom reported on college football as brilliantly as anyone in the profession, and both of whom believed that Notre Dame's coach, Ara Parseghian, had purposefully played for a tie. Such a strategy on Parseghian's part, in retrospect, appears both pragmatic and brilliant to the detached observer: Notre Dame had found itself perfectly matched by the East Lansing Spartans, and unlike Michigan State, it needed only a tie to play in a major bowl game when the season ended. The November 16 game was Michigan State's last of the season, and it *had* to play to win: it had no bowl to go to, "no chance for redemption, no overtime." Notre Dame, on the other hand, was scheduled to play the University of Southern California the following week, a game that it stood in a very good stance of winning, and thus had some maneuverability in its strategy: a tie against Michigan State, followed by a victory against Southern Cal, would still insure a bowl game for Notre Dame.[5]

But for the Fighting Irish faithful, who have been accused of many things but never of being detached observers, even the prospect of Our Lady's team playing for a tie came close to defining the "Sin against the Holy Spirit." The headline of Murray's column in the *Los Angeles Times* became the responsorial verse for the requiem of disgruntled Domers ever since: " 'Tis a Pity When the Irish 'Tie One for the Gipper.' " Murray's wrath, poured out in a column that was to achieve cult status among football aficionados, was quoted from coast to coast for weeks after the contest, and is still well-known enough to be quoted, at length, by current fans: "The Four Horsemen indeed! The Four Rabbits! The Four Mice! Outlined against a blue-grey October sky, the Four Mice went into hiding again today. May George Gipp never hear of it."[6]

Even today, over thirty years later, the "inglorious tie of 1966" represents something like a blot on the honor of an institution that many American Catholics believe represents the shock troops of Catholicism's "holy war" on America's Protestant culture. Notre Dame's "athletic tradition" (as coaches and administrators in South Bend like to phrase it) emerged in the era of rabid anti-Catholicism, so that the national prominence of Knute Rockne's teams from an obscure and penurious Catholic school in one of the most Protestant states in the Union became a source of both pride and group esteem for millions of American Catholics who never set foot on the campus, as well as the target of scorn and distrust by other Americans. While the exact morphology of the title "Fighting Irish" has engendered an impressive historical literature of its own, it can be documented that during its first decade of intercollegiate contests the team was identified by a number of sobriquets that help to explain the blending of ethnicity and religion that has marked it since: the football team was identified by various Midwestern sports writers as the Notre Dame "Papists," the "Horrible Hibernians," the "Dumb Micks," and the "Dirty Irish."[7]

Rockne, the Founding Father of the "invincible" athletic tradition marking the school since the 1930s, although a Protestant, had come to South Bend as an undergraduate because of the school's reputation as a "poor boy's institution, a place where students with little money but a willingness to work could succeed." But it was Notre Dame's reputation as a "poor boy's" place tied up with another fact, one so obvious that it is often overlooked by pundits explaining the "mystique" of the place: for over half a century Notre Dame football teams generally won. And their victorious football seasons — stretched back-to-back for so many years — helped to make the Notre Dame "Victory March" ("Cheer, cheer, for old Notre Dame, Wake up the echoes cheering her name") one of the nation's four best-known songs, along with the "Star-Spangled Banner," "God Bless America," and "White Christmas."[8]

In a very real and generally acknowledged sense, the "Notre Dame Tradition" was quite self-consciously invented by Rockne shortly after he was named the Fighting Irish head coach in 1918. Already, by the early 1920s, the football team was bringing Notre Dame profits averaging around $200,000 a year, reaching a pre-Depression high of over half a million dollars in the 1929 season. Rockne thus inherited a "going concern" perched on the cusp of athletic greatness and micro-managed the team into a national presence: from the beginning, he sought perfection in every play, in every movement of his team. Rockne substituted grace and speed for sheer mass on the front line and perfected the forward pass (actually "invented" at Stanford) as the hallmark of Notre Dame's amazingly successful offense. But Rockne paid careful attention to appearance as well as substance: he replaced the team's canvas pants with gold satin. As Rockne's chief hagiographer noted in his 1931 encomium, the new coach recognized that the "lustre and fit of this material made a striking combination with the blue or green of the jersey." Thus, on a number of levels (strategy, public relations, adolescent psychology, and even aesthetics) Rockne's genius lay in his recognition immediately after World War I that

> the conditions at Notre Dame were ideal for the growth of the athletic idea. Fraternities were prohibited. There was no coeducation. Everybody lived in dormitories on the campus. You can't

put boys together like this for 24 hours of the day without some college spirit brewing among them. It was this spirit that took them in a cheering noisy body to the games. The [football] field was made a laboratory in which they were to create a new system.... Such was the background of perhaps the best college spirit in America.[9]

Notre Dame's unique formula for representing the fortunes of millions of American Catholic "poor boys" thus mixed together a number of sociological, theological, and economic factors: the rich athletic culture of the school's all-male student body; emotional fan identification based on both ethnicity and religion; a long tradition of innovative and charismatic coaches; a phenomenal win-loss record against more culturally "established" schools like Michigan and Princeton; and a quite self-conscious theological cast to playing football, represented by the team's visits to the Grotto of Our Lady behind the university church before home games, attending Mass before away games, and quantifying grace in "eucharistic receptions" among the Notre Dame student body, so that the eucharistic "intentions" of hundreds of young men receiving Holy Communion were directed toward a victory for the team: nothing had ever been seen like it, anywhere else, at any time, in American collegiate sports history.[10]

Whatever the final evaluation of the intentions and strategy of Coach Parseghian on that fateful November afternoon in 1966 — himself a passionate perfectionist and a Protestant, like the Golden Dome's most famous coach and perfecter of the forward pass, Knute Rockne — the commotion generated by The Game might actually have to be delegated to a secondary concern, listed after *another,* less well-known but arguably more important incident that same year at Notre Dame, an incident with more far-reaching importance for American Catholic higher education than The Tie. For in April of 1966, the opening gambit in a decades-long debate about "Catholic identity" in higher education was played out in — of all unlikely places — the pages of Notre Dame's own pious journal, *Ave Maria.*[11]

In the April 16 issue of *Ave Maria,* Ralph Martin — himself a 1964 graduate of the university and one of its "best and brightest," having gone off to Princeton on a Woodrow Wilson Fellowship to study philosophy — offered an open letter to Father Theodore Hesburgh about the desultory state of Catholicism at the "new Notre Dame." On leave from Princeton to help organize the then-emerging Cursillo movement in the United States and soon to emerge as one of the national leaders of the Catholic Pentecostal phenomenon in the late 1960s, Martin lamented in his letter that "as I was exposed to the best that Notre Dame had to offer as a student in the College of Arts and Letters, I grew farther and farther away from Christianity; it ceased having a practical influence in my life."[12]

The "new Notre Dame" had been decades in the making, using both the fame and the revenues generated by the football team to parlay the school into a serious research (and resolutely Catholic) national university. The figure who presided over Notre Dame's "arrival" among the front-rank national schools was Father Theodore Hesburgh: if anyone had "invented" the "new" Golden Dome, it was he, and it was at his feet that Martin laid his lament:

> Those who were really thriving on the new Notre Dame, on academic excellence, seemed more and more to be focusing precisely on that: on the university part of [a] Christian university. Many of the national fellowship winners in the classes of '64 and '65 — I know almost every one personally — are not *practicing* Catholics. In the course of four years at Notre Dame, my own Catholicism dissolved.... "All the action" seemed to be in the academics, and many of us drew the practical implications and went where the action was. In my opinion, many of the best students that Notre Dame "produces" are no longer Catholics by the time they graduate.[13]

Martin's fear was that the "trajectory Notre Dame seems to be traveling in" would eventuate, in the not too distant future, in a complete secularization of the institution: "Notre Dame will no longer be a Christian university in any way other than Yale or Harvard are Christian universities." His letter noted that this "secularization" in South Bend revealed itself in a number of ways: in the "vocational" and instrumentalist attitude of its students, in the drop in vocations generated by the school, in the serious decline of student devotionalism, and in the "demoralization" of so many of its priests. The end result of all of this was that "Notre Dame is becoming more and more like the pagan and secular modern world, rather than asking the world to become more and more like the Kingdom of God."[14]

Among many other things, Martin's lament represented the opening salvo in a decades-long debate about how the words "American," "Catholic," and "university" might appear in meaningful relationship to each other, a debate that has shown little signs of abating three decades later. Notre Dame, the wealthiest and most visible Catholic university in the nation, had, by the mid-1960s, long since ceased to be in fact a "poor boy's institution, a place where students with little money but a willingness to work could succeed." It was much closer to being defined as a "J. Crew catalogue with crucifixes" — a resolutely upper-middle-class institution dominated by affluent children of Catholics from the Chicago suburbs, who possessed both the financial means and the SAT scores to attend a quite selective (and expensive) university. "Ethnic" Notre Dame's sons (and soon, daughters) might have been, but not in the sense embodied in the school's student body in the first century of its existence, or probably in the sense understood by many working-class Catholics who remained passionate supporters of the Fighting Irish but who couldn't afford to send their own children there. In 1966, Notre Dame most assuredly retained a different (and recognizably nonmainstream) "feel" to it that set it apart from eastern Ivys or prestigious Midwestern institutions like Oberlin and Northwestern: it was, in fact, precisely that "feel" that enabled its fans to continue to perceive it as the standard-bearer of the "good fight" against "godless" places like Michigan State. The home of the "Fighting Irish" remained, in that sense, recognizably "ethnic." But somehow ethnicity, athletics, and Catholicism at Notre Dame had become reconfigured by the mid-1960s, significantly aided by the "coaching" of Theodore Hesburgh, into something very different from the configuration portrayed in the James Cagney/Ronald Reagan film, *Knute Rockne – All American.*[15]

Ethnicity and Catholicism

The debate over the meaning of "ethnicity" in U.S. culture and history, of course, has spawned a vast literature generating as much heat as light; but it can be (and has been) cogently argued that the category of "ethnicity" offers a helpful way of understanding both the success story of the Golden Dome and the tale of Catholics in the United States at mid-century. As Harold Abramson has observed in the magisterial *Harvard Encyclopedia of American Ethnic Groups,* "the equation of *religion* with *ethnicity* has been common"; thus a major Catholic participant in the discussion about ethnicity, Andrew Greeley, has convincingly argued that American Catholics are, in fact, "an ethnic group, in the general sense of the term, as well as being a group of ethnic groups, in the specific use of the word 'ethnic' as meaning descendants of European immigrants." Greeley's starting point for such an assertion is the recognition that American Catholicism represents a "collectivity" that is, in certain crucial respects, different from the "host" culture in America: Catholics represent a "group within the larger society, and are *perceived* both by others and by themselves to be different to some extent.[16]

Greeley's own assertion about Catholicism as an "ethnic group" in the United states is built on the work of a number of sociologists of American culture, scholars like Milton Gordon, who defined ethnicity as a "sense of peoplehood." From Philip Gleason's perspective (writing on "American Identity"), Gordon's definition "is the simplest and most satisfactory yet proposed." But Greeley also builds on the insights of Richard Schermerhorn, who has defined "ethnicity" as

> a collectivity within a larger society having real or putative common ancestry, memories of a shared historical past, and a cultural focus on one or more symbolic elements defined as the epitome of their peoplehood.... A necessary accompaniment is some consciousness of kind among members of the group.[17]

From Greeley's perspective, ethnicity has proven to be a useful and productive construct, both for American Catholicism as it navigated its way from the margins of American society into middle class affluence and social/political arrival, and for students of that religious tradition attempting to understand that journey. "Ethnicity" as a primary category of self-identification for American Catholicism, Greeley argues, was not used as an excuse for *withdrawing* from the rest of society so much as a strategy for "dealing oneself into it." "Ethnicity" provided Catholicism in the United States a "rationale for self-definition," as well as providing the congeries of ethnic groups within American Catholicism with considerable political, social, economic, and psychological advantages, serving as a context for preserving and passing on certain skills, traits, and characteristics brought from the "Old World" and useful in the New. "Ethnic differentiation," then, turned out to be both a safe and inexpensive way for immigrant Catholics in America to define themselves "over against" a collectivity that perceived them (in some sense) as "different," and as a strategy for dealing with each other in their "differentness."[18]

By 1996, the majority of American Catholics — and certainly the majority of Notre Dame students — were no longer "ethnic" in the earlier economic and sociological sense of being deprived or marginalized, just as most of the players on Notre Dame's varsity had long since ceased to be Irish, fighting or otherwise. Thus, while the two decades after World War II witnessed the solidification of the "ecological move" of U.S. Catholics from the margins to the affluent mainstream of the culture, a high percentage of Catholics remained "ethnic" in the sense of retaining self-conscious and voluntary affiliation with a recognizable "collectivity" within the larger culture, if no longer in the working-class urban conclaves of the nineteenth century. Indeed, in this quite specific sense of the term "ethnic," Notre Dame's football team can serve as a useful metaphor for American Catholics poised on the cusp of what is now known as the "Sixties."

Catholics were, by 1966, more likely to have more years of education and have a higher income than the national average, despite the media propagation of stereotypes of hard-hat "urban ethnics" supporting the war in Vietnam and beating up on "long-hairs"; American Catholics were more likely to vote for liberal and progressive political candidates than "mainstream" Protestants; they were more likely to support social programs for the social welfare of the poor. They were, in short, identifiably "different" from the Protestant mainstream — and thus "ethnic" in Greeley's broad sense — but in a quite specific way that may have surprised the Gipper. The Fighting Irish, for the surprisingly many Americans who still recite their "Hail Marys" for them, constitute the front ranks of an ethnic "holy war against the Protestant majority in the United States," but in a way that the Midwestern nuns of the 1930s and 1940s never dreamed. The prayer remained the same: "Hail Mary, full of grace, Notre Dame's in second place." It was both the meaning and the combatants in the "Holy War" that had changed rather dramatically since the Gipper.[19]

John O'Hara and "Notre Dame du Lac"

If there was ever a time when the University of Notre Dame actually *was* a "football school," marked by a resolutely masculine, athlete culture and noisy, unintellectual religion — an institutional identity fiercely contested by faithful Domers — it was arguably between 1924 and 1934, when Notre Dame's famous prefect of religion given to the quantification of grace for the purposes of athletic victory — John O'Hara — set a tone of manly spirituality that would become every Midwestern Catholic schoolboy's dream after seeing *Knute Rockne – All American*. Perhaps more than any other individual, O'Hara molded the widespread American Catholic perception of the Golden Dome as the epicenter of "Our Lady's Legions." Under O'Hara's reign as prefect, the fusion of ethnicity, religion, and masculine culture was perhaps as potent as it would ever become at "Notre Dame du Lac."

During those Depression years, Notre Dame was understood by most Americans as a "home of masculine Catholicism." It was marked by a "macho image, of good boys becoming good men." Under that institutional persona, it appealed to Catholic high school teachers across the nation to send it recruits.[20]

There was nothing theological, and probably little that could even be described as "doctrinal," about O'Hara's gospel during his ten years as prefect of religion — the official charged with the ghostly life of undergraduates. O'Hara was known as the most dynamic prefect of religion Notre Dame had ever seen, promoting a "manly piety" that saw frequent Communions and devotion to the Blessed Mother as evidences of a healthy masculine identity. His cherished vision was to make the Golden Dome a "City of the Blessed Sacrament," with young men receiving Communion at every hour of the morning. His message was simple: "By receiving Communion frequently you will be better men, better students, and better athletes." One of his main targets for his message were members of the football team, and his chief means of evangelization was the *Religious Bulletin*. At first simply a one-page collection of church notices, advice, and short phrases about the spiritual life, the *Bulletin* was posted around campus on dormitory doors and kiosks. But the *Bulletin* would grow in both size and influence between the years 1924 and 1934, eventually being slipped under the door of every dorm room on campus. The "theology" evinced on those sheets might fairly be termed rather "thin" by contemporary academic standards — especially the almost-overt quantification of spiritual acts for athletic purposes — but it was a "theology" that most of Notre Dame's young men understood instinctually. Thus, in his October 3, 1930, *Bulletin,* O'Hara announced that it was a "pious tradition at Notre Dame" to remember the football team during "Holy Communion on the morning of every game. Most of the members of the squad have already started daily Communion: we want no accidents to mar the season." The Catholic identity of "Notre Dame du Lac," established to fuse American identity, "healthy manhood," and Marian piety into one package, never seemed more secure.[21]

Founded in 1842 by a group of French priests of the Order of the Holy Cross led by Father Edward Sorin on 524 acres in the Indiana countryside (on the site of the mission outpost of Theodore Badin, the first Catholic priest ordained in the United States), the school reflected both the European educational beliefs and the nineteenth-century French (as distinct from Irish) piety of its founders: the vision of Sorin and the French priests with him included both a center of sound Catholic formation for young men on the western border of Indiana and a center of Marian piety that would reach throughout the United States. As a recent, insightful student of "material culture" has observed about the place, Sorin

> claimed the land on which Notre Dame sat, transforming it from wilderness into an ordered, sacred space. Catholics would be nurtured not only through proper education but also through living in a Catholic "natural" environment. Toward this end, a series of shrines was built at Notre Dame to promote visitation not only by students but also by Catholics from the surrounding area. The eventual construction of the now well-known replica of the Lourdes grotto in 1896 capped off a past tradition of shrine building at Notre Dame.[22]

Sorin and his French fellow priests thus began building a large Gothic pilgrimage church — "Our Lady of the Sacred Heart," now the University Church and the spiritual heart of the campus — in the 1860s, several years after completing the first of the Marian shrines on campus. The first grotto to "Our Lady of Lourdes" (a devotion just nineteen years old at the time) was completed in 1877, soon to be followed by several others. The now-famous grotto shrine to Our Lady of Lourdes, built on the gently sloping hill immediately behind the Gothic Sacred Heart Church, was completed in 1896, and soon became a campus shrine visited by students before exams, during personal crises, and (later) by the entire football team before home games. Both the bucolic setting and the religious architecture of Sorin's institution thus conspired to ring quite a few changes on the "mystic chords of memory" of adolescent boys, lending the place an almost mystical glow.[23]

It was, appropriately enough, during O'Hara's reign as prefect of religion that the most famous death-bed scenario of a football star — suffused with genuine pathos, athletic bonding, and Catholic angelology — took place. In a tableau made famous by an actor destined to become the president of the United States, George Gipp — described by Knute Rockne's biographer as the "greatest [football] player Notre Dame ever turned out — lay dying of pneumonia with "The Rock" and other members of the squad close by his side. As Rockne himself later described the moment, someone at Gipp's bedside observed that "it's pretty tough to go":

"What's tough about it?" Gipp smiled at us feebly. "I've no complaint." He turned to me: "I've got to go, Rock. It's all right. I'm
not afraid." His eyes brightened in a frame of pallor. "Sometime,
Rock, when the team's up against it, when things are wrong and
the breaks are beating the boys, tell them to go in there with all
they've got and win just one for the Gipper. I don't know where
I'll be then, but I'll know about it and I'll be happy."[24]

The death-bed conversation between Gipp and Rockne — part of the
collective unconscious of Midwestern parochial school boys for several generations, at least before "Gipp" became president — evinced
the type of "eschatological athleticism" that abetted the broad cultural
perception of the Notre Dame football team as defender of American
Catholicism's honor. No intellectual himself, O'Hara as prefect (and
later president) was "suspicious of intellectualism [sic] as dangerous
to faith and religion. He wanted no truck with abstractions, had small
use for philosophy, [and] thought of theology almost wholly in terms
of apologetics."[25]

Given O'Hara's anti-intellectualism, then, it is one of those delicious ironies of history that, on being named acting president of
the school in 1934, he became the founder of the *University* of
Notre Dame: O'Hara played the critical role in founding the graduate school (establishing the graduate program in philosophy in 1936,
in physics and math in 1938, and in political science in 1939) and
appointed a scholar's scholar, Father Philip Moore, to run it; he
instituted a "visiting scholars" program that brought some of the
brightest stars of the British and Irish intellectual firmament to South
Bend; he lured an impressive group of European academics fleeing
Hitler — Waldemar Gurian, Karl Menger, Arthur Haas, Yves Simon — to come to Notre Dame as professors and sponsored the
frequent presence on campus of the two greatest neo-Thomists in
the Catholic world, Etienne Gilson and Jacques Maritain; he oversaw
the founding of Notre Dame's perhaps most prestigious publication,
the *Review of Politics;* he provided the finances for scholarly conferences for which the school would shortly become famous. In just
five years (in 1939 O'Hara left Notre Dame to become a bishop and
military chaplain and was later named cardinal archbishop of Philadelphia), O'Hara laid the solid foundations for the emergence of Notre
Dame as a "serious" national academic institution. Thus, the tradition of parlaying the school's athletic success, "ethnic" identity, and
masculine piety into something considerably more intellectually de-

manding had begun by 1939. O'Hara's successors would build on his foundations.[26]

O'Hara's immediate successor in the president's office, Father Hugh O'Donnell, himself one time center on the school's varsity football team, worked closely with the federal government during the war years to make Notre Dame one of the most important military training centers in the nation, lending concrete embodiment to the motto carved on the entrance to the university church: "God, Country, Notre Dame." In 1947 O'Donnell was succeeded by O'Hara's hand-picked successor as prefect of religion, John Cavanaugh — a onetime businessman and executive at Studebaker before entering the Holy Cross order. As a result of its wartime experience of working closely with the federal government and the broadening of horizons that experience engendered, the institution Cavanaugh inherited was poised to move into the world of serious academic research and scholarship.[27]

Cavanaugh can be credited as the founder of the "University of Notre Dame Foundation" — an office originally intended to coordinate the activities of the alumni association with the office of public relations, but which quickly evolved into a permanent fund-raising institution with a full-time staff. The Foundation set as its first major challenge the raising of two million dollars for a new science building (subsequently dedicated in 1952), and has, in the half century since then, made Notre Dame the wealthiest Catholic educational institution in the nation. Cavanaugh oversaw the explosion of numbers in the student body following World War II, set off in large part by the GI Bill of Rights: to meet the new, more mature intellectual and spiritual needs of ex-servicemen, he endorsed the "General Program of Liberal Studies" in 1950 — a kind of "four year college within a college" organized around a "great books" approach to learning closely resembling the undergraduate core program instituted by Cavanaugh's friend Robert Maynard Hutchins at the resolutely intellectual University of Chicago. The aim of Notre Dame's "General Program" was to form undergraduates in an "integral Catholic humanism" through seminars on the Great Books, language tutorials, and other specialized courses — all carried out under the careful eye of Thomistic philosophers and theologians. The new program in South Bend was launched in the shadow and with the benediction of Robert Hutchins, and the assistant of one of Hutchins's closest intellectual lieutenants, Mortimer Adler, was brought in to direct the program. Hutchins, as chancellor of the University of Chicago, had played a key role in getting that school to scuttle its high-profile football program in order to marshal all of its forces for the "life of the mind" and had recently made headlines throughout the Catholic academic world by accusing American Catholic educational institutions of betraying the "oldest intellectual tradition in the West" by buying into the American university shibboleths of "athleticism, collegiatism, vocationalism, and anti-intellectualism," while simultaneously failing to emulate their non-Catholic counterparts in dedication to research and high academic standards. Cavanaugh's presidency thus laid the crucial foundations for Notre Dame's "takeoff" into the ranks of first-class educational institutions after mid-century.[28]

Father Theodore Hesburgh — who became Notre Dame's fifteenth president in 1952, at the tender age of thirty-five — thus inherited a "university ready for takeoff." The *New York Times* would, within a decade of his assuming office, write that "as an educator, he has brought Notre Dame from the forefront of the nation's football factories to the forefront of the nation's universities." By 1966, Hesburgh would be favorably compared to his only other rival as *paterfamilias* among university presidents in the United States: "Yale's Kingman Brewster, Jr. has been called the 'Protestant Hesburgh' only a little less often than Father Hesburgh has been called the 'Catholic Brewster.' "[29]

In the very first year of his presidency Hesburgh realized that the revolution sweeping higher education in America after World War II — with its quantitative standards of professorial excellence, its heightened emphasis on the "hard sciences" in the heat of the Cold War, and its renewed emphasis on academic freedom after the constraints of wartime ideology — "threatened to leave theology and philosophy attached to the academic body like a kind of vermiform appendix, a vestigial remnant, neither useful nor decorative. If this happened, Catholic universities might become great, but they would no longer be Catholic." Hesburgh thus determined that Notre Dame's aim of acceptance into the ranks of elite academic institutions would not be bought at the price of its religious identity. In 1952, within months of his arrival in the president's office, Hesburgh initiated a self-study of the College of Arts and Letters that resulted in a three-hundred-page, single-spaced document, advocating the [intellectual] "integration of the college" around a core of courses in neo-scholastic philosophy and theology.[30]

Just nine years later, in 1961, Hesburgh initiated a new self-study "to suggest ways for improving the intellectual substance of the College of Arts and Letters." The latter self-study was initiated, in part, by the heated debate on Catholic intellectual life taking place among the

Notre Dame faculty (and among Catholic intellectuals more broadly) about the role of "synthesizing norms" in "Catholic education," as well as proceeding from the desire of departments for more autonomy. While the 1961 self-study, in the event, produced little in the way of concrete influences on the core in South Bend, it did witness to Hesburgh's constant concern about the role of theology in "Catholic mission" of Notre Dame.

By 1962, Notre Dame's "efflorescence" — holding on to its ethnic, Catholic, and athletic traditions while demanding a place at the table of the academic powerhouses — moved Chicago's Hutchins to call its rise "one of the most spectacular developments in higher education in the last 25 years." During the first ten years of his presidency, Hesburgh put up twelve new buildings, increased faculty salaries by 90 percent, tripled endowment to $25 million, multiplied science spending tenfold, and began building a new library in South Bend that would have five times more book space than the old. All of this formed part of Hesburgh's "Program for Excellence," a ten-year, $66 million race to academic distinction.[31]

Hesburgh likewise realized that "overobedience" and passive learning had been among the chief criticisms brought to bear against students in Catholic colleges, typified by places like Notre Dame, where lights and electricity had been cut off in student rooms at 11:00 p.m. and where students had had to "sign in" for Mass with prefects stationed outside hall chapels three mornings a week. By 1962 Hesburgh had dropped both restrictions (Mass attendance remained the same for several years), and revised the eleven-page handbook of student rules to a two-page list of guidelines and expectations: clearly a "new Notre Dame" was in the offing.[32]

Hesburgh's devotion to the cause of academic distinction, however — revealed in strategies like his "Program for Excellence" — followed the path of his predecessors in *not* eschewing the school's athletic tradition (as was the case at places like the University of Chicago) or in downplaying Notre Dame's strong Catholic popular identity (as some would later accuse places like Georgetown); rather, the young president in South Bend held on to the singular blending of all three that distinguished the "Notre Dame Tradition" while simultaneously refashioning that tradition into something recognizably different from other institutions (and Catholic). The triumphant 1953 Fighting Irish football season (the first full season of Hesburgh's presidency) thus offered instructive signals of athletic things to come: Notre Dame would finish the 1953 season with a brilliant record under the driven coaching of Frank Leahy, the man credited with the "audacity to drop the Notre Dame box shift in favor of the 'T-Formation.' " Leahy's teams served as "near-models of perfection" that produced four Heisman Trophy winners: he amassed the second highest winning percentage of games (85.5 percent) of any American collegiate coach (after Rockne himself) and won more national titles than anyone (including Rockne).[33]

Leahy's almost-paranoid "passion for perfection" had already earned him legendary status among Notre Dame's fans (and enemies), although one could wonder what the good fathers — especially one good father in the president's office with a quite distinct vision of what Our Lady's school should stand for — made of it all: Leahy regularly drove both his teams and himself beyond their limits, delivering Rockne-style locker room orations "with a mist in his eyes that was at once both ingenuous and guileful." He hired security guards to patrol the second floor of campus buildings overlooking the practice fields to prevent spying from the "opposition." An unconfirmed legend reported that Leahy chartered a plane to patrol the areas surrounding the practice fields in order to discover "clandestine agents" from other teams hiding in the trees.[34]

All of this must have come very close to "the edge" for Father Hesburgh; the edge was crossed during the Notre Dame–Iowa game in November 1953, when Leahy instructed one of his players to feign an on-field injury near the end of the first half when the Fighting Irish were out of "time-outs." Notre Dame secured the needed time to score as a result of the ruse and ended the game with a tie. But the following Saturday the *New York Times* led its story about the Notre Game game that afternoon with the title "Leahy Will Miss Notre Dame Game." Not for Father Hesburgh the gridiron antics of the previous Saturday, bespeaking a football factory praised for its wily tactics in barrooms across the land. Leahy's brilliant record notwithstanding, pleading failing health the seasoned and successful coach was replaced in the 1954 season by a green young alumnus of unknown promise, Terry Brennan. The record of the next few football seasons under Brennan and his immediate successor were undistinguished compared to Leahy's triumphs, but a line in the sand had been drawn: "football factory" was not a phrase Notre Dame's president ever wanted to hear spoken in his presence.[35]

Even on Saturday afternoons in South Bend, with the band playing "Onward to Victory" and the proceeds of sports concessions booming, Hesburgh knew that Notre Dame needed more money — lots of it — to "play with the big boys" of academics like the Ivys and state behemoths like Michigan and Wisconsin. Certainly the money generated by Notre Dame's sports teams could (and was) used for resolutely academic ends, but considerably more was needed. Another possible (new and heretofore untapped) source was foundation grants: by 1960, after painstaking coordination with the university's own "Foundation" office, Notre Dame was one of six universities in the U.S. awarded a six-million-dollar "matching grant" by the Ford Foundation for academic scholarships, faculty development, and new academic buildings. The only Catholic institution to be awarded such a grant in Ford's program to help six "regional universities of outstanding promise" — the others were Johns Hopkins, Vanderbilt, Brown, Stanford, and the University of Denver — Hesburgh not only "matched" the Foundation's grant but immediately launched a new campaign ("Challenge II") that financed a new athletic and conference center on campus. "Challenge II," in turn, generated funds that helped fuel a $62 million campaign (SUMMA) to endow distinguished professorships, graduate student scholarships, and Hesburgh's "special projects" that buttressed the school's Catholic ethos, like the Institute for Advanced Religious Studies. Already, by 1960, Hesburgh revealed his strategy of utilizing Notre Dame's much-vaunted "athletic tradition" for other, more serious purposes, about which the Golden Dome's far-flung "straphanger alumni" neither knew nor cared about. "Cheer, Cheer for Old Notre Dame" was still being sung by thousands of voices on Saturday afternoons as new science labs and a computer building were being built around the stadium.[36]

In 1963 Hesburgh and Notre Dame at last found a football coach in the Rockne-Leahy tradition but comfortable with the direction of the "new Notre Dame": an Armenian Presbyterian at Northwestern University, Ara Parseghian would later describe both the excitement and fear he felt as he drove up the drive toward the Golden Dome for his official on-campus interview — excitement because of the athletic tradition he stood in chance of inheriting, and fear because, like Rockne, he would be a Protestant in the very epicenter of American Catholicism. In the event, Parseghian would resurrect the tradition (and victories) of that earlier Protestant while also displaying an instrumentalist devotion to the "larger picture" that must have warmed the heart of administrators: in his first season he amassed a 9–1 record, with record-making profits from the football team that went to the university and not to the athletic department.[37]

By the time of the "Game of the Century" several years later, both

Hesburgh and Parseghian had crafted a Notre Dame whose reality was somewhat different from the perception of both fans and critics, a place where successful football teams were merely a metaphor for other, more serious, pursuits. If Edward Sorin's dream had been of a great Catholic university (with emphasis on both words), then Hesburgh (and Parseghian) made it come true. As the chronicler of "The Game" would later put it:

> By 1966, Notre Dame no longer had to take students and athletes wherever it could find them. Now athletes sought out the school, and not all of them found that athletic talent alone was enough to get them in. There was still a blue-collar flavor to the school, but now there was also a feeling of superiority that the university encouraged. . . . Big-time football at schools like Yale, Harvard, and Princeton was considered antithetical to a quality education. But Notre Dame felt that if it was going to do something it was going to do it right and be the best at it. Football was the metaphor for that determination. The university's president agreed with that feeling, but he also felt that there was a lot more to life than the successful application of the 2-minute drill.[38]

If football under Parseghian in 1966 was a serious business (and all of his players agreed it was), so was the academic world presided over by Hesburgh. By the year of "The Game" Notre Dame's twelve-hundred-acre campus boasted sixty buildings, half of which had been built under Hesburgh, and significant pedagogical reforms had been implemented to mirror the significant architectural changes on campus: the dormitories on campus had become "residence halls" so that real communities of students emerged; curfews for undergraduates had been abolished, and the priest-rectors who had ruled student dorms by fiat now contended with democratically elected student representatives who were given a significant voice in running the halls.[39]

Conservative alumni and Catholic traditionalists did not go gentle into the good night foreshadowed therewith, however: parents of "Domer" students received (anonymous) mailings in the early 1960s decrying the "new Notre Dame," and a Chicago-based group, calling itself the "Advocates of Our Lady," mailed out thousands of letters charging the administration of the place with permitting "liturgical aberrations" in some residence hall masses. Likewise, the Advocates warned that the "radical move" to allow freedom of speech on campus "could only lead to the erosion of Catholicism" inside the very fortress of Our Lady. And it was not only religious reactionaries who took up the cry: Dr. Robert Hassenger, of Notre Dame's sociology department, reported a survey he had taken among alumni showing that, except for the classes of 1916 and 1961, most graduates wanted the rules on campus *tightened,* not "loosened" — which appeared to be the direction Hesburgh was taking.[40]

Catholicism's "Holy War" in the U.S.

Ralph Martin's letter in *Ave Maria,* then, hardly constituted lightning in a clear blue sky: well before April 1966, conservative Catholics and those who saw Notre Dame as the front legion of Catholicism's "holy war" in the U.S. raised questions about a Catholic flagship institution in which academic excellence stood at the top of the value system. The difference was that Martin was not one of the "old boys" remembering the days of Rockne and prayers at the grotto; nor was he an anti-intellectual smarting from the implementation of the reforms of Vatican II: he was a notably talented young man, the winner of Notre Dame's own Dockweiler Award in Philosophy, who had won a Woodrow Wilson Fellowship to Princeton. His *confessio* thus appeared to voice a profound concern about how the revered institutions of "ethnic Catholicism" would fare in the brave new world of postimmigrant America:

> In junior year I stopped practicing. The vitality and honesty of that small part of the student body and faculty who were thriving on academic excellence seemed much more attractive and alive than Christianity at the university.... Each year Notre Dame graduates over a thousand persons, very few of whom have been personally converted to Jesus Christ, very few of whom are concerned with making Christ a real part of their lives and work. A practical paganism pervades each graduating class. The practical axis of most Notre Dame students' lives lies in "getting ahead," "being a success" — not in giving witness to their Lord.[41]

Labeling the problem more "pastoral" than "academic," Martin argued that most of Notre Dame's faculty "do not or cannot make the painful attempt to relate their discipline" to the faith of their students. The situation, moreover, was becoming more critical "with the policy of hiring non-Catholic faculty members now in force." The end result was that Notre Dame stood in danger of "becoming part of the problem rather than contributing to the solution; as if it were gaining the whole world, yet suffering the loss of its soul."[42]

Hesburgh's "Reply," printed in the same issue of the magazine and immediately following Martin's open letter, offered the "old" answer to Martin's plaint and also adumbrated a future vision of Catholic education in which "ethnic" would continue to define the American Catholic experience, but in a significantly different way. Manifesting no desire to repudiate Notre Dame's traditional emphasis on "moral formation" in educating young people, Hesburgh nonetheless drew on perhaps the most venerable theologian in the English-speaking world, John Henry Newman, in offering a fresh vision of an old task:

> At an earlier age in this country, there was an enormous emphasis in Catholic universities on moral formation, and this was accepted both by students and parents, at times, as the very meaning of the university. And perhaps it was. Universities were often put in the same category as seminaries. Certainly there has to be an element of moral formation in the total educational process. But at the same time one has to always hold, as Cardinal Newman did, that the primary purpose of the university is intellectual formation, involving a philosophical and theological sophistication in the total teaching and learning process.[43]

American Catholic educators, of course, had always claimed Newman's epochal work, *The Idea of a University,* — as the textual "classic" for understanding how the words "university" and "Catholic" might be used in the same phrase; Hesburgh, however, was the first American Catholic educator to actually have a shot at implementing Newman's vision of a rigorously academic and resolutely Catholic liberal arts education in one place, and he evinced a fierce determination that nothing, not even salutary impulses on students' part like community service, get in the way of that vision:

> There is certainly an enormously greater interest in social action than there was in the past. And I would say that this is not entirely a good thing. It leads to too much of a concern for action at a time when we should be laying the intellectual foundation on which this action is going to be effective. . . . It doesn't help in the long run, I think, if students are distracted from what they can do only during their college years.[44]

Thus, some Catholic institutions had to be committed to a quite specific kind of formation — *intellectual* formation — as the pearl of great

price for which earlier generations had sacrificed. A rigorous grounding in the intellectual, academic questions of Catholicism was at least
as appropriate a task for Catholic higher education as that of "moral
formation." The task for Catholic institutions like Notre Dame, Hesburgh remarked in the "Reply," was to pass on to students the *habitus*
of "how to think theologically, how to get at the roots of an *understanding* of the faith, how to create an *intellectual formation* that
won't be overturned by emotionalism or by the fad of the day."[45]

Hesburgh's vision of a great "Catholic university," elucidated in his
1966 reply to Ralph Martin, never dimmed during the next twenty
years of his presidency: in a 1977 interview Hesburgh was asked
by a reporter to respond to the recurrent criticism that "something
has been lost at Notre Dame because of the emphasis on academic
achievement...that the Catholic tradition has become something like
a subculture." The president observed that "my deepest conviction is
that Notre Dame won't make it unless it stays Catholic. If we lose our
Catholic character we will not be very successful in getting people to
support this place." Indeed, Notre Dame's singular success in several
decades of fund-raising, he noted, was "because people believe there
ought to be a great Catholic university." And during his final year in
office, in an article entitled "Facing Life Without Father," Hesburgh
was eulogized (somewhat prematurely) for his

> courage to act on his wonderful dream of a great Catholic uni-
> versity. While he worked to enhance its academic reputation, he
> strove mightily to insure that Notre Dame would never lose its
> Catholic soul. For all of us he set an example by ending his
> workdays here unfailingly with a visit to the Grotto.[46]

In a sense Hesburgh's solution to the dilemma of Catholic higher education in the latter half of the twentieth century displeased both
"sides" to the debate: Catholic critics maintained that his emphasis
on academic excellence was won at the expense of the older privileg-
ing of "moral formation," while secular critics observed that Notre
Dame was still altogether too "Catholic" to *really* fit the standards
of American mainstream research institutions. But it was precisely in
the interstices of these criticisms that Hesburgh discerned (brilliantly, it
turned out) Notre Dame's ecological "niche" in the world of American
higher education: Notre Dame's success in becoming and remaining an
academic institution of the first rank would depend, ironically enough,
on its remaining resolutely "ethnic" in ethos, constituency, and commitment; but its ethnicity would be redefined, along with the culture

in which it found itself. One can only wonder what Orestes Brownson, the mid-nineteenth-century intellectual famous for his crusade for "Americanization" and the "inculturation" of the church in the United States, made of it all from his grave in the crypt of Notre Dame's Sacred Heart Church.

"Ethnic" Catholicism at Century's End: Triumph and Irony

Notre Dame's story in the two decades following the close of the Second World War was one of triumph and irony, arguably much like that of American Catholicism itself. The "answer" offered by Notre Dame to the long-debated dilemma fought between assimilationists (the "Americanists" of the nineteenth century and the "liberals" of the twentieth) and those fearful of the culture (the "ultramontanists" of the nineteenth century and the "conservatives" of the twentieth) was: *sic et non,* — that is, both yes and no. Notre Dame would strive (and largely succeed) in becoming a research university of the first rank, competing with the very best educational institutions in the United States on their own terms. But at the same time, Notre Dame would remain palpably different from places like Harvard and the University of Chicago, its very landscape bespeaking "ethnic" allegiances differentiating it from the religiously sanitized "pluralism" of those elite educational institutions. Pluralism there certainly is (and always was) at Notre Dame: some of the figures who had brought it national athletic glory even in the days of its most parochial identity — figures like Rockne in his early career — had been Protestants, and its "winningest" coach of the post-Rockne era, Ara Parseghian, stood outside "The Faith." Concrete realizations of Hesburgh's academic vision for the place, like its Institute of Jewish-Christian Relations, proclaimed intellectual loyalties well beyond the fears and prejudices of an earlier immigrant ghetto. A stroll around a campus redolent of affluence and laboratory research dispelled any notion of the place as a "poor boys' school," full of first-generation college students reveling in Robert Hutchins's cardinal sins of "athleticism" and anti-intellectualism. Its standardized test scores placed it in the elite company of perhaps twenty-five other schools in the nation, and the quality of its academic journals was anything *but* "parochial." But its emergence as a serious research institution, taken seriously by even the most secular of academics, depended on its maintaining loyalties with a quite specific "subgroup" in the culture, for its pluralism was, and is, of a quite

distinct and limited variety. And it is here that Andrew Greeley's redefinition of "ethnicity" helps to uncover the story of Notre Dame
(and of the faith it proclaimed) at mid-century.

The Catholic community in the United States, Greeley has observed,
represents a "group which is in some respects different from the host
culture":

> There are boundaries between Catholics and others in the United
> States. These boundaries are not legal, for the most part, al-
> though there are boundary-setting consequences of laws or judi-
> cial decisions.... [For] the boundaries among religious groups in
> American society are cultural and social for the most part; they
> are implicit and unofficial.[47]

These implicit and unofficial "boundaries" between Catholics and
"others," he asserts, help to account for the resurgence of anti-
Catholicism in American culture in the 1960s and 1970s — in the
wake of Vatican II, when it might have been reasonably expected
that Catholics would be more welcome in the culture than ever before. For, despite the great promise of the ecumenism endorsed by the
Second Vatican Council, Catholics kept their schools and their "divisive" attitudes on abortion: "they did not stop being 'strange' as the
price for ecumenical dialogue. They have not yet been assimilated."
Thus the "new" anti-Catholicism in the latter half of the twentieth century would be voiced by public intellectuals and academics
rather than by hooded patriots, for "part of the official 'melting pot'
model of acculturation to American society is that the differences
ought to go away." The fundamental assumption of "professional"
acculturationists, Greeley argues, is that the forces working for "homogenization" — for the eventual amalgamation of all subgroups in
the culture into a common and largely undifferentiated mass — are
so powerful as to be irresistible. But, in fact, the example of Notre
Dame (specifically) and of American Catholicism (more generally)
would appear to raise profound questions about the likelihood of total
homogenization anytime in the near future:

> Processes of homogenization and differentiation are going on
> simultaneously. We are, to put the matter in popular terms, be-
> coming more like one another and more different at the same
> time.... The acculturation perspective does not take into account
> the fact, noted by many historians, that ethnicity was perceived
> by the immigrants as a way of becoming Americans. The hy-

phen in the hyphenate American was a symbol of equality, not
inequality. In an urban environment where everyone, including
the native American, was a something-else-American, one had to
be ethnic to find one's place on the map.[48]

Greeley thus presses the point that the "creation" of ethnic subgroups
in the United States — of not being "Milanese" or "Florentine" in
America but "Italian" — was a way for the immigrant population
to plan for its present and future in America, rather than hold on
to its past in the Old World. In a complex society like that of the
U.S., marked by what he terms "unstable pluralism," one had to be
"something" if one were going to be "anybody." Ethnicity thus revealed itself as a relatively safe form of differentiation. While there
might be conflict and competition among various ethnic groups, the
conflict was rarely violent; indeed, American society implicitly *legitimated* ethnic differentiation, if not required it, providing protocols
and processes whereby any potential conflict was minimized. Ethnicity, in such a cultural circumstance, represented *not* a residual social
force, gradually disappearing, but rather a dynamic, flexible social
mechanism transformed and transmuted into various shapes to meet
changing situations and circumstances.[49]

In the U.S. and indeed in virtually all Western industrialized countries, according to Greeley, religious groupings operate as "quasi-
ethnic groups." Catholicism in these societies provides for its adherents both a worldview and a self-definition; it passes on certain
behavioral traits and personality characteristics in a process that is
normally quite un-selfconscious. But the "Catholic collectivity" in
America is far more tightly defined than it is in a country like Italy,
where virtually everyone is Catholic "in some fashion." To be Catholic
in the U.S.

> means to be different. Catholicism offers you a potentially im-
> portant form of self-definition, a social location in which you can
> define yourself by those very differences as separate from the rest
> of society, but the separateness need not and usually does not im-
> ply hostility or major conflict; it is rather a way of carving out a
> piece of social turf for yourself. It is ground around which one
> can wander more or less as one pleases, so there is no reason for
> yielding this useful means of social location and self-definition as
> a price for participating in the larger society. On the contrary, it
> is viewed as a means *of participating* in the larger society.[50]

If Greeley is correct in applying the definition of "ethnicity" to contemporary religious groupings like Catholics in the U.S. (and this study
obviously accepts as axiomatic that his reading of the cultural circumstance is presciently correct), then much about almost-fanatical loyalty
and enthusiasm engendered in fans by the Fighting Irish football team
in their "holy war" fought on autumnal Saturday afternoons — as well
as the singular success of Theodore Hesburgh in building a small parochial school in the Midwest into a prestigious national university —
falls into place.

All those blue and gold flags bearing only the letters "ND" waving
from front porches from coast to coast during football season proclaimed the *Americanness* of their owners, but an Americanness of a
particular stripe and "denomination" (as it were). The "Fighting Irish"
in the decades after World War II would continue to elicit the ethnic loyalties of millions of fans who never set foot on the South Bend
campus precisely because Notre Dame *was,* in some palpable if often-
times misunderstood way, "ethnic"; but in the years after mid-century
this "ethnicity" had little or nothing to do with social or educational
marginalization or economic deprivation.

Notre Dame's remarkable rise, under the guiding genius of Theodore Hesburgh, into the rarefied company of elite American educational institutions was built on the solid recognition that its raison
d'être — its niche in the ecological landscape of American higher education — was a quite distinctive "take" on the American Dream. Part
of that dream certainly involved the astonishingly victorious athletic
tradition of Rockne and Leahy and Parseghian, with the Fighting Irish
football team taking the field on glorious Midwestern fall afternoons
while Domer fans sang themselves hoarse to the words of "Onward
to Victory"; most assuredly another part of that dream was tied to
its bucolic campus, chock-full of fake-Gothic buildings connected by
hundreds of acres of lakes and lush green landscape — precisely the
kind of architectural "set" that high school seniors thought of when
the word "college" came to mind. Still another part of that dream
involved the "mystic chords of memory," recalling "good boys (and,
in time, good girls too) becoming good men and women" by working hard to achieve their parents' hopes. But one would miss the
"juice" — the power and the ineluctable attraction — of Notre Dame's
charisma if one were to focus on any of those things as the "answer"
to its remarkable ascent into the fold of what college guides refer to
as "first tier" institutions. *The* answer to Notre Dame's remarkable
charisma and success in attracting money, students, and very good

football players is the combination of all of these things with another, disarmingly obvious, factor: its quite self-conscious and unapologetic identity as an American Catholic university — arguably *the* American Catholic university if one were judging by endowment, selectivity, or name-identification.

The ironic, late twentieth-century resolution to the battles between "Americanists" and "ultramontanists" of the previous century — evinced in the institutional history of the University of Notre Dame and its famous football team — was one that neither side could have foreseen. American mainstream standards of academic excellence, state-of-the-art facilities, and institutional monies devoted to research were all realized with a vengeance at the home of the "Dumb Micks" in the decades after World War II. And yet the place remained recognizably "ethnic" in fact and by plan and elicited "ethnic loyalties" from its supporters long after the number of descendants of Irish immigrants on its football squad could be easily counted on one hand. Indeed, one might reasonably argue that its continued institutional "ethnicity" was precisely the thing that made possible its high academic standards, state-of-the-art facilities, and impressive monies devoted to research. The very thing that so frightened the Americanists — the continued devotion to a recognizable and distinctive subculture within the larger cultural discussion — was *the* thing that allowed the realization of their dream.

The year 1966 proved to be a benchmark for the Fighting Irish and their president: the calculated "use" that Notre Dame made of its football team for its own institutional purposes was revealed with breathtaking clarity in Ara Parseghian's shepherding of the team during the "Game of the Century" on its way to yet another bowl game. A quite healthy, Niebuhrian sense of instrumentalist calculation guaranteed yet another victorious pigskin season, as the Fighting Irish "did what they had to do" during their battle against Michigan State — winning with a tie, as it were. The revered president of the place was no less Niebuhrian in discerning what made people support his institution: Hesburgh's letter to Ralph Martin in 1966 — published, appropriately enough, in the pages of the parochially sold *Ave Maria* — announced clearly and publicly that Notre Dame was and would always remain (insofar as he had anything to do with it) a resolutely and unapologetically Roman Catholic institution, "ethnic" to the core.

The "Horrible Hibernians," the "Fighting Papists" had arrived — socially, economically, and now educationally — in no small part due to their clear ethnic loyalties: but, as Hesburgh recognized with what might (at first) appear cold calculation but on closer scrutiny can be recognized as Niebuhrian wisdom, "if we lose our Catholic character we will not be very successful in getting people to support this place." If Mass and lights out at eleven were no longer imposed, Catholicism would nonetheless still remain palpably present, in ethos, curriculum, faculty, and even in landscape architecture. While all of these things appeared less than substantial to Hesburgh's critics, they nonetheless assured a sacramental "feel" about the place that both Catholics and others immediately recognized. The "Fighting Irish" (although not predominantly or even significantly Irish in the years after mid-century) would still take the field to win a mind-numbing percentage of their football games, even under the direction of Armenian Protestant coaches, while fans in the mammoth stadium "at the Dome" and across the country rang out the words to "Onward to Victory."

Conclusion

Magnalia Christi Americana

"The Lord will be our God and delight to dwell among us as his owne people, and will cammaund a blessing upon us in all our ways, soe that wee shall see much more of his wisdome, power, goodness and truthe than formerly we have beene acquainted with."

— JOHN WINTHROP, "Modell of Christian Charitie,"
Aboard the *Arbella*, 1630[1]

"The Mighty Works of Christ in America"

At least since 1702, when Cotton Mather invented the historical genre that scholars now call "American religious history" by publishing his *Magnalia Christi Americana,* theologians and students of American culture have sought to chronicle and interpret God's "mighty works" in the New World. Some of Mather's successors chose to follow his lead in offering what is termed "doxological history" — that is, studies of the North American past that emphasize and celebrate white, Protestant America's unique "covenant" with the Holy One, as well as its "getting right" what corrupt (Catholic) Europe had largely "gotten wrong." These studies of religion in the United States, in Mather's footsteps, have tended to focus on the *culture* itself, as opposed to some religious institution, as the locus of grace in North American history. For these scholars, it is American culture itself — not a church or institutional presence set over against the culture — that promises redemptive action in history. In that technical sense, American "church" history since Mather tends, overall, to bow to American "religious" history as the organizing matrix of the most insightful and creative studies of the role of religion in North America.[2]

Consistently portrayed as the "city upon a hill" in this tradition of religious history writing, North America's pure — and therefore, by definition, Protestant — *culture* was uniquely suited to "redeem the world," both by being true to its original covenantal promises *and* by making good on those promises by exporting them abroad. Thus, two of the most important subtexts of this master narrative in doxology might be termed the "covenantal" and "exceptionalist" themes. The covenantal theme in this genre of religious history devotes itself to illustrating how the "covenant" made between the Holy One and the first generation of nonseparating congregational Puritans in *New England* was faithfully kept on the human side from the seventeenth century to the present, with the political/cultural result (in Woodrow Wilson's perhaps too effusive phrase) that "America had the infinite privilege of fulfilling her destiny and saving the world."[3]

The "exceptionalist" strand of this revered narrative tradition consists in proving that religion in the American colonies (and, after 1776, in the United States) could not simply be reduced to European Christianity transplanted to a new place: North American Christianity is something unique and pure — "exceptional" in every sense. Marked by a voluntary spirit in organization, an activistic "can do" spirituality that eschews mysticism and meditation, a democratic distrust of academic theology, and a missionary expansionism alarmingly analogous to cultural imperialism, such Christianity bears the same relationship to the religion of the "Old World" as Emerson's "party of the future" bore to the "party of the past." Such Christianity announced — and, in nineteenth-century domestic and foreign missions, *claimed* — a religious "manifest destiny" to remake the world in its own fresh image.[4]

Reinhold Niebuhr's mid-twentieth-century reinterpretation of this revered historical genre spawned by Cotton Mather — a reinterpretation published in 1952 as *The Irony of American History* — was certainly not the first modern questioning of this "great tradition" of American salvation history; but it *was,* arguably, the most influential of such reinterpretations. Niebuhr's book outlined a more sober, less comfortable theological reading of the history and culture of the United States that would have profound effects in politics and the academy, and not just in the seminary. The ways of grace, Niebuhr opined, did not form straight lines in history; historical actors — even, and perhaps especially, "righteous" actors — took part in a comedy for which they had only part of the script. God's redeeming ways could not be reduced to the platform or intentions of any ecclesial/political party or group. If indeed America *was* called to "redeem the world," it was called to do so as part of a much larger eschatological party — the "children of light" — whose purposes and destiny finally transcended ecclesiastical, tribal, and nationalistic categories altogether. Indeed, Niebuhr's "problematizing" of America's redemptive destiny limned both sin and grace working in the "children of darkness" no less than in light's children, making American culture's corporate state of grace problematic — at best.[5]

Building on his earlier theological reflections on the dichotomy between individual altruism and virtue over against group selfishness, Niebuhr offered a chastened, less triumphalistic reading of salvation history: all groups claiming to work for God's purposes in history — including the Protestant-inspired culture of the world's newest superpower in the years after World War II — battled for righteousness using sinful, coercive means. Grace and sin, wisdom and folly, mingled freely and richly in the intentions and outcome of all human efforts, even efforts like that of the United States in battling Hitler and Stalin to "redeem the world." Precisely because the American situation in the mid-twentieth century constituted a particularly vivid symbol of the ironies of a Christian "read" of history,

> the degree of American power tends to generate illusions to which a technocratic culture is already too prone. This technocratic approach to the problems of history, which erroneously equates the mastery of nature with the mastery of historical destiny, in turn accentuates a very old failing in human nature: the inclination of the wise, or the powerful, or the virtuous, to obscure or deny the human limitations in all human achievements and pretensions.[6]

In Niebuhr's estimation, sin-filled and selfish human motives intermingled with the purposes of divine grace to effect a redemption that was eschatological, not historical: the "glory" of God's "mighty works" can not be glimpsed in history, but only beyond history — in that "age which is to come." No human culture can claim to be completely (or even primarily) "Christian" over against a historical "evil empire" of Satan's legions. The "mighty works of Christ in America," in Niebuhr's reading of the situation in the decade after Hiroshima, eventuated *not* in a triumphant army of righteous Americans robed in white, but in traces of divine purpose glimpsed in power politics and congressional compromises that witnesses (however dimly and incompletely) to a "redemption" beyond history's vagaries.[7]

Niebuhr's brilliant rereading of American history was primarily aimed, of course, at the "Protestant Establishment" in the United States at mid-century — that congeries of Protestant-based families, institutions, and denominational networks which had always claimed (and took) responsibility for American culture since Cotton Mather had penned his history. As preceptor to both the "meaning" and "destiny" of the United States, this Protestant Establishment had believed that by the early twentieth century it had successfully fused its religious values with American culture itself, with a resultant "culture religion" that provided American culture with transcendent meaning. This Protestant culture religion, however, had undergone a series of nasty shocks between the end of the Civil War and 1945 — both intellectual shocks provided by Darwin, Freud, and assorted other "god killers," as well as social crises that exposed genuine cultural pluralism for the first time in North American history. Further, in the decades after the Second World War, what sociologist Robert Wuthnow has termed a "restructuring" occurred in American religion, so that the old religious Establishment "lost" in terms of both absolute numbers and in cultural influence, while "others" — Catholics being among the most visible — "won" in influence and institutional growth.[8]

Self-consciously marching under the banner of a new theological movement that he and others termed "Christian Realism," Niebuhr sought an interpretive tool that would make sense of the serendipitous course of grace in American religion, politics, and foreign policy in the light of Christian redemptive claims. But the sheer brilliance of Niebuhr's revisionist reading of America's past in 1952 failed to recognize at the time (ironically enough) that the "post-Protestant era of American religious history" was already well under way. This new era was witnessed to (among other ways) in the "restructuring" recognized by Wuthnow, in the generic "religiosity" promoted out of the nation's capital in the "Piety on the Potomac" of the Eisenhower years, by the interreligious postwar revival preached by Rabbi Liebman, Monsignor Sheen, and the Reverend Mr. Peale, and by the sheer secularity — what later commentators would call the "naked public square" — of American political and popular culture.[9]

It has been argued in these pages that, in ways that neither Reinhold Niebuhr nor American Catholics could fully understand in 1952, the historical/theological interpretation offered by *The Irony of American History* uncovers patterns of sin and grace in the North American Catholic community, then emerging as a "major player" in the postwar culture, at least as well as in the older Protestant Establishment. This "ironic" reading of the place of Catholics in the ecology of postwar U.S. religion rests, then, on a newfound Catholic confidence and willingness to speak *to* and *for* the mainstream culture in the years after 1945. In doing so, a culturally visible and increasingly affluent segment of American Catholics inherited the conflicted load of that heavy mantle, and in becoming part of the mainstream produced mixed results — unexpected, unintended outcomes. The heady promises of postwar affluence / The Sixties / Vatican II did not eventuate in anything remotely like a Catholic Kingdom of God in America so feared by Paul Blanshard. Rather, a more sober, chastened, but still-sympathetic account of postimmigrant Catholic culture can serve to balance an ancient Christian belief in the Providence of God in history with a candid admission that things did not exactly turn out as planned. Though God's purposes and grace are not foiled or nullified by well-intentioned but fallible human actors, this Niebuhrian account of our situation suggests, at the very least, that "we walk by faith, and not by sight."

American Freedom and Catholic Power

Sheltered by high walls from the intellectual and social blasts that had withered the confidence of the Protestant mainstream, the many American Catholics who emerged from the parochial world of the local parish demonstrated a resilient self-confidence at mid-century and began to claim and redefine the millennial and exceptionalist strands of the "doxological" tradition stretching back to Mather. As the largest, most unified, and most institutionally organized Christian tribe in mid-twentieth century America, these spiritual descendants of the believers so hated by Oliver Cromwell and his American Puritan cousins appeared to have inherited the millennial kingdom in the years after World War II.

By 1960 American Catholics alone, as John Courtney Murray and others less brilliant pointed out, retained the natural law language and worldview of America's founding documents and became the best expositors of the "truths" Americans all hold. Catholics alone knew what belonged to Caesar and what to God, how to balance devotion to, and critique of, a culture too easily loved. "God, Country, Notre Dame" could be chanted without the self-conscious smirk that "For God, For Country, and For Yale" produced on a sea of singing faces during the annual Harvard-Yale game. The forest of lawns across the country balancing the flag with the Madonna bespoke confident identity, pride, and purpose. *They* were (as Catholics always knew they were) the true "insiders," and the city on the hill was now safely in their keeping. *They* were now the guardians of the covenant, with a high priest in the presidency to prove it.[10]

The careers of both Leonard Feeney and Joe McCarthy — however unwittingly and problematically — announced and abetted the emergence of a newly confident, culturally hegemonic style of Catholicism that felt at home in, and would come to make claims on, the affluent middle-class culture of postwar America. Feeney and McCarthy mark the end of the dominant parochial/tribal style of immigrant Catholicism—a style that had overwhelmed the even earlier Anglo-American "Maryland Tradition" by the mid-nineteenth century — announcing in the process that Communion breakfasts, city-wide high school football championships, and contests for the best "Catholic poetry" no longer defined the horizons of American Catholic culture. The emergence of a culturally confident American Catholicism at mid-century, however, contained within itself the conflicts inherent in all forms of "culture religion" — conflicts that would be played out in the final quarter of the century.

One of the most delicious ironies of the postwar Catholic story was that the style of "otherness" that came to be most respected among many of its co-religionists and "others" — Dorothy Day's pacifist and personalist Catholic Worker movement—itself reflected the communitarian, perfectionist impulses of canonical American figures like Emerson and Thoreau, which claim "insiderhood" precisely *by* being radical "outsiders." Offering a distinctively Catholic analogue to the perfectionist gospels of Puritan John Winthrop and Transcendentalist Ralph Waldo Emerson, as well as an analogue to the utopian communal experiments of Bronson Alcott and John Humphry Noyes, Day and Peter Maurin crafted a singularly "American" form of Catholic antinomianism, proclaiming its "Americanness" in the very act of critiquing the culture. The very discomfort that Day and her movement inspired helps to account, no doubt, for her "canonization" among her co-religionists long before her death in 1980. As George Bernard Shaw once remarked of Joan of Arc, saints are more easily canonized and memorialized in stained-glass windows than lived with. The very radicalness of Day's movement helped legitimate the "suburban captivity" of many of Catholics: see, American Catholics could now say, we can produce an American prophet too. Day was as radical as any New England abolitionist or Transcendentalist communitarian. Having successfully produced a prophet and a saint, Catholics could then return to more immediate concerns, like crabgrass and Little League.

Day's fellow convert Thomas Merton and media celebrity Fulton Sheen both uncovered the rich resources of the Catholic traditions of spirituality and neo-scholastic theology for postwar America, making those traditions accessible and popular to millions of Americans sated with the "busyness" and materialism of the Age of Anxiety. Merton's Eriksonian recognition that the "truth of his experience" was also the truth of many others' permitted him to offer a mature, sophisticated "take" on the Catholic tradition to fellow believers just then moving out of the parochial ghetto, while the user-friendly Catholicism of Sheen and his "Little Angel" on the new medium of national television helped to de-fang "America's oldest intellectual tradition" (as Arthur Schlesinger, Jr., termed anti-Catholicism). The very popularity of such Catholic preceptors, however, offering the democratic access of mass culture to the mysteries of sin and grace, would also subvert the explicitly apologetic purposes that initially informed both of their creative efforts. Neither Merton nor Sheen, at least in the years immediately following the war, sought cultural acceptance or the "mainstreaming" of American Catholicism as the primary end of their public careers. Indeed, its very "otherness" — marked by plainchant and neo-scholastic categories — guaranteed Catholicism's claims as preceptor and judge of human culture, American culture at the head of that tutorial list.

Winning the holy grail of American politics in 1960 turned out to be yet another of the ironies of the postwar years for U.S. Catholics. The brief but dramatic presidency of John F. Kennedy has been touted by historians and cultural commentators as announcing the "arrival" of Catholics into the U.S. political and economic mainstream, as well as marking the stylish realism and mature "toughness" of a New Frontier that eschewed petty prejudices of all kinds, religious prejudice among them. But the grail was won at an exceedingly high price, a price that Catholic intellectuals and church authorities at the time and later denounced as a lamentable trend toward secularity. As was asserted by Kennedy critics with various agendas, no Catholic in good conscience — or serious believer of any kind, for that matter — can assent to a hard and fast "wall of separation" between religious belief and political principles, however expedient such an assent might be. The conundrum of personal belief in a pluralist society could not be relaxed by collapsing the rigorous demands of the former into the irenic needs of the latter. The fact that it was a Roman Catholic candidate for the nation's highest office who outlined such a "wall of separation" leads one to sober Niebuhrian reflection on the vagaries of sin and grace (and divine humor) in history.

The implementation of the Second Vatican Council's mandates on liturgy and on religious life likewise, ironically, achieved what, at the time, would be considered unthinkable. An ecumenical council gathered under the impulse of the Holy Spirit itself (at least from the viewpoint of Catholic faith) unleashed several decades of ecclesial turmoil over guitars, banners, and the hemlines of nuns' habits. Holy Mother Church herself, under the Spirit's gracious if humorous guidance, sponsored the guidelines for a revolution it would come to lament and denounce. In "tinkering" with the public worship of the church — especially its central, defining act, the Liturgy of the Eucharist — the good bishops of Vatican II proved the truth of Prosper of Aquitaine's ancient dictum. A new *lex orandi,* in the event, did indeed appear to sponsor a new and disturbing *lex credendi,* disturbing at least from the standpoint of the bishops who so overwhelmingly had a hand in crafting the "smoking gun" — the council's Constitution on the Sacred Liturgy. The "People of God," laity as well as clergy, now demanded a hand in carrying out the *liturgia,* the "work of the *whole* people," to the surprise and dismay of many of those charged with shepherding them.

That same Vatican Council's call for the renewal of religious life found most obedient (if not docile) ears among the Immaculate Heart of Mary sisters in Los Angeles. Breaking through the dead hand of convent routinization and historically inappropriate forms of apostolic life, they found the charismatic Spirit leading them into a nasty public dispute with their own ordinary (an "ordinary Ordinary" as Sister Corita Kent once so whimsically put it), Cardinal McIntyre. The historical upshot of that ecclesiastical civil war offered problematic results for both the diocese of Los Angeles and for the IHMs themselves. All talk of "winners" and "losers" in the Los Angeles "IHMs Case" appears both inappropriate and heavy-handed: where, indeed, the Spirit's guidance of Holy Church?

Perhaps the "Tie of the Century" — the moniker given Notre Dame's famous football battle against Michigan State University in 1966 — best summarizes the results of Catholicism's "holy war" in U.S. culture during the two and a half decades following World War II. Clammering for a century to move beyond its identity at the margins of the mainstream culture, a significant section of American Catholicism (and the University of Notre Dame as well) discovered at mid-century that "ethnicity" itself proved to be a not unhelpful tool for ecological location in the dense forest of twentieth-century American culture. Perhaps — as Father Hesburgh had recognized so well in a South Bend landscape marked by Marian shrines and "Touchdown Jesus" — "otherness" was what the Holy Spirit had been calling American Catholics to all along: not the paranoid otherness of Fr. Feeney and Joe McCarthy, but (ironically enough) something more along the lines of the densely textured, complex, and Spirit-filled humanity of Catholic Workers, Gethsemani Monastery, and the Notre Dame football team (at least in certain "winning" years.)

What, Then, Must We Do?

This study of selected figures/events in the American Catholic community in the middle of the twentieth century does not offer itself as a new "master narrative" or cohesive synthesis of a rambunctious but faithful group of people organized as the "American Catholic Church" in the second half of the twentieth century. Indeed, one of the (not so hidden) subtexts of this study has been the profound suspicion that such master narratives of "The Big Picture" — as a genre — are now problematic in a perhaps permanent way. Written from the standpoint of historical theology in conversation with social science, this study *has* attempted to uncover the sometimes heroic, often humorous, but always interesting workings of grace in the lives Catholics attempting to "walk by faith" amid the challenges of modern America. Each of the stories recounted here, of course, has its own integrity and pattern that is irreducible to any other's; but it is the central contention of this study that a larger pattern — transcending their individual ones — does indeed emerge in the middle years of the twentieth century, a pattern best discerned using Niebuhr's lens of "irony" to understand how what might be termed "public Catholicism" moved from the margins to the center stage of American culture in the years after World War II, with mixed results from a theological point of view.

Many "styles" of twentieth-century Catholicism in North America — the Hispanic Catholicism of the Southwest, the Italian Catholicism of the Northeast, the Slovak Catholicism of central Pennsylvania, etc. — were not represented in any of the stories presented in these pages. The involvement of these vibrant Catholic groups in the previous tale probably spanned the spectrum from minimal to nonexistent. Their absence in this tale in no way implies the unimportance of *their* stories. Indeed, their absence necessitates the stories already being told about them by other students of North American Catholic culture, stories that enrich and broaden our understanding of the Catholic tribes. For the genuine pluralism of the American Catholic community — the "manyness" of the lived reality of American Catholicism balancing the dogmatic "oneness" of the Catholic Tradition — is what led this study to embrace Niebuhrian irony as a revealing interpretive framework in the first place. It is precisely *because* of this tension between the unity and the diversity of the North American Catholic tradition(s) — a tension recognized half a century ago by the great Catholic historian Thomas McAvoy — that permits and perhaps demands the use of irony as a lens to recognize divine grace working in the often serendipitous story that has resulted.[11]

The story recounted here — which began with Leonard Feeney and his "Slaves of the Immaculate Heart" in Boston and ends with "Touchdown Jesus" in South Bend, Indiana — represents an interesting journey by any standard. And yet, of course, the story does not really "end" there at all: the years from 1945 to 1968, in fact, represent the background era to contemporary American Catholicism, in which the decisions made, fault lines discerned, and stands taken have been played out with equal measures of heroism, wisdom, and folly in the final decades of the twentieth century.

Some American Catholics now remember the tribal cohesion of their Faith in the late 1940s and 1950s as constituting a happier and more desirable ecclesial identity (even granted its perhaps too effusive confidence) — an identity more durable and resistant to the acids of modernity than the current one, which they would describe as heading in the direction of a "culture religion" not much different from the Protestant one that unraveled earlier in the century. Other Catholics feel mostly relief that the walls of the Catholic ghetto came tumbling down in the decades after World War II and see in their less confident and more fractious community a faith truer to that of the early church: "on pilgrimage" with their Master amid the vicissitudes of history. This study, conflicted like its author, feels genuine sympathy with both points of view. As a result of precisely this conflicted sense, the interpretive lens of "irony" offered by Reinhold Niebuhr has been presented as a fruitful stance for balancing both the good-willed but fallible decisions and actions undertaken by people of faith in a confusing world, and the work of grace — often cooperating with them, sometimes pushing against them — in building a kingdom in but not of this world.

Historians, to judge from the record of previous practitioners of the field, make lousy prognosticators of the future. And yet if I were a betting person, I would put my money on the rich category of "ethnicity" as described by Andrew Greeley and discerned by Theodore Hesburgh as providing the most promising identity for American Catholics navigating the treacherous rapids of a new century in an even more pluralistic land. "An ethnic group of ethnic groups," porous but distinct, is a good place to start in constructing studies of the North American Catholic community as it faces a new millennium.

Perhaps, finally, the best that a historical theologian can do in recounting the story of grace working in historical communities is to tell the tale in light of the wisdom of Scripture, which has seen many human communities come and go, offering Light on an often shadowy path: "The One who sits in Heaven laughs; but blessed are they who put their faith in God."

Notes

Introduction: "Oh, the Irony of It All"

1. Paul Blanshard, *American Freedom and Catholic Power,* 11th ed. (Boston: Beacon Press, 1950). Back of title page for printing dates. Maria Monk, *Awful Disclosures of the Hotel Dieu Nunnery* (New York: Published by Maria Monk, 1836). Lyman Beecher, *A Plea for the West* (Cincinnati: Truman and Smith, 1835). Quote from Blanshard, *American Freedom,* 5; italics in original. The classic studies of anti-Catholicism as part of broader nativist patterns in nineteenth- and early twentieth-century America are Ray Billington, *The Protestant Crusade 1800–1860: A Study of the Origins of American Nativism* (New York: Macmillan, 1938), and John Higham, *Strangers in the Land: Patterns of American Nativism, 1850–1925* (New Brunswick, N.J.: Rutgers University Press, 1955).

2. See especially chapter 12 of Blanshard's *American Freedom* for an interesting exposition of this fear about "Roman" control of decent American Catholics. See also Norman Vincent Peale's statement about the Kennedy presidential candidacy in 1960 in chapter 6 of this work.

3. Garry Wills, *Bare Ruined Choirs: Doubt, Prophecy, and Radical Religion* (Garden City, N.Y.: Doubleday, 1971), 15, 16.

4. Charles R. Morris, *American Catholic: The Saints and Sinners Who Built America's Most Powerful Church* (New York: Times Books, 1997), ix. Morris's book is perhaps the finest study of the century-long movement of Catholicism from "ministate" to the largest denomination in the United States. Wills, *Bare Ruined Choirs,* 17.

5. Wills, *Bare Ruined Choirs,* 39, 42.

6. Ibid., 42–43.

7. The phrase "when Catholic lambs ate ivy" is a gloss on a famous editorial that appeared in *America* magazine in the 1950s entitled "Should Catholic Lambs Eat Ivy," a discussion of the growing numbers of Catholic undergraduates attending Ivy League universities.

8. For a fine discussion of postwar Catholicism, see Jay P. Dolan, *The American Catholic Experience: A History from Colonial Times to the Present* (Garden City, N.Y.: Doubleday, 1985), 361–83; 407–17.

9. I am indebted to David Hackett, an undergraduate American Studies major in Fordham College, for the phrase "BVM in a bathtub," referring to the familiar sight on lawns across the country of a statue of the "Blessed Virgin Mary" in a shallow grotto resembling a bathtub. "Areas of second urban settlement" is from Dolan, *American Catholic Experience,* 357. "Redeemer Nation" is the title of Ernest Lee Tuveson's fine study, *Redeemer Nation: The Idea of*

America's Millennial Role (Chicago: University of Chicago Press, 1968), which examines the political, biblical, and diplomatic history of America's "millennial" sense of identity. The best and most reasoned argument for Catholics being in the best position to understand and direct the American experiment is John Courtney Murray's *We Hold These Truths: Catholic Reflections on the American Proposition* (New York: Sheed and Ward, 1960), a book published in the year of John F. Kennedy's presidential race. The quote at the end of the paragraph is from Morris, *American Catholic*, ix.

10. Jay Dolan, *American Catholic Experience*, 357–62. Andrew Greeley, *The Church and the Suburbs* (New York: Sheed and Ward, 1959), 52. Dino Cinel, *From Italy to San Francisco: The Immigrant Experience* (Stanford, Calif.: Stanford University Press, 1982), 125–30. Douglas T. Miller and Marian Nowak, *The Fifties: The Way We Really Were* (Garden City, N.Y.: Doubleday, 1977), 133.

11. On the early history of "English Catholicism" in Maryland and the American colonies, see James Hennesey, S.J., *American Catholics: A History of the Roman Catholic Community in the United States* (New York: Oxford University Press, 1981), 46–115. On the "Americanist Crisis," see the classic account: Thomas McAvoy, C.S.C., *The Great Crisis in American Catholic History, 1895–1900* (Chicago: University of Chicago Press, 1957). "Ultramontanism" — based on the Latin words *ultra mons,* literally "over the mountains" — refers to an understanding of Catholicism that looked "over the mountains" (i.e., beyond the local circumstances) to Rome; it is thus a resolutely centralized, hierarchical model of Catholicism hostile to the idea of local "adaptation." "Hibernarchy" is a phrase that refers to the overwhelmingly Irish character of the Roman Catholic hierarchy in America. My observation that the "heroes" of American Catholic historiography have tended to be the accommodationists is borrowed from R. Laurence Moore, *Religious Outsiders and the Making of Americans* (New York: Oxford University Press, 1987).

12. William Halsey, *Survival of American Innocence* (Notre Dame, Ind.: University of Notre Dame Press, 1979); Peter A. Huff, *Alan Tate and the Catholic Revival: Trace of the Fugitive Gods* (New York: Paulist Press, 1996), 7–24. The phrase "voluntary establishment" is used by Robert Handy to describe the real but nonlegal reality of evangelical Protestantism constituting the "religious establishment" in the United States from 1776 until the 1930s, when the "Second and real dis-establishment" of religion in America took place. See Robert Handy, *A Christian America: Protestant Hopes and Historical Reality* (New York: Oxford University Press, 1971), Introduction.

13. See Jay Dolan's *The Immigrant Church: New York's Irish and German Catholics, 1815–1865* (Baltimore: Johns Hopkins University Press, 1975), for an insightful and lively account of Catholic social and devotional life in the first half of the nineteenth century. For the social and political commitments of American Catholicism in the pre–World War II years, see Aaron Abell, *American Catholicism and Social Action: A Search for Social Justice* (Garden City, N.Y.: Hanover House, 1960); on the church's involvement in working-class movements, see Henry Browne, *The Catholic Church and the Knights of Labor* (Washington, D.C.: Catholic University of America Press, 1949). On the "German Triangle,"

see Philip Gleason, *The Conservative Reformers: German-American Catholics and the Social Order* (Notre Dame, Ind.: University of Notre Dame Press, 1968).

14. Andrew Greeley, *The American Catholic* (New York: Basic Books, 1977). A major exception to this Irish story is the German Catholicism of the Midwest; see Coleman Barry, *The Catholic Church and German Americans* (Washington, D.C.: Catholic University of America Press, 1953), and Philip Gleason, *The Conservative Reformers*.

15. The "seven sisters" is the name applied by William Hutchison to those seven Protestant denominations that made up the Protestant Establishment in America: the Congregational, Presbyterian, Methodist, Episcopalian, Northern Baptist, Christian (Disciples of Christ), and Lutheran Churches. See William Hutchison, *Between the Times: The Travail of the Protestant Establishment in America, 1900–1960* (New York: Cambridge University Press, 1989), 6. Will Herberg, *Protestant, Catholic, Jew* (Garden City, N.Y.: Doubleday, 1955).

16. H. Richard Niebuhr, *Christ and Culture* (New York: Harper & Row, 1951), chapter 3, "Christ of Culture," 83–115. Arthur Schlesinger, Jr., in his classic essay "A Critical Period in American Religion, 1875–1900" (*Proceedings of the Massachusetts Historical Society* 61 [1932]) argued that the last quarter of the nineteenth century represented a "critical period" for mainstream American Protestantism because of the latter's close identification with the culture itself: as the culture underwent a series of intellectual and social challenges from Darwinism, higher criticism, the new study of world religions, the "new immigration," urbanization, etc., the religious mainstream itself suffered the same challenges.

17. For changing demographic, cultural, and ideological patterns in American Catholicism in the decades after World War II, see Robert Wuthnow, *The Restructuring of American Religion* (Princeton, N.J.: Princeton University Press, 1988), 33–34, 73–75, 84–88.

18. The phrase "nation with the soul of a church" is from G. K. Chesterton. See Catherine Albanese, *Corresponding Motion* (Philadelphia: Temple University Press, 1977); *Sons of the Fathers* (Philadelphia: Temple University Press, 1976); *America: Religions and Religion* (Belmont, Calif.: Wadsworth, 1981); Robert Orsi, *The Madonna of 115th Street* (New Haven: Yale University Press, 1985); *Thank You, St. Jude:* (New Haven: Yale University Press, 1996); Colleen McDannell, *Material Christianity: Religion and Popular Culture in America* (New Haven: Yale University Press, 1995).

19. Reinhold Niebuhr, *The Irony of American History* (New York: Charles Scribner's Sons, 1952), preface, viii. Emphasis is my own.

20. Ibid., 155–56.

21. My use of the term "Protestant Establishment" derives from the definition offered by William Hutchison in his book *Between the Times: The Travail of the Protestant Establishment in America, 1900–1960*. Hutchison writes: "When historians have used terms like establishment or mainline in a more-than-regional sense they almost always have meant Congregationalists, Episcopalians, Presbyterians, and the white divisions of the Baptist and Methodist families. For the decades since 1900, the Disciples of Christ and the United Lutherans have been added" (chapter 1, "Protestantism as Establishment," 4).

22. For a magisterial discussion of the problem of a "post-Protestant Amer-

ica," see Sidney Ahlstrom, *A Religious History of the American People* (New Haven: Yale University Press, 1972). See especially chapter 1: "American Religious History in the Post-Protestant era." On the question of the arrival of the "Catholic moment," see Richard John Neuhaus, *The Catholic Moment: The Paradox of the Church in the Modern World* (San Francisco: Harper & Row, 1987).

23. H. Richard Niebuhr has posed the tension between the demands of the Christian message and the demands of human accommodation to the world in terms of "Christ and Culture," the title of one of his most seminal works. In that work Niebuhr presents five basic models for understanding the tension between these two sets of "demands." See *Christ and Culture,* Introduction.

24. "Decent poverty" was Dorothy Day's own term for what she herself lived and demanded of her fellow workers: enough food and money to live on and serve others, but a "doing without superfluities to let others have the necessities." See Dorothy Day, *Houses of Hospitality* (New York: Sheed and Ward, 1939). The "corporal works of mercy" were traditionally defined in Catholic theology as charitable acts that witnessed to the theological virtue of Christian love: feeding the hungry, clothing the naked, visiting the imprisoned, etc.

Chapter 1: Boundary Maintenance

1. The quotation is taken from the Associated Press wire service, reporting on a Feeneyite who ran onto the field during a 1953 Notre Dame football game. John Deedy, "Whatever Happened to Father Feeney?" *The Critic* 31 (1973): 22.

2. *The Pilot,* September 6, 1952. The letter was published on the front page, first in Latin and then in English translation.

3. Ibid. The quotation is from the ninth paragraph of the letter (*Quare nemo salvabitur*). While allowing for "implicit desire," however, the letter ended by announcing that such cases were exceptions to the more general rule that "submission to the Catholic Church and to the Supreme Pontiff is required as necessary to salvation."

4. Catherine Clarke, *The Loyolas and the Cabots* (Boston: Ravengate, 1950), 300. Deedy, "Whatever Happened?" 19–20.

5. The only other rival for this heretical crown — the set of beliefs denounced by *Testem Benevolentiae* in 1899 and usually labeled "Americanism" — has been considered by many Catholic historians a "phantom heresy." The papal letter in 1899 declared that it accused no one of the doctrines condemned, but merely pointed out "certain excesses to be avoided," while all the parties involved in the debate thanked the pope for the clarification that the letter offered. Thomas McAvoy, offering what became the standard interpretative line, argued that the theological (as opposed to cultural) tendencies condemned by the letter were really to be found in the French Church at the end of the nineteenth century, especially those surrounding a group of French Catholics who had proclaimed themselves "Americainistes" for ecclesiastical political reasons. See Thomas McAvoy's *The Americanist Heresy in Roman Catholicism, 1895–1900* (Notre Dame, Ind.: University of Notre Dame Press, 1963), 300–322. For a lively revisionist reading, arguing that there was indeed an American "theological imperialism" afoot, see Thomas Wangler, "The Birth of American-

ism: 'Westward the Apocalyptic Candlestick'" *Harvard Theological Review* 65 (1972): 415–36.

6. Both Deedy ("Whatever Happened?") and Mark Silk (*Spiritual Politics: Religion and America since World War II* [New York: Simon & Schuster, 1988]) offer fine examples of the sociological explanation of the Feeney affair. For a classic discussion of the sectarian model, see Ernst Troeltsch, *The Social Teaching of the Christian Churches*, 2 vols. (New York: Macmillan, 1949), 2:461.

7. By "accommodationist" here I mean an epistemological presupposition that modern culture itself is revelatory of divine purpose, or at least of the "direction" of history. Modern culture, therefore, represents the norm to which traditions, religious and other, must adapt in order to lead people to God, understand the direction of history, uncover the true sources of culture, etc. For a fine discussion of such accommodationism in the context of theological modernism, see William Hutchison's *The Modernist Impulse in American Protestantism* (Cambridge, Mass.: Harvard University Press, 1976), 2. Perhaps the most famous and critical study of the post–World War II religious revival that took precisely this understanding of "cultural accommodation" to task is Will Herberg's *Protestant, Catholic, Jew* (Garden City, N.Y.: Doubleday, 1955).

8. Emile Durkheim, *The Division of Labor in Society,* trans. George Simpson (Glencoe, Ill.: Free Press, 1947), 102. Kai T. Erikson (*The Wayward Puritans: A Study in the Sociology of Deviance* [New York: Wily, 1966], 4–12) offers a particularly lucid exposition of this theory.

9. Erikson, *Wayward Puritans,* 67–159. Paul Boyer and Stephen Nissenbaum, *Salem Possessed: The Social Origins of Witchcraft* (Cambridge, Mass.: Harvard University Press, 1974), 179–216.

10. Mary Douglas, *Natural Symbols* (London: Barrie & Rockliff, 1970), ix. See also idem, *Purity and Danger: An Analysis of Concepts of Pollution and Taboo* (New York: Praeger, 1966), chapters 1 and 2.

11. Douglas, *Natural Symbols,* viii, ix.

12. Ibid. See especially chapter 7, "The Problem of Evil."

13. Clarke, *Loyolas and Cabots,* 3–4.

14. Deedy, "Whatever Happened?" 17.

15. Avery Dulles, "Leonard Feeney: In Memoriam," *America,* February 25, 1978, 135.

16. Catholic periodicals throughout the 1940s debated whether Catholic students should attend non-Catholic, and especially Ivy League, colleges; the famous article addressing this issue in *America* magazine was entitled "Should Catholic Lambs Eat Ivy?" See Clarke, *Loyolas and Cabots,* 3–4, 6.

17. Deedy, "Whatever Happened?" 17.

18. Silk, *Spiritual Politics,* 71–72.

19. Dulles, "Leonard Feeney: In Memoriam," 135.

20. Silk, *Spiritual Politics,* 72. Clarke, *Loyolas and Cabots,* 45: "We waited and we listened, but no strong voice arose above the noise of the world. There was only the jubilant announcement of a new age, the atomic age, born out of the abandonment of a Christian principle!"

21. Clarke, *Loyolas and Cabots,* 45.

22. Ibid.

23. John Deedy, "Whatever Happened?" 17.

24. Avery Dulles, "On Keeping the Faith," *From the Housetops* 1 (1946): 60–62. Mark Silk, *Spiritual Politics*, 74, refers to this quotation.

25. The phrase is from the encyclical of Boniface VIII's *Unam Sanctam*, who "declared, defined, and pronounced" it in 1302. Feeney also loved to quote the famous oath sworn by all participants at the First Vatican Council, who professed allegiance to the "true Catholic faith, outside of which no one can be saved." See also Deedy, "Whatever Happened?" 19.

26. Deedy, "Whatever Happened?" 19.

27. Clarke, *Loyolas and Cabots,* 50–51.

28. William O'Connell, "The Catholic Priest and the Catholic School," *Sermons and Addresses* (Boston: Pilot, 1931), 10, 51–53.

29. *Boston Globe,* February 16, 1948. Cushing went to dinner at Harvard's Lowell House at the invitation of house master Perkins to discuss the conversion of Temple Morgan, a Harvard undergraduate living there. Morgan — the scion of a prominent family and member of the elite Porcellian Club — had been converted by Feeney's preaching, baptized by Feeney, and promptly withdrew from Harvard to enroll at St. Benedict's own school. Rumor had it that the consternation over Morgan's withdrawal had reached Harvard's Board of Overseers, which had discussed the case at some length. Silk, *Spiritual Politics,* 78.

30. Clarke, *Loyolas and Cabots,* 100, 112.

31. Ibid., 139–41. British Catholic novelist Evelyn Waugh visited the center that fall on the advice of Mrs. Clare Boothe Luce ("a saint and apostle on no account to be missed"). Waugh's account is itself classic: "I found him one morning surrounded by a court of bemused youth of both sexes & he stark raving mad.... He fell into a rambling denunciation of all secular learning which gradually became more and more violent.... It seemed to me that he needed an exorcist more than an alienist. A case of demonic possession & jolly frightening." Mark Amory, ed., *The Letters of Evelyn Waugh* (New Haven: Tickner & Fields, 1980), 292–93.

32. Clarke, *Loyolas and Cabots,* 144–62.

33. Silk, *Spiritual Politics,* 81. See chapters 20 and 21 in Clarke's *Loyolas and Cabots* for an insider's view of these events.

34. Quoted in Silk, *Spiritual Politics,* 81.

35. "A Letter from the Holy Office," *American Ecclesiastical Review* 127 (1952): 307–15.

36. *Roma locuta, causa finita* ("Rome has spoken, the case is finished") had guided Feeney's calls to Rome until the fatal pronouncement on August 8: thereafter, Feeney believed that liberalism infected even the Vatican itself. Clarke, *Loyolas and Cabots,* 247–66, 300–301.

37. Deedy, "Whatever Happened?" 20–23. There is further irony in Feeney's move to Harvard, Massachusetts. His new "monastery" there abutted the site of "Fruitlands," the nineteenth-century commune of transcendentalist Bronson Alcott, which itself represented precisely the kind of "fuzzy Christianity" that Feeney targeted with disdain.

38. Joshua Liebman's best-selling *Peace of Mind* (New York: Simon and

Schuster, 1946), was among the first of an interdenominational genre of religious/therapeutic best-sellers, including Fulton J. Sheen's *Peace of Soul* (New York: McGraw-Hill, 1949) and Norman Vincent Peale's *Power of Positive Thinking* (Englewood Cliffs, N.J.: Prentice-Hall, 1956). Donald Meyer has convincingly argued that this new form of popular theology really eschewed questions of theology that might accentuate differences in order to offer a therapeutic "fix" to the American religious psyche. See his *The Positive Thinkers* (Garden City, N.Y.: Doubleday, 1965).

39. Silk, *Spiritual Politics,* 84.

40. *Lumen Gentium,* the Second Vatican Council's dogmatic statement on the church, offered the new definition. See "The Dogmatic Constitution on the Church," in Austin Flannery, ed., *Vatican II, The Conciliar and Post-Conciliar Documents* (Collegeville, Minn.: Liturgical Press, 1983), 359.

41. On the American "distinctive tradition" that maintained Roman loyalty and cultural identification, see James Hennesey, "The Distinctive Tradition of American Catholicism," in Philip Gleason, ed., *Catholicism in America* (New York: Harper & Row, 1970); and Thomas McAvoy, *The Formation of the American Catholic Minority, 1820–1860* (Philadelphia: Fortress, 1967). On Americanism, see Wangler's "The Birth of Americanism."

42. On the Catholic claim to "insider status," see William Halsey's *Survival of American Innocence* (Notre Dame, Ind.: University of Notre Dame Press, 1979). Perhaps the classic text in elucidating this claim is John Courtney Murray's *We Hold These Truths: Catholic Reflections on the American Proposition* (New York: Sheed & Ward, 1960).

43. See J. M. Muldoon, "Innocent III," *The New Catholic Encyclopedia,* 7:521–24.

44. See F. X. Lawlor, "The Church (Theology of)," *The New Catholic Encyclopedia,* 3:683–93.

45. *The Pilot,* September 6, 1952, 1: "It is beyond understanding how a member of a religious institute, namely, Father Feeney, presents himself as a 'Defender of the Faith' and at the same time does not hesitate to attack the catechetical instruction proposed by lawful authorities, and has not even feared to incur grave sanctions threatened by the sacred canons because of his serious violations of his duties as a religious, a priest, and an ordinary member of the church."

46. For the classic discussion of the distinction between "church" and "denomination," see H. Richard Niebuhr, *The Social Sources of Denominationalism* (New York: Henry Holt & Co., 1929).

Chapter 2: Young Man Merton

1. Merton's later reflection on experiencing his first liturgy at Gethsemani Monastery on April 7, 1941. See Thomas Merton, *The Seven Storey Mountain* (New York: Harcourt, Brace, 1948), 324. Emphasis in the second sentence is my own.

2. For the details behind the publication of *The Seven Storey Mountain* (hereafter "*SSM*"), See Michael Mott, *The Seven Mountains of Thomas Merton* (Boston: Houghton, Mifflin, 1984), 231. The quote as to Merton's significance

is from David Tracy, "Thomas Merton, Symbol, and Synthesis of Contemporary Catholicism," *Cistercian Studies* 12 (1977): 283.

3. The number one and two best-sellers for 1948 were *The White Collar Zoo* and a book on canasta (Donald Grayston, *Thomas Merton: The Development of a Spiritual Theologian* [New York: Edwin Mellen Press, 1985], 16). For the publication statistics for *SSM*, see Mott, *Seven Mountains*, 247–48.

4. For the quotes from Greene and Luce, see Mott, *Seven Mountains*, 243. See also Gerald Twomey, "Thomas Merton, an Appreciation," in *Thomas Merton: Prophet in the Belly of a Paradox*, ed. Gerald Twomey (New York: Paulist Press, 1978), 4.

5. Merton, *SSM*, 419. For a perceptive critique of the putative "religious revival" going on in America after World War II, see Will Herberg, *Protestant, Catholic, Jew* (Garden City, N.Y.: Doubleday, 1955).

6. For a classic consensus account of American Catholic history in which the liberals/accommodationists are portrayed as the "heroes" of the story, see John Tracy Ellis, *American Catholicism* (Chicago: University of Chicago Press, 1955). For a more recent revisionist account that seeks to nuance that story, see R. Laurence Moore, *Religious Outsiders and the Making of Americans* (New York: Oxford University Press, 1986), chapter 2.

7. For the classic texts of Protestant neo-orthodoxy (more properly termed "crisis theology"), see Karl Barth, *The Epistle to the Romans*, first Eng. ed. (London: Oxford University Press, 1933), and Reinhold Niebuhr, *Moral Man and Immoral Society* (New York: Charles Scribner's Sons, 1932).

8. For the "third-generation immigrant" phenomenon, often explained according to "Hansen's Law," See Herberg, *Protestant, Catholic, Jew*, 201.

9. Joshua Liebman, *Peace of Mind* (New York: Simon & Schuster, 1946); Fulton J. Sheen, *Peace of Soul* (New York: McGraw-Hill, 1949); Norman Vincent Peale, *The Power of Positive Thinking* (New York: Prentice-Hall, 1952). The quote is from Donald Meyer, *The Positive Thinkers: Religion as Pop Psychology from Mary Baker Eddy to Oral Roberts* (New York: Pantheon, 1965). See especially chapter 23 ("Social Anesthesia") and Postscript II ("Mind Cure among Catholics and Jews").

10. Quote from Jean Leclercq, preface to Merton's *Contemplation in a World of Action* (Garden City, N.Y.: Doubleday, 1971), 17.

11. Some of these excellent studies include Mott, *The Seven Mountains of Thomas Merton*; Edward Rice, *The Man in the Sycamore Tree* (Garden City, N.Y.: Doubleday, 1970); the excellent collection of essays in Twomey, *Prophet in the Belly of a Paradox*; Donald Grayston, *Thomas Merton: The Development of a Spiritual Theologian* (New York: Edwin Mellen Press, 1985); Walter Capps, *Hope against Hope: Moltmann to Merton in One Theological Decade* (Philadelphia: Fortress, 1976); Henri Nouwen, *Pray to Live: Thomas Merton, a Contemplative Critic* (Notre Dame, Ind.: Fides, 1972).

12. Erik Erikson, *Young Man Luther: A Study in Psychoanalysis and History,* 9th ed. (New York: William Norton, 1962).

13. George Lindbeck, "Erikson's *Young Man Luther*: Historical and Theological Reappraisal," in *Encounters with Erikson: Historical Interpretation and*

Religious Biography, Walter Capps, ed. (Santa Barbara, Calif.: Scholars Press, 1977), 16. Emphasis in the last line is my own.

14. For Erikson's technical, Durkheimian use of the term "ideology," see *Young Man Luther,* 42ff. Much of my reading of Erikson in this paragraph derives from Lindbeck's "Erikson's *Young Man Luther:* Historical and Theological Reappraisal," in *Encounters with Erikson,* 16–18.

15. Merton, *SSM,* 3ff.; 118ff.; 126; 138ff.

16. Ibid., 190, 204.

17. Ibid., 172–73.

18. Ibid., 216. On the role of Gilson's book in his conversion, Merton wrote: "When I had put this book down, I began to have a desire to go to church, a desire more sincere and mature and deep-seated than I had ever had before" (172, 175).

19. "Conditional baptism" is performed for a non-Catholic Christian being received into the Roman Church whose previous baptism is either uncertain or non-Trinitarian in formula. Merton's conversations with Lax and the quote are both in *SSM,* 237.

20. Merton's first stay at Gethsemani was April 7–14, 1941 (*SSM,* 310, 321).

21. Merton, *SSM,* 379–80.

22. Mott, *Seven Mountains,* 201, 202. "Merton's vocation was clear: he was not called to be a priest, or a member of a religious order. These were possible ways, but not the end. In the end, he sought to be a saint. As Leon Bloy had said, the greatest sadness was not being a saint" (185).

23. Because of a famous reform of the order in La Trappe, France, that returned it to its original fasts and penances, Cistercians of the Strict Observance are popularly known as "Trappists." On Merton's feeling of liberation in the monastery, see Mott, *Seven Mountains,* 206, 207.

24. Letter of Thomas Merton to James Laughlin, March 1, 1946, James Laughlin Archives, Norwalk, Connecticut. Laughlin was the founder and director of *New Directions,* who had published *Thirty Poems,* Merton's first collection of poems.

25. The *Nihil obstat* (meaning literally "nothing stands in the way") is the permission granted by church authorities to Catholic authors for any book published on Catholic theology. Mott, *Seven Mountains,* 235.

26. Mott, *Seven Mountains,* 235, 247.

27. Ibid., 244, 248. Merton, *SSM,* 419.

28. Merton, *SSM,* 85.

29. Henri Nouwen, *Pray to Live: Thomas Merton, a Contemplative Critic* (Notre Dame, Ind.: Fides, 1972), 14; Lawrence Cunningham, "The Pursuit of Marginality," *Christian Century* 95 (December 1978): 1183; Jean Leclercq, preface to Merton's *Contemplation in a World of Action* (Garden City, N.Y.: Doubleday, 1971), 18; Capps, *Hope against Hope,* xx.

30. The root meaning of the Latin word *traditio* is, of course, "to pass on." On Merton's role in "revealing" American Catholicism to itself, see Elena Malits, "Thomas Merton: Symbol and Synthesis of Contemporary Catholicism," in Grayston, *Merton,* 285. The block quote is from Jean Leclercq, "Merton and History" in Twomey, *Thomas Merton: Prophet in the Belly of a Paradox,* 215.

31. George Lindbeck, "Erikson's *Young Man Luther,*" 16.

32. Ibid., 14, 22.

33. Erikson, *Young Man Luther,* 15; Lindbeck, "Erikson's *Young Man Luther,*" 21.

34. Lindbeck, "Erikson's *Young Man Luther,*" 18.

35. For a lively narrative of Catholics after 1945, see Jay Dolan, *American Catholics* (Garden City, N.Y.: Doubleday, 1985), chapters 14 and 15.

36. For an excellent discussion of the "piety on the Potomac" school of piety, whose chief priest was President Dwight David Eisenhower, see Sydney Ahlstrom, *A Religious History of the American People* (New Haven: Yale University Press, 1972), chapter 56: "World War II and the Post-War Revival."

37. Both the quote and much of the argument for this paragraph derive from Richard Bushman's insightful article, "Jonathan Edwards as Great Man: Identity, Conversion, and Leadership in the Great Awakening," in *Encounters with Erikson,* (242).

38. Among those "ironies" is Merton's own death (by electrocution in a bathtub) in 1968, the same year as the death of Karl Barth, thousands of miles away from his monastery in Bangkok while attending an international ecumenical conference. See Mott, *Seven Mountains,* 505ff.

Chapter 3: Catholicism as a Cultural System

1. *Wheeling Intelligencer,* February 10, 1950, quoted in Thomas C. Reeves, *The Life and Times of Joe McCarthy* (New York: Stein and Day, 1982), 222–23.

2. *Wheeling Intelligencer,* February 10, 1950. Copies of the "original" Wheeling speech (the contents of which have been disputed by both McCarthy and his critics) can be found in U.S. Senate, Subcommittee of the Committee on Foreign Relations, *State Department Employee Loyalty Investigation Hearings,* 81st Congress, 2d session, 1950, 1758–67.

3. Reeves, *The Life and Times of Joe McCarthy,* 222–23.

4. *Wheeling Intelligencer,* February 10, 1950; Reeves, *Life and Times,* 224.

5. Reeves, *Life and Times,* 226–27; *Washington Star,* April 5, 1954.

6. For contemporary discussions of McCarthy's relationship to the Catholic Church (among a host of works), see Paul Blanshard, *Communism, Democracy, and Catholic Power* (Boston: Beacon Press, 1951); "McCarthy and the Catholics," *Christian Century* 67 (May 31, 1950): 667; William F. Buckley, *McCarthy and His Enemies: The Record and Its Meaning* (Chicago: H. Regnery, 1954); William R. Bechtel, "Protestants and Catholics," *New Republic* 128 (July 27, 1953): 11–12; "Catholics and McCarthy," *Commonweal* 61 (December 10, 1954): 276; "The Church and Politics," *Newsweek* 42 (October 19, 1953): 100; Vincent DeSantis, "A Catholic View of McCarthy," *New Republic* 130 (June 7, 1954): 22; "Freedom of Catholic Opinion," *America* 91 (June 5, 1954): 261; "McCarthy Resorts to Religious Test," *Christian Century* 70 (November 18, 1953): 311.

7. The first Gallup poll's statistics can be found in *Gallup Poll Number AIPO 454* (March 1950).

8. Donald Crosby's *God, Church, and Flag: Senator Joseph R. McCarthy and the Catholic Church* (Chapel Hill: University of North Carolina Press,

1978), is undoubtedly the best monograph examining McCarthy's ambivalent relationship to the Catholic Church. Chapter 1 is an especially fine contextualization of McCarthy within the church's anti-communism crusade. For two somewhat biased discussions of the "Father Walsh rumor," see I. F. Stone, *The Haunted Fifties* (New York: Random House, 1963), 39ff.; and Richard H. Rovere, *Senator Joseph McCarthy* (New York: Harcourt, Brace, 1959), 122–23.

9. Crosby, *God, Church, Flag*, 4, 11–16. See also Aaron Abell, *American Catholicism and Social Action: The Search for Social Justice, 1865–1950* (Notre Dame, Ind.: University of Notre Dame Press, 1963), 275–78; David O'Brien, *American Catholics and Social Reform: The New Deal Years* (New York: Oxford University Press, 1968), 96ff.

10. Crosby, *God, Church, Flag*, 158–67; the text of Bishop Sheil's most famous speech against McCarthy can be found in the *Chicago Daily News,* April 9, 1954. The letter to *Commonweal* is in "Fortieth Anniversary Symposium," *Commonweal* 81 (November 20, 1964): 261. The text of Senator Chavez's speech is found in U.S. Congress, The Senate, *Congressional Record,* 81st Congress, 2d Session, 1950, 6969–75.

11. Sheil's remarks can be found in the *Chicago Daily News*, April 9, 1954.

12. Clifford Geertz, "Religion as a Cultural System," in *The Interpretation of Cultures* (New York: Basic Books, 1973).

13. Ibid., 90.

14. Ibid., 89. This landmark essay was originally published in M. Banton, ed., *Anthropological Approaches to the Study of Religion* (London: Tavistock, 1966), 1–46.

15. Ibid., 96, 108.

16. Ibid., 96–97; quote from 122.

17. Jack Anderson and Ronald May, *McCarthy: The Man, the Senator, the Ism* (Boston: Beacon Press, 1953), 8. The quote about the religious life of the McCarthy family is from Crosby, *God, Church, Flag*, 26. The *Marquette Tribune*, October 16, 1930.

18. Reeves, *Life and Times*, 27–30. For contemporary reflections on the import of McCarthy's campaign, see the Appleton (Wisconsin) *Post-Crescent,* April 4, 1939, and the *Milwaukee Journal*, October 28, 1940. Rovere, *Senator Joseph McCarthy*, 91.

19. For an unsympathetic account of the "war injury," see Reeves, *Life and Times*, 47–51. See also Anderson and May, *McCarthy*, 58–61. Robert Griffith, *The Politics of Fear: Joseph R. McCarthy and the Senate* (Lexington: University Press of Kentucky, 1970), 9ff. McCarthy defeated LaFollette by 207,935 votes to 202,557. See the *Milwaukee Journal*, August 14, 1946.

20. *Madison Capitol Times*, October 25, 1946.

21. James M. O'Neill, *Catholics in Controversy* (New York: Declan X. McMullen, 1954), 173–74. Crosby, *God, Church, Flag*, 31.

22. Roy Cohn, *McCarthy* (New York: New American Library, 1968), 8–10. For the "literally overnight" account, see Reeves, *Life and Times*, 198.

23. According to Pearson, "likeable young Senator McCarthy" had asked his dinner guests for a winning campaign issue: "The man who urged this latter advice, Fr. Edmund Walsh of Georgetown University, is not happy at the out-

come" (*Washington Post,* March 14, 1950; I. F. Stone, *The Haunted Fifties* [New York: Random House, 1963], 39). Donald Crosby, on the other hand, has convincingly argued that "it is unlikely that Walsh urged McCarthy to go on a crusade with subversives. The story's foundations are extremely shaky and completely bereft of documentary support" (*God, Church, Flag,* 51, 52). On Walsh's presence at the dinner and subsequent break with McCarthy, see the *New York Times,* November 1, 1956.

24. Committee on Foreign Relations, *State Department Employee Loyalty Investigation Hearings,* 81st Congress, 2d Session, 1950, 1758. The quotations are from Reeves, *Life and Times,* 223; Griffith, *The Politics of Fear,* 48–49.

25. McCarthy named Alger Hiss, John Stewart Service, Mary Jane Kenney, and H. Julian Wadleigh by name in the course of the Wheeling speech; Reeves, *Life and Times,* 223–24. McCarthy made five more references to both the letter and the figure ("205") on the remainder of his Lincoln Day Tour: in Denver, Salt Lake City, Reno, Los Angeles, and Milwaukee, although twice he referred to "207 traitors." See the discussion of the fluctuating number of traitors in Reeves, *Life and Times,* 225–26.

26. *Denver Post,* February 11, 1950. The incident at the Denver Airport is described in hilarious detail by Reeves, *Life and Times,* 227.

27. *Congressional Record,* 81st Congress, 2d session, February 22, 1950, 2129–50. *New York Times,* February 23, 1950.

28. *Madison Capitol Times,* March 21, 1950. *Washington Post,* March 29, 1950.

29. Quote from the Tydings Committee Report from the *New York Times,* July 18, 1950. Description of the report as "scorching" from Reeves, *Life and Times,* 304.

30. Reeves, *Life and Times,* 287, 288.

31. *Congressional Record,* 82d Congress, 1st Session, June 14, 1951, 6556–6603; 6557. Description of the speech in Reeves, *Life and Times,* 372.

32. *Brooklyn Tablet,* March 4, 1950. For McGinley's denunciation of Chavez, see New York's *Catholic News,* May 20, 1950. Joseph Breig in the *Los Angeles Tidings,* May 26, 1950.

33. Crosby, *God, Church, Flag,* 59–60. *Ave Maria* 72 (September 20, 1950): 419.

34. George Higgins, "The Yardstick," *NCWC News Release,* June 5, 1950. On Cronin, see Crosby, *God, Church, Flag,* 56.

35. Vincent Kearney, "Wedermeyer versus McCarthy," *America* 85 (June 30, 1951): 323; Francis Downing, " 'Patriots' and Controversial Figures," *Commonweal* 55 (November 7, 1951): 90. Statement of the National Conference of Catholic Bishops, November 1951, United States Catholic Conference, Washington, D.C. On the 1951 meeting of Catholic bishops, see Crosby, *God, Church, Flag,* 87.

36. McCarthy's "slip of the tongue" referred to Alger Hiss, then being investigated for communist sympathies. McCarthy's supporters had paid $78,000 for thirty minutes of air time for the Palmer House address. For a lively account of the Palmer House speech, see *New York Times,* October 28, 1952.

37. Robert Hartnett, S.J., "Pattern of GOP Victory, "*America* 88 (Novem-

ber 22, 1952): 208–10. "Letters," Senator Joseph McCarthy, *America* 88 (December 13, 1952): 316.

38. Crosby, *God, Church, Flag,* 123. The description of Hartnett as "stubborn and resourceful" is from Crosby, *God, Church, Flag,* 101. Blanshard — perhaps the most notable "professional anti-Catholic" of the twentieth century — argued that McCarthy's "campaign of disgraceful vilification" had received wide support and acclaim from the Catholic press. See Paul Blanshard, *Communism, Democracy, and Catholic Power* (Boston: Beacon Press, 1951), 298.

39. *Our Sunday Visitor,* July 26, 1953; *Boston Pilot,* June 6, 1953. Joseph B. Matthews, "Reds and Our Churches," *American Mercury* 453 (July 1953): 3–13, 3. For the Catholic-Protestant tensions caused by Matthews's article, see William Bechtel, "Protestants and Catholics," *New Republic* 128 (July 27, 1953): 11–12; "The Church and Politics," *Newsweek* 42 (October 19, 1953): 100; "McCarthy Resorts to Religious Test," *Christian Century* 70 (November 18, 1953): 311; "Senator McCarthy's New Critics," *New Republic* 129 (August 3, 1953): 3.

40. *Los Angeles Tidings,* July 10, 1953. Spellman's remark is reported in the Madison (Wisconsin) *Capitol Times,* August 6, 1953. Nelson's remarks about Spellman are reported in the *New York Times,* October 25, 1953. The Gallup poll for January 1954, cited in William V. Shannon, *The American Irish* (New York: Macmillan, 1966), 381. On the three Protestant leaders see the *New York Times,* March 1, 1954, 13. On Pike and Sayre, see the *New York Times,* March 22, 1954, 21.

41. *New York Times,* March 1, 1954, 13. George Ford, *A Degree of Difference* (New York: Farrar, Straus & Giroux, 1969), 150ff.

42. The Army-McCarthy Hearings were a full public inquiry, announced by the House Un-American Activities Committee (HUAC) on March 16, 1954, in response to McCarthy's charges in September 1953, that the Army had distributed "clear-cut Communist propaganda" to its own personnel in a document entitled "Psychological and Cultural Traits of Soviet Siberia." McCarthy had told reporters that "if you read this and believed it, you would move to Russia" (*Madison Capitol Times,* September 10, 1954). In its turn, the Army formally rendered twenty-nine charges against McCarthy to the congressional subcommittee charged with evaluating the evidence on April 14, 1954, eight days before the hearings were to begin; the Army rested its case on May 26, and one week later — on June 1 — Senator Ralph Flanders rose on the Senate floor to deliver an impassioned denunciation of McCarthy in light of the Army's evidence, referring to McCarthy as "Dennis the Menace" (Reeves, *Life and Times,* 591–624). On the mail received by *America* regarding McCarthy, see Crosby, *God, Church, Flag,* 179–82. Robert Hartnett, S.J., to Wilfred Parsons, S.J., April 7, 1954, Parsons Papers, Georgetown University, Washington, D.C. See the letter of Joseph T. Prentiss to *America* 91 (April 10, 1954): 44. McCarthy's use of the letter from the unidentified Army Intelligence officer violated Army Regulation 380–10 as well as the Internal Security Act of 1950. See Hartnett, " 'Peaceful Overthrow' of the U.S. Presidency," *America* 91 (May 22, 1954): 210.

43. Robert Hartnett, " 'Peaceful Overthrow,' " 211.

44. John McMahon, William E. Fitzgerald, and William F. Maloney, letter of May 29, 1954, to Robert Hartnett. "McCarthy Editorial" folder, Jesuit Archives, Fordham University. McMahon noted in his letter that "we do not wish you to interpret this Directive as a vote of no confidence. It is not that.... But in the present heated state of public opinion, particularly among Catholics, we think silence for two months would be golden."

45. Cohn, *McCarthy,* 208; Joseph N. Welch, "The Lawyer's Afterthoughts," *Life* 37 (July 26, 1954): 100. Gallup Poll No. AIPO 537, September 1954, quoted in Crosby, *God, Church, Flag,* 196.

46. *New York Times,* June 10, 1954, 15. U.S. Congress, Senate, Committee on Government Operations, Special Subcommittee on Investigations, *Special Senate Investigation of Charges and Counter-Charges Involving: Secretary of the Army Robert T. Stevens, John G. Adams, H. Struve Hensel, and Senator Joe McCarthy, Roy M. Cohn, and Francis P. Carr: Hearings,* 83d Congress, 2d Session, March–June 1954, 1920. Crosby, *God, Church, Flag,* 189–90. Frank Gibney, "After the Ball: The Cohn Dinner," *Commonweal* 60 (September 3, 1954): 532–33.

47. U.S. Congress, Senate, Committee on Rules and Administration, Subcommittee on Privileges and Elections, *Select Committee to Study Censure Charges: Hearings... on S.R. 301.* 83d Congress, 2d Session, September 1954. U.S. Congress, Senate, *Congressional Record,* 83rd Congress, 2d Session, 1954, 16329, 16389–81. *The Wanderer,* December 9, 1954. "McCarthy Censure," *America* 92 (December 8, 1954): 309; Francis J. Keenan, "Censure of Senator McCarthy," *Commonweal* 61 (December 31, 1954): 356, 358.

48. Geertz, "Religion as a Cultural System," 89, 97.

49. Ibid., 104.

Chapter 4: "Life Is Worth Living"

1. Fulton J. Sheen, *Peace of Soul* (New York: McGraw-Hill, 1949), 1.

2. For a description of the opening show, see the cover story of *Time* magazine, "Microphone Missionary," April 14, 1952, 72. On the history of the show, see "Life Is Worth Living," in Tim Brooks and Earle Marsh, *The Complete Directory to Prime Time Network TV Shows* (New York: Ballantine, 1992), 512.

3. Kathleen Riley Fields, "Bishop Fulton J. Sheen: An American Catholic Response to the Twentieth Century," Ph.D. dissertation, University of Notre Dame, 1988 (Ann Arbor, Mich.: UMI, 1988), 113–23. "Microphone Missionary," 72. Graham quote in Jay Dolan, *The American Catholic Experience* (Garden City, N.Y.: Doubleday, 1985), 393.

4. D. P. Noonan, *Missionary with a Mike: The Bishop Sheen Story* (New York: Pageant Press, 1968), 4–6. The *agrégé* is a prestigious "postdoctorate" awarded by Louvain for extraordinarily promising and impressive doctoral work. Louvain awarded him its prestigious Mercier Prize for his dissertation published as his first book, *God and Intelligence.* For examples of Sheen's disdain for psychiatric answers to the anxiety of his time, see Sheen, *Peace of Soul,* 7, 20, 69ff.

5. Gretta Palmer, "Bishop Sheen on Television," *Catholic Digest* 17 (February 1953): 75–81, 75.

6. For a sampling of the broadly theological but nonsectarian nature of his television broadcasts, see Fulton J. Sheen, *Life Is Worth Living, First Series* (New York: McGraw-Hill, 1953): "Science, Relativity, and the Atomic Bomb," chapter 3, 19ff.; "The Philosophy of Communism," chapter 7, 62 ff. All five seasons of the TV show were recorded and transcribed, being subsequently published by McGraw-Hill as *Life Is Worth Living, First* through *Fifth Series.*

7. "The Death of Stalin," chapter 15, 157ff., in Sheen, *Life Is Worth Living, First Series.* For a description of the popular reception given his "Stalin" broadcast, see Brooks and Marsh, *Complete Directory,* 512.

8. Brooks and Marsh, *Complete Directory,* 512.

9. Will Herberg, *Protestant, Catholic, Jew* (Garden City, N.Y.: Doubleday, 1955), 68; "A Jew Looks at Catholics," *Commonweal* 57 (May 22, 1953): 174.

10. Donald Meyer, *The Positive Thinkers: Religion as Pop Psychology from Mary Baker Eddy to Oral Roberts* (New York: Pantheon Books, 1980), 332; William McLoughlin, *Revivals, Awakenings and Reform* (Chicago: University of Chicago Press, 1979), 186; Martin Marty, *Pilgrims in Their Own Land* (Boston: Little, Brown, 1984), 414; Donald Crosby, S.J., *God, Church, and Flag: Senator Joseph McCarthy and the Catholic Church* (Chapel Hill: University of North Carolina Press, 1978), 15; Fields, "Bishop Fulton J. Sheen," Abstract.

11. H. Richard Niebuhr, *Christ and Culture* (New York: Harper & Row, 1951).

12. Ibid., 120–21, 144–47.

13. Ibid., 93.

14. The phrase "gospel of social anesthesia" is from Meyer, *The Positive Thinkers.*

15. For an account of the degree being awarded "with highest distinction," see his autobiography: Fulton J. Sheen, *Treasure in Clay* (Garden City, N.Y.: Doubleday, 1980), 22ff.; Fields, "Bishop Fulton J. Sheen," 4–9. Ken Crotty, *Boston Post* reporter and the author of a series of articles on Sheen that ran from May 7 to 18, 1953, in the *Post,* was the first to question Sheen's account of his name change, claiming that it occurred considerably after his grammar school education, and was done so at Sheen's own instigation. See Fields, "Bishop Fulton J. Sheen," 2.

16. Sheen was awarded the Mercier Prize in 1926 for his *agrégé,* subsequently published as *God and Intelligence in Modern Philosophy: A Critical Study in the Light of the Philosophy of St. Thomas Aquinas* (New York: Longmans, Green, 1928). For his year as a parish priest in Peoria, see Fields, "Bishop Fulton J. Sheen," 9.

17. Sheen's "scholastic" works include his series of articles in *The New Scholasticism* published between 1927 and 1929, as well as *Religion without God* (New York: Garden City Books, 1954, originally published in 1928), *The Life of All Living* (New York: Garden City Books, 1951, originally published in 1929), and *The Philosophy of Science* (Milwaukee: Bruce, 1934). His more popular works include *The Divine Romance* (New York: Garden City Books, 1950, originally published in 1930), *Old Errors and New Labels* (New York: Cen-

tury, 1931), and *The Eternal Galilean* (New York: Garden City Books, 1950, originally published in 1934). Statistics on requests for transcripts of Sheen's talks is from Fields, "Bishop Fulton J. Sheen," 103. For the citation of "outstanding achievement," see *Commonweal,* October 1, 1930. Sheen being made a monsignor: *Catholic Action* 16 (August 1934): 13.

18. Fields, "Bishop Fulton J. Sheen," 109; 111.

19. Ibid., 272; *Communism and the Conscience of the West* (Indianapolis: Bobbs-Merrill, 1948). Crosby, *God, Church, Flag,* 15; Sheen quote in Sr. Mary Jude Yablonsky, "A Rhetorical Analysis of Selected Television Speeches of Archbishop Fulton J. Sheen on Communism," Ph.D. dissertation, Ohio State University, 1979).

20. *New York Times,* July 16, 1948; *Scholastic* 96 (February 11, 1955). David O'Brien, *American Catholics and Social Reform: The New Deal Years* (New York: Oxford University Press, 1968), 96.

21. David O'Brien, *The Renewal of American Catholicism* (New York: Paulist Press, 1972), 138. Winthrop Hudson, *Religion in America* (New York: Charles Scribner's Sons, 1973), 403. For publication information on *Peace of Soul,* see Fields, "Bishop Fulton J. Sheen," 327ff.

22. For an example of the "mind cure" interpretation, see Meyer, *The Positive Thinkers,* 332ff. Fields, "Bishop Fulton J. Sheen," 322. For Sheen's debates with the psychiatric profession, see *New York Times,* "Sin and Confession," March 10, 1947, and Sheen's letter on the Op/Ed pages of the *New York Times,* July 21, 1947.

23. O'Brien, *The Renewal of American Catholicism,* 138. Sheen, *Peace of Soul,* (New York: McGraw-Hill, 1949). Fields, "Bishop Fulton J. Sheen," 314.

24. Fields, "Bishop Fulton J. Sheen," 315. The quote is from Herberg, *Protestant, Catholic, Jew,* 161.

25. Lawrence H. Hughes, "Bishop Sheen's Sponsor," *Catholic Digest* 20 (May 1956): 17–21. Sheen's salary from the show was donated to the Society for the Propagation of the Faith, Blessed Martin de Porres Hospital in Mobile, Alabama, and the Mission Humanity, Inc., the last being a foundation directed by Sheen himself. Fields, "Bishop Fulton J. Sheen," 352.

26. On the expectations of the Dumont Network in approaching Sheen for a TV show, see "Video Debate," *Time,* February 25, 1952, 72. The Dumont Television Network operated from 1946 until 1955, when it went out of business. Sheen's program was carried by Dumont from 1952 until 1955, when it moved to the American Broadcasting Company (ABC): Brooks and Marsh, *Complete Directory,* 350.

27. "Microphone Missionary," *Time,* 72.

28. Theater and network statistics from "Microphone Missionary," *Time,* April 14, 1952; Jack Gould, "Bishop Fulton J. Sheen Preaches Absorbing Sermons in 'Life Is Worth Living' Series," *New York Times,* February 27, 1952. Quote from James C. Conniff, *The Bishop Sheen Story* (Greenwich, Conn.: Fawcett Publications, 1953), 5. The estimated audience for the 1955 season quoted from the *New York Times,* April 22, 1955, in Fields, "Bishop Fulton J. Sheen," 355.

29. Palmer, "Bishop Sheen on Television," 76. Italics in original.

30. "Life Is Worth Living," 4, in Sheen, *Life Is Worth Living, First Series; From the Angel's Blackboard: The Best of Fulton J. Sheen,* ed. Patricia Kossmann (Liguori, Mo.: Triumph Books, 1995), 40; on "Eve," see "Knowing and Loving," *Life Is Worth Living, First Series,* 71; on the "lifeboat," see *From the Angel's Blackboard,* 51; quote about the theory of relativity on "Science, Relativity, and the Atomic Bomb," *Life Is Worth Living, First Series,* 25.

31. Quote from A. Roy Eckhard, "Bishop Fulton J. Sheen Tells the Story of the Birth of Christ," *Christian Century* 71 (January 20, 1954): 80; see also "Bishop Cloys as Critic," *Christian Century* 73 (December 5, 1956): 1413. For critiques of Sheen's pretelevision career, see *Christian Century* 65 (May 19, 1948): 468; 65 (July 21, 1948): 726.

32. Fields, "Bishop Fulton J. Sheen," 337.

33. Sheen, *Peace of Soul,* 1; Fulton J. Sheen, *Guide to Contentment* (New York: Simon and Schuster, 1967), 26.

34. Val Adams, "The Bishop Looks at Television," *New York Times,* April 6, 1952. "The Philosophy of Communism," in Sheen, *Life Is Worth Living, First Series,* 65.

35. Palmer, "Bishop Sheen on Television," 76.

36. David O'Brien, *Public Catholicism* (New York: Macmillan, 1985). "Life Is Worth Living," in *Life Is Worth Living, First Series,* 8. On education, see *Life Is Worth Living, Second Series* (New York: McGraw-Hill, 1954), 153–54.

37. Fulton J. Sheen, "Liberal or Reactionary," *Life Is Worth Living, Second Series,* 46.

38. Perhaps the best-known work that advances this portrait of Sheen is Will Herberg's *Protestant, Catholic, Jew;* a more balanced and nuanced scholarly presentation of the same position can be found in Donald Meyer's *The Positive Thinkers.*

39. "Microphone Missionary," *Time,* April 14, 1952, 78. Conniff, *The Bishop Sheen Story,* 5; italics my own. For Sheen's disclaimers about "preaching" on his show, see Joseph Roddy, "A Talk with Bishop Sheen," *Look* 17 (January 27, 1953): 76. Sheen, *Life Is Worth Living, First Series,* frontispiece; ibid., 18.

40. Sheen, *Life Is Worth Living, Second Series,* 84. Sheen, "Psychoanalysis and Confession," *Peace of Soul,* 114.

41. Adams, "The Bishop Looks at Television," *New York Times.* "Most influential voice" from Conniff, "Bishop Sheen Story," 5.

Chapter 5: "The Downward Path"

1. Dorothy Day, *Houses of Hospitality* (New York: Sheed and Ward, 1939), 275. This chapter takes as axiomatic the history of Day and the Catholic Worker movement recounted by William D. Miller in *A Harsh and Dreadful Love: Dorothy Day and the Catholic Worker Movement* (New York: Liveright, 1973).

2. Dorothy Day, "Where Are the Poor? They Are in Prisons, Too" *Catholic Worker* 22 (July–August 1955): 1. The event is also recounted in Dan Wakefield, *New York in the Fifties* (Boston: Houghton Mifflin, 1992), 82; Miller, *Harsh and Dreadful Love,* 284–85. The phrase at the end of the paragraph is a gloss on the title of Robert Coles's insightful and moving study of the movement, *A*

Spectacle unto the World: The Catholic Worker Movement (New York: Viking Press, 1973). See also Coles's moving tribute to Day in "Remembering Dorothy Day" in *Harvard Diary: Reflections on the Sacred and the Secular* (New York: Crossroad, 1988), 5–6.

3. Day, "Where Are the Poor?" 8.

4. Ibid., 1. See also the statement on the front page of this issue of the *Catholic Worker* entitled "10th Anniversary of Hiroshima," which declared (among other things) that "we the undersigned, openly refuse to pay our income taxes, because more than 80 percent go for war. We are doing this as Christians, as Catholics, whose aim is to obey the teaching of Christ as given in the Sermon on the Mount" (1).

5. Dorothy Day, "CW Editors Arrested in Air Raid Drill," *Catholic Worker* (July–August 1956): 1, 8; "Dorothy Day among Pacifists Jailed," special edition, *Catholic Worker* (July 17, 1957): 1. See "A Lesson in Civil Defense," *Commonweal* 62 (July 1, 1955): 31, for a description of "Operation Alert" in 1955.

6. Wakefield, *New York in the Fifties*, 82; Miller, *Harsh and Dreadful Love*, 284–85.

7. "Personalism" is the term applied to the ideas of a group of post–World War I French philosophers who argued that all historical change (political, economic, social) must begin with the human person and not with institutional/structural reform. Maurin and Day thus resolutely opposed almost all forms of "collectivism," by which they meant everything from Stalinist Russia to the New Deal under Roosevelt. As the *Catholic Worker* itself described it, such collectivism "implicitly or even explicitly made the *group* a sort of higher order individual," which perverted social reality and led almost ineluctably to totalitarianism. The Worker's brand of personalism included a commitment to decentralization of government, voluntary and "decent poverty," the performance of the "corporal works of mercy," and the "restoration of the human person to the center of the social order." See Tom Cain, "Personalism: The One Man Revolution," *Catholic Worker* 22 (February 1956): 1. "First children" in David O'Brien, "The Pilgrimage of Dorothy Day," *Commonweal* 107 (December 19, 1980): 711–15, 711.

8. James T. Fisher, *The Catholic Counter-Culture in America: 1933–1962* (Chapel Hill: University of North Carolina Press, 1989), 1. Day's quote from the broadcast script of "Still a Rebel," *Bill Moyer's Journal*, WNET, 1973.

9. Dorothy Day, editorial, *Catholic Worker* 1 (May 1933): 1, 7. Mel Piehl's *Breaking Bread* (Philadelphia: Temple University Press, 1982) offers one of the best critical studies of the spirituality/philosophy informing the day-to-day operations of the movement.

10. I am using the classical Greek term *polis* here as meaning the public sphere or common good — the reason why human beings form communities. My understanding of the Worker's economic/political "take" on personalism has followed the convincing arguments of Michael Baxter, "Notes on Catholic Americanism and Catholic Radicalism: Toward a Counter-Tradition of Catholic Social Ethics," in *American Catholic Traditions: Sources for Renewal*, ed. Sandra Yocum Mize and William Portier (Maryknoll, N.Y.: Orbis Books, 1997),

53–71; see especially 53–55, 65–68. For a lucid exposition of the Worker's espousal of "localist politics," see Robert Coles, *Dorothy Day: A Radical Devotion* (Reading, Mass.: Addison Wesley, 1987). On p. 107, Coles defines the Catholic Worker understanding of "localist politics" to be "Christian anarchism," which constitutes "an advocacy of certain kinds of government — de-centralized, self-governing, participatory modes of government, and not — as many wrongly assume — opposition to government *per se.*" "Christologically shaped politics" is from Paul Furfey, *Fire on the Earth* (New York: Macmillan, 1936), 117. For Day's approval of the English distributists, see *The Long Loneliness* (New York: Harper & Row, 1963), 56. Quote by Day from *Houses of Hospitality,* 259.

    11. Miller, *Harsh and Dreadful Love,* 9. One of the best sources for understanding Day's own perception of the spiritual influences on her life is her autobiography, *The Long Loneliness.* See, for example, her lucid reflections on the importance of retreats on her spiritual life on pp. 247ff.

    12. Fisher, *Catholic Counter-Culture,* 28. Quote about Day being the "most significant" is from David O'Brien, "The Pilgrimage of Dorothy Day," 711.

    13. Fisher, *Catholic Counter-Culture,* 24, 63. Marc Ellis, *Peter Maurin: Prophet to the Twentieth Century* (Ramsey, N.J.: Paulist Press, 1981).

    14. Miller, *Harsh and Dreadful Love,* 25.

    15. Frederick Bauerschmidt, "The Politics of the Little Way: Dorothy Day Reads Therese of Lisieux," in Mize and Portier, *American Catholic Traditions,* 79–91; quote from 79. See also the Introduction to Dorothy Day's *Therese,* 2d ed. (Springfield, Ill.: Templegate Publishers, 1979), for her reflections on coming to understand Therese.

    16. Fisher, *Catholic Counter-Culture,* 1; Miller, *Harsh and Dreadful Love,* 85.

    17. James T. Fisher, "Dorothy Day, an Ordinary American," 72–75, in Mize and Portier, eds. *American Catholic Traditions,* 75.

    18. Victor Turner, *The Ritual Process: Structure and Anti-Structure* (Chicago: Aldine Publishing Company, 1969), 96–97, 106.

    19. Ibid., 97.

    20. Ibid., 128.

    21. "Antinomian" here refers to those left-wing Puritan impulses — embodied in the teaching of New England figures like Anna Hutchinson and Roger Williams — which took the Calvinist tendencies inherent in English Reformed thought to their radical conclusion. Antinomian Puritans taught that if, indeed, Christians were "saved by faith" and not by works, and if "no one is saved by the works of the law," then true Christians could ignore (indeed, *should* ignore) mere human authority for the sake of following the promptings of the Spirit. While both Hutchinson and Williams were expelled from the Massachusetts Bay Colony for false teaching and civil disturbance, both have come to be seen as forcing English Puritan thought on grace and works to their logical — if socially unquieting — conclusions. This new understanding of figures like Hutchinson and Williams has helped to sponsor a revolution in Puritan historiography and in understanding the "Puritan origins of the American self": in the revision-

ist school of Puritan scholarship, these "outsiders" who questioned the ends of the New England experiment's emphasis on order and legality were themselves as important to the experiment as John Winthrop, governor of Massachusetts Bay Colony. See Sacvan Bercovitch, *The Puritan Origins of the American Self* (New Haven, Conn.: Yale University Press, 1975); Janice Knight, *Orthodoxies in Massachusetts: Rereading American Puritanism* (Cambridge, Mass.: Harvard University Press, 1994); Philip Gura, *A Glimpse of Zion's Glory: Puritan Radicals in New England, 1629–1660* (Middletown, Conn.: Wesleyan University Press, 1984). For the older, magisterial understanding of the relationship of Hutchinson and Williams to the mainstream Puritan experience — which considered both well beyond the pale of true Puritan thought, to the extent of even denying the name "Puritan" to them — see Perry Miller, *Orthodoxy in Massachusetts* (Boston: Beacon Press, 1955); *The New England Mind,* 2 vols. (Cambridge, Mass.: Harvard University Press, 1939, 1953).

22. Dorothy Day, editorial, *Catholic Worker* 1 (December 1933): 4.

23. Fisher, *Catholic Counter-Culture,* 25, 28. See also Dorothy Day, "I Remember Peter Maurin," *Jubilee* 1 (March 1954): 34–39, for Day's memories of the French philosopher.

24. Dorothy Day, *From Union Square to Rome* (Silver Spring, Md.: Preservation of the Faith, 1938), 74–75; Fisher, *Catholic Counter-Culture,* 12.

25. Day's older brother Donald would become a foreign correspondent for the *Chicago Tribune,* while her brother Sam worked at the *New York Journal American.* See Nancy Roberts, *Dorothy Day and the Catholic Worker* (Albany: State University of New York Press, 1984). Miller, *Harsh and Dreadful Love,* 36–39, 44–53, 46.

26. Dorothy Day, *The Eleventh Virgin* (New York: A. C. Boni, 1924). Day, *From Union Square to Rome.* Quote from Coles, *A Spectacle unto the World,* 29; Day, *The Long Loneliness,* 139.

27. Fisher, *Catholic Counter-Culture,* 14. Fisher is quoting Philip Slater, *The Pursuit of Loneliness,* 4.

28. Fisher, *Catholic Counter-Culture,* 14–15.

29. Day, *The Long Loneliness,* 143; *From Union Square to Rome,* 134–38. The quote at the end of the paragraph is from Fisher, *Catholic Counter-Culture,* 18.

30. Day, *The Long Loneliness,* 139, 149.

31. Charles R. Morris, *American Catholic: The Saints and Sinners Who Built America's Most Powerful Church* (New York: Times Books, 1997), 143.

32. Piehl, *Breaking Bread,* 65. Goldman quote in O'Brien, "The Pilgrimage of Dorothy Day," 712.

33. Morris, *American Catholic,* 144.

34. Miller, *Harsh and Dreadful Love,* 13–14.

35. Ibid., 67, 72–73.

36. Day, *Houses of Hospitality,* 258ff.

37. The letter to Day is cited in Miller, *Harsh and Dreadful Love,* 85.

38. Wakefield, *New York in the Fifties,* 8.

39. Wakefield quotes Michael Harrington's *Fragments of a Century* in ibid., 77–78. See also Morris, *American Catholic,* 143.

40. Wakefield, *New York in the Fifties*, 73, 75.

41. O'Brien, "Pilgrimage of Dorothy Day," 712–13.

42. Miller, *Harsh and Dreadful Love*, 198.

43. Wakefield, *New York in the Fifties*, 83.

44. Ibid., 284. "H-Bomb Tests and Human Survival," *Catholic Worker* 22 (January 1956): 1. In the same issue, see "Holy Father Pleads for Nuclear Ban," 2. "Individual Income Tax: War's Chief Supporter," *Catholic Worker* 22 (March 1956): 1.

45. Dorothy Day, "CW Editors Arrested in Air Raid Drill," 8.

46. "Dorothy Day among Pacifists Jailed," special edition, *Catholic Worker* 24 (July 17, 1957): 1. Miller, *Harsh and Dreadful Love*, 285.

47. Turner, *The Ritual Process*, 94. Turner acknowledges that his understanding of the entire *rites de passage* was shaped by the great cultural anthropologist Arnold van Gennep.

48. Ibid.

49. "Liminality" (from the Latin, *limen, limina*, doorway or gate) refers to an individual or group standing on the edge or margins (literally, "at the gate"). While such marginality involves exclusion from the mainstream, it also allows the individual/group to define the "inside" precisely by drawing the line of where the "outside" begins. See chapter 1, especially the discussion of Mary Douglas's ideas regarding "deviance."

50. Turner, *The Ritual Process*, 102. The Latin phrase *servus servorum Dei* means "servant of the servants of God."

51. Ibid., 96–97.

52. Ibid., 127–28.

53. Fisher, "Dorothy Day, an Ordinary American," 75; O'Brien, "The Pilgrimage of Dorothy Day," 712.

54. On "outsidership," see R. Laurence Moore, *Religious Outsiders and the Making of Americans* (New York: Oxford University Press, 1986), xi, xii.

55. O'Brien, "The Pilgrimage of Dorothy Day," 711.

56. Ibid., 712.

Chapter 6: A Catholic for President?

1. John F. Kennedy, "On Church and State: Remarks of John F. Kennedy Addressed to the Greater Houston Ministerial Association," in *The Kennedy Reader*, ed. Jay David (Indianapolis: Bobbs-Merrill, 1967), 363, italics added.

2. Theodore H. White, *The Making of the President, 1960*, 2d ed. (New York: Atheneum Publishers, 1969), 260. For an overtly hostile account of the Houston Speech, see Victor Lasky, *JFK, the Man and the Myth* (New York: Macmillan, 1963), 490.

3. "On Church and State: Remarks of John F. Kennedy," 364, 365.

4. Albert Menendez, *John F. Kennedy: Catholic and Humanist* (Buffalo, N.Y.: Prometheus Books, n.d.), 31ff.

5. Jacqueline Kennedy's remark reported in ibid., 2. For a secular reading of Kennedy's "faith," see Bruce Miroff, *Pragmatic Illusions: The Presidential Pol-*

itics of John F. Kennedy (New York: David McKay, 1976), 5–9, 10. Sorensen's recollection is in Theodore Sorensen, *Kennedy* (New York: Harper & Row, 1965), 19.

6. The phrase "error has no rights" was a dictum of the 1917 Code of Canon Law. During the 1960 presidential campaign, well over three hundred different anti-Catholic tracts — aimed specifically at the Kennedy ticket and much of it scurrilous — were sent out to over twenty million homes by Protestant groups organized against Kennedy because of his religion. Likewise, Dr. George Ford of the National Association of Evangelicals attempted to make "Reformation Sunday" on October 30, 1960 — nine days before the election — into an event that would feature anti-Kennedy sermons in Protestant churches across the land. Sorensen, *Kennedy,* 194, 195.

7. Kennedy received 34,221,463 votes (49.7 percent of the number cast), while Richard Nixon received 34,108,582 votes (49.6 percent), making Kennedy's the closest presidential election in American history. See White, *Making of President,* 350. On the "American Way of Life" as the *real* American religion, see Will Herberg, *Protestant, Catholic, Jew* (Chicago: University of Chicago Press, 1960), chapter 5.

8. On the history of the "Judeo-Christian Tradition" as a cultural and political term in America, see Mark Silk, "Notes on the Judeo-Christian Tradition in America," *American Quarterly* 36 (1984): 64–85, especially 74ff. On the "suburban captivity of the churches," see Gibson Winter, *The Suburban Captivity of the Churches: An Analysis of Protestant Responsibility* (New York: Macmillan, 1962). On the piety of the 1950s "revival" abetting the mind cure gospel of "social anesthesia," see Donald Meyer, *The Positive Thinkers: Religion as Pop Psychology from Mary Baker Eddy to Oral Roberts,* 2d ed. (New York: Pantheon Books, 1980), chapter 23: "Social Anesthesia." On "Piety on the Potomac" as a political/religious phenomenon during the Eisenhower presidency, see Sydney Ahlstrom, *A Religious History of the American People,* 7th ed. (New Haven: Yale University Press, 1977), 954.

9. In his Second Inaugural, Lincoln offered a distinctly religious content to the "bonds of affection" that bound North and South together: "Both read the same Bible, and pray to the same God." See Sidney Mead, "Abraham Lincoln's 'Last, Best Hope of Earth': The American Dream of Destiny and Democracy," 73, in *The Lively Experiment: The Shaping of Christianity in America* (New York: Harper & Row 1976 [1963]). In calling for American support for the 14 Points after World War I, Woodrow Wilson had announced that "America had the infinite privilege of fulfilling her destiny and saving the world." See Ernest Lee Tuveson, *Redeemer Nation: The Idea of America's Millennial Role* (Chicago: University of Chicago Press, 1968), frontispiece, 173–75, 209–13, 224–25. An excellent discussion of the implications of President Eisenhower's famous statement can be found in Herberg, *Protestant, Catholic, Jew,* 16.

10. Peter Berger, *The Sacred Canopy: Elements of a Sociological Theory of Religion* (New York: Doubleday, 1967), 133–34.

11. There is, of course, a daunting mass of social scientific literature addressing the question of just what "secularization" might mean, and how it has (or hasn't) affected modern American culture. This chapter will take as ax-

iomatic Peter Berger's classic definition of "secularization" as the "privatization of religious impulses" and their marginalization from public discourse.

12. Berger, *The Sacred Canopy,* 134. See Sidney Mead, *The Nation with the Soul of a Church* (New York: Harper & Row, 1975), 48. The phrase "nation with the soul of a church" was coined by G. K. Chesterton in answer to his question, "What Is America?" — the title of one of his essays.

13. Menendez, *Kennedy: Catholic and Humanist,* 25; Lasky, *JFK,* 173–79; White, *Making of the President,* 241.

14. White, *Making of the President,* 241; Sorensen, *Kennedy,* 81.

15. Lasky, *JFK,* 180–81. See also Appendix B: The "Bailey Report," 587–88, 591ff.

16. Sorensen, *Kennedy,* 83. Lasky, *JFK,* 181–82. *Christian Century* 33 (August 15, 1956): 941. For an editorial reflection on the "import" of the Democratic Party's decision in 1956 not to run Kennedy as vice president, see "Senator Kennedy and the Convention," published in *America,* September 4, 1956, in *The Kennedy Reader,* 359–61.

17. "A Catholic in 1960," *Look* Magazine, March 3, 1959; emphasis my own.

18. "Catholic Censure of Kennedy Rises," *New York Times,* March 1, 1959; "Cushing Backs Kennedy on Church-State Replies," *New York Herald Tribune,* March 10, 1959; "On Questioning Catholic Candidates," *America,* March 7, 1959; James A. Pike, *A Roman Catholic in the White House* (Garden City, N.Y.: Doubleday, 1960), 39.

19. Pike, *A Roman Catholic in the White House,* 39; Sorensen, *Kennedy,* 19.

20. Sorensen, *Kennedy,* 112.

21. The "religion issue" was hotly debated throughout February and March 1960, including in the "liberal" religious press. For a sampling, see Robert Michaelsen, "Religion and the American Presidency, I," *Christian Century* (February 3, 1960): 133–35. Sorensen, *Kennedy,* 122, 127; quotation on 128.

22. Sorensen, *Kennedy,* 137.

23. Ibid., 137, 139.

24. Ibid., 142.

25. "The Responsibility of the Press: Address to the American Society of Newspaper Editors, Washington, D.C., April 21, 1960," in *"Let the Word Go Forth": The Speeches, Statements, and Writings of John F. Kennedy,* ed. Theodore Sorensen (New York: Delacorte Press, 1988), 126, 128.

26. Sorensen, *Kennedy,* 143.

27. Ibid., 144.

28. Ibid.

29. Ibid., 146.

30. Ibid., 154–55; 159–61.

31. "Religious Affiliation," *Christian Century* (August 17, 1960): 939–40.

32. *Charleston Daily Mail,* April 14, 1960, quoted in Carol V. R. George, *God's Salesman: Norman Vincent Peale and the Power of Positive Thinking* (New York: Oxford University Press, 1993), 195.

33. George, *Peale,* 200–201. The "Statement of Purpose" of the group is

from a letter from Donald Gill to Norman Vincent Peale, August 29, 1960, in the Norman Vincent Peale Manuscript Collection at Syracuse University.

34. *New York Times,* September 8, 1960, reported in George, *Peale,* 202; Sorensen, *Kennedy,* 188.

35. David, *Kennedy Reader,* 363, 364.

36. Ibid., 364–65.

37. Ibid., 365.

38. Ibid. The emphasis in the quotation is my own.

39. Ibid., 366.

40. Winthrop Hudson, "The Religious Issue in the Campaign," *Christian Century* 177 (October 26, 1960): 1239.

41. Lasky, *JFK,* 326.

42. Sorensen, *Kennedy,* 190.

43. John Courtney Murray, *We Hold These Truths: Catholic Reflections on the American Proposition* (New York: Sheed and Ward, 1960). Murray had observed in his book that "the inspiration of this democratic monism is partly a sentimental mystique — the belief that power vested in the people, in distinction from all other powers, is somehow ultimately inevitably benevolent in its exercise. [But] Christianity has always regarded the state as a limited order of action for limited purposes, to be chosen and pursued under the direction and correction of the organized moral conscience of society, whose judgments are formed and mobilized by the [Catholic] Church" (202–3).

44. In scholastic thought, the "thesis" represented the ideal social and political situation, while the "hypothesis" sought to address actual social circumstances. Thus, Catholic scholars had argued during much of the nineteenth and early twentieth centuries that, while Catholics were the minority in the United States (the "hypothesis"), they could and should support freedom of religion and separation of church and state; but should Catholics ever become the majority of citizens (the "thesis" situation), they would have a moral obligation to establish the Catholic Church as the official religion of the country. A classic statement of this argument can be found in John A. Ryan and Moorhouse F. X. Millar, *The State and the Church* (New York: Macmillan, 1922). See especially Ryan's "Comments on the Christian Constitutions of States," 26–61.

45. Letter of John Courtney Murray to Mrs. J. M. Devine, May 19, 1967, in the Murray Papers, Woodstock College Collection, Georgetown University, Washington, D.C.

46. Quotation in the paragraph from Peter Berger, *The Heretical Imperative: Contemporary Possibilities of Religious Affirmation* (Garden City, N.Y.: Anchor Press, 1970), xi, 17; block quote from *The Sacred Canopy,* 151–52.

47. Berger, *Sacred Canopy,* 147.

48. One of Reinhold Niebuhr's most famous and influential works was *The Irony of American History* (New York: Charles Scribner's Sons, 1952). The phrase "American democratic faith" was coined and defined by Ralph Henry Gabriel in *The Course of American Democratic Thought: An Intellectual History since 1815* (New York: Ronald Press, 1940).

Chapter 7: "Into Uncertain Life"

1. *Information Catholique Internationale* 183 (January 1, 1963): 1. The title for this chapter is from Garry Wills, *Bare Ruined Choirs: Doubt, Prophecy, and Radical Religion* (Garden City, N.Y.: Doubleday, 1971), 21.

2. Frederick McManus, "Vatican Council II," *Worship* 37 (February 1963): 146–48; Daniel O'Hanlon, S.J., "The Development of Worship at the Second Vatican Council," *Worship* 40 (March 1966): 130–36. The twenty-one universal councils of the Roman Catholic Church are usually referred to as "ecumenical" (from the Greek *oekumene,* meaning "worldwide" or "universal"), as bishops from around the world are invited to gather and consider ecclesiastical questions for instruction or legislation. "Introduction," *Documents of Vatican II,* ed. Walter Abbott, S.J. (New York: Guild Press, 1966), xv.

3. *Peritus (periti* in the plural) is Latin for "expert" or "scholarly counselor." James D. Crichton, *Changes in the Liturgy: Considerations on the Instructions of the Sacred Congregation of Rites for the Proper Implementation of the Constitution on Sacred Liturgy, Issued on September 26, 1964* (Staten Island, N.Y.: Alba House, 1965), 4–6. For the epochal definition of the church as the "People of God," see "The Dogmatic Constitution on the Church," *Documents of Vatican II,* chapter 2, 24ff.

4. George Devine, *Liturgical Renewal: An Agonizing Reappraisal* (New York: Alba House, 1973), 45. Frederick R. McManus, "The New Rite of Mass," *Worship* 39 (February 1965): 69. McManus's article offers the clearest explanation of the practical changes that parishes faced as result of the "September Instruction." Luis Maldonado, "Liturgy as a Communal Enterprise," in *The Reception of Vatican II,* ed. Guiseppe Alberigo, Jean-Pierre Jossua, and Joseph Komonchak (Washington, D.C.: Catholic University of America Press, 1987), 309–21. John Henry Newman, *The Letters and Diaries of John Henry Newman,* ed. C. S. Dessain and T. Gornall (Oxford: Oxford University Press, 1979), 25:175.

5. Josef Jungmann, S.J., "What the Sunday Mass Could Mean," *Worship* 37 (December 1962): 21–29, especially 23–26. Crichton, *Changes in the Liturgy,* 5–9. Devine, *Liturgical Renewal,* 17ff. This and many of the following paragraphs were informed by the second chapter of Devine's book, "The Anatomy of Renewal: The 20th Century to 1963."

6. Paul B. Marx, O.S.B., *Virgil Michel and the Liturgical Movement* (Collegeville, Minn.: Liturgical Press, 1957), 73–74. The title of the new journal revealed much about the aims of the movement itself: *Ecclesia Orans,* or "the church prays."

7. Ibid., 407–8; Devine, *Liturgical Renewal,* 27–28.

8. Marx, *Michel,* 36–37, 56, 87–88. St. John Abbey's influential journal on liturgy, *Orate Fratres,* became known as *Worship* by the time of Vatican II, a journal that still cuts a broad swathe in the academic and pastoral worlds of liturgical theology. In November 1950, the editor of the *Catholic Journalist* said of *Orate Fratres,* "In proportion to its circulation, no Catholic magazine ever exercised so great an influence on American Catholic life" (Marx, *Michel,* 407). On the September 3, 1958, "Instruction" on the "Dialogue

Mass," see William J. Leonard, ed., *The Instruction for American Pastors on Sacred Music and the Sacred Liturgy* (Boston: McLaughlin & Reilly, 1959). For the excitement of the earlier revival in Gregorian chant, read the Introduction in Nicola A. Montani, *The Saint Gregory Hymnal* (Philadelphia: St. Gregory Guild, 1940).

9. Wills, *Bare Ruined Choirs.* In chapter 1, "Memories of a Catholic Boyhood," 17, 21. *In saecula saeculorum* is the Latin conclusion of most "collect" prayers in the Roman Rite, meaning "forever and ever."

10. Ibid., 2, 21.

11. "Foreword," vii, *The Reception of Vatican II,* ed. Alberigo, Jossua, and Komonchak, vii. On Pius V's 1570 missal, see Bard Thompson, *Liturgies of the Western Church* (New York: New American Library, 1961), 42–49. See also Hubert Jedin, *A History of the Council of Trent* (New York: Thomas Nelson & Sons, 1957), 1:130. For a critical, revisionist evaluation of the "standardization" of Pius's missal, see John Bossy, "The Counter-Reformation and the People of Catholic Europe," *Past and Present* 47 (May 1970): 51–70, especially 67–69.

12. "Vernacular Warning: Scandal in Hurried, Undignified Use," *National Catholic Reporter* (November 4, 1964): 3. Robert W. Hovda, "The Mass of the Future," *The Critic* 23 (October/November 1964): 29.

13. Wills, *Bare Ruined Choirs,* 65. Dale Francis, "The Mood of the Laity: How Are Catholics Reacting to the New Liturgy?" *The Critic* 24 (February/ March 1965): 57.

14. "Backlash Gets Organized: Ask Referendum on Liturgy," *National Catholic Reporter* 1 (April 7, 1965): 1.

15. The term "liberal" Catholic in the pre–Vatican II Roman Church had a very different set of connotations than its current set of meanings. A Catholic liberal in the pre–Vatican II church was obsessed with neither authoritarian clerical structures nor with the neuralgic issues surrounding the sixth and ninth commandments. Rather, "liberals" in that preconciliar context sought a church and liturgy "purified" of crass American culture religion and "Main Street" sentimentality. Thus, such a liberal despised his own parish church, less for being irrelevant to the trends of the culture than for being a "fund-raising operation, school board, and Eucharist-dispensary. The liberal became a lay priest. He bought a priest's breviary, and learned to recite the Divine Office. . . . Obscure rites and signs were unearthed from Dom Prosper Gueranger's fifteen-volume *Liturgical Year,* and pilgrimages were made — e.g., to Monsignor Hellriegel's church in St. Louis — to see what *real* ceremonies looked like. Each of these trips made the return to one's own parish enervating — the Latin mumbled unintelligibly, the choir's performance exactly suited to its syrupy repertoire, the statues meretricious, the stations of the cross both lugubrious and laughable." Such liberals undoubtedly welcomed the new liturgical changes, not because they made the Mass "relevant," but because they promised escape from the less than moving celebrations of the Tridentine rite that occurred in most American parishes every week. Wills, *Bare Ruined Choirs,* 42–43.

16. The letter published in the spring of 1965 ("I fail to see . . . ") was by Larry Michaels, "Commotion about the New Mass?" *National Catholic Reporter* 1 (April 28, 1965): 4; emphasis added. Msgr. J. D. Conway, "Question

Box," *National Catholic Reporter* 1 (November 25, 1964): 4. Joseph T. Nolan, "Questions and Answers by a Pastor Not at All Happy with Half-Vernacular Mass," *National Catholic Reporter* 1 (January 6, 1965): 6.

17. Among those lamenting the new liturgy was Victor Turner, the renowned cultural anthropologist, and himself a devout Catholic. He would later write in *Worship* magazine: "These comparative considerations have induced me to regard 'certain features of the recent liturgical changes with a wary eye. In many ways depth has been abandoned for breadth.... I do not wish to sound uncharitable towards sincere and devout individuals, but science must have a say, and the comparative study of cultures has already some valid findings to its credit.... The [new] liturgy has been conceived as a suitable 'expression' or 'reflection' of contemporary social structures and processes, even fashions and fads. Rituals which represent the *fine fleur* of generic human experience understood in the light of the gospel have been jettisoned in favor of sometimes jaunty verbal formulations which are thought to be 'relevant' to the experience of 'contemporary man.' Behind all this is the notion that the 'ordinary faithful' can only appreciate the 'sacred' when it is packaged in 'secular' wrappings" ("Ritual, Tribal and Catholic," *Worship* 50 [November 1976]: 504–25). For an account arguing that the changes were part of a much broader, longer history, see Joseph Komonchak, "The Local Realization of the Church," in *The Reception of Vatican II*, ed. Alberigo, Jossua, and Komonchak, 77–90. Also Frederick McManus, "Liturgy," *The Critic* 21 (August–September 1962): 23–25.

18. Emile Durkheim, *The Elementary Forms of the Religious Life*, 4th ed., trans. Joseph Ward Swain (London: George Allen & Unwin, 1957), 416.

19. Ibid., 416, 417; emphasis added.

20. Ibid., 417, 418.

21. The phrase *lex orandi lex credendi* is a shortened form of the phrase *legem credendi lex statuit supplicandi* and is usually attributed to a fifth-century theologian and papal secretary, Prosper of Aquitaine. Scholars date its first appearance to somewhere between 435 and 442. A disciple of St. Augustine, Prosper wrote against the heresy of semi-pelagianism, arguing that the apostolic injunction to "pray at all times" (which the church obeys in its daily cycle of prayer) proved that the obligation "to believe" is, from first to last, a work of grace, as both were grace-inspired injunctions made possible by the work of the Holy Spirit. While Prosper's intent was, arguably, to prove that "praying" and "believing" always proceeded from the same source ("the law of praying *is* the law of believing"), his dictum has come to be interpreted by Catholic theologians in causative terms ("the law of praying *forms or causes* the law of believing"). See Geoffrey Wainwright, *Doxology: The Praise of God in Worship, Doctrine, and Life* (London: Epworth Press, 1980), 224–27. See also Catherine LaCugna, *God for Us: The Trinity and Christian Life* (San Francisco: HarperCollins, 1973), 112.

22. "Statement on the Ecumenical Council's Constitution on the Sacred Liturgy," *Catholic Messenger* 82 (December 12, 1963): 12; "The Decree of April 2, 1964, On the Use of English in the Mass," *The Jurist* 24 (July 1964): English text: 358–62; Latin text: 360–62; "The Liturgical Reform: The American Bishops' Committee on the Liturgy," *Catholic Mind* 62 (May 1964): 51–54.

23. Crichton, *Changes in the Liturgy,* 4–6.

24. McManus, "The New Rite of Mass," 65–76; Frederick McManus, "The Implementation and Goals of Liturgical Reform," *Worship* 39 (October 1965): 482ff. *In persona Christi* is a Latin phrase meaning "in the person of Christ," a much-debated theological description of priests: does it mean "modeling" Christ to others? In the "place of" Christ to the church? etc.

25. "Here's How the Mass Will Change," NCWC News Service, *National Catholic Reporter* 1 (October 28, 1964): 1, 3, 5.

26. Jim Castelli and Joseph Gremillion, eds. *The Emerging Parish: The Notre Dame Study of Catholic Life since Vatican II* (San Francisco: Harper & Row, 1987), 129. As the editors wryly remark about congregational singing in the two decades after Vatican II: "introducing music is one thing; getting Catholics to sing en masse is another. More than two-thirds of the congregation joined in hymn-singing in only 30 percent of the masses observed. The pattern seems to be that the general level of singing the seasonal parts of the Mass is far from impressive" (129).

27. "Sweeping Changes at the Altar," *National Catholic Reporter* 1 (October 28, 1964): 5, 7. Crichton, *Changes in the Liturgy,* 44–48.

28. Dale Francis, "The Mood of the Laity: Confused, Frustrated, and Bewildered," *The Critic* 24 (February/March 1965): 56. Francis himself was a columnist for *Our Sunday Visitor,* a widely read Catholic newspaper sold at the entrances to Catholic parishes that would emerge in the next decade as a right-of-center organ criticizing liturgical (and general Catholic) "excesses."

29. Quote from Devine, *Liturgical Renewal,* 48.

30. "Sweeping Changes at the Altar," 5.

31. Ibid., 1.

32. "Getting Serious about the Liturgical Renewal," *National Catholic Reporter* 1 (May 12, 1965): 3.

33. Ibid.

34. "Merton Asks for a Gentle Touch in Liturgy Changes," *National Catholic Reporter* 1 (November 25, 1964): 2.

35. "Restorationism" here refers to the Catholic theological movement that emerged in the postconciliar era that seeks a restoring of church identity and Catholic piety by what might be termed a "move to the center." The "classic text" of the entire movement might very well be the *Catechism of the Catholic Church* (Liguori, Mo.: Liguori Press, 1994), read by many as an attempt to capture the "moderate reform" that animated most of the bishops who attended the Second Vatican Council while simultaneously eschewing the liturgical and disciplinary "excesses" that emerged in the decade after the council's close. Led by many former conciliar and postconciliar progressives like Joseph Cardinal Ratzinger (*Gospel, Catechesis, Catechism: Sidelights on the Catechism of the Catholic Church* [San Francisco: Ignatius Press, 1997]; *Introduction to the Catechism of the Catholic Church* [San Francisco: Ignatius Press, 1994]) and Pope John Paul II himself (*Veritatis Splendor* [Washington, D.C.: United States Catholic Conference, 1993]), the movement comes close to defining the official papal/curial "take" on the Second Vatican Council.

36. Wills, *Bare Ruined Choirs,* 21.
37. "Dogmatic Constitution on the Church," *The Documents of Vatican II,* 14–96. See especially the fine introduction to this document by Avery Dulles, S.J., 9–13.
38. Cardinal Bellarmine's classic institutional, papal-centered model of the church can be found in his *Disputationes de Controversiis Christianae Fidei adversus huius temporis haereticos* (Igolstadt, 1586, 1588, 1593); James Broderick, S.J., *The Life and Work of Blessed Robert Francis Cardinal Bellarmine* (London, 1928). See also John Hardon, S.J., *A Comparative Study of Bellarmine's Doctrine on the Relation of Non-Catholics to the Catholic Church* (Rome: Gregorian University, 1951).
39. "Dogmatic Constitution on the Church," chapter 2, "The People of God," 31, in *Documents of Vatican II,* ed. Abbott.
40. Durkheim, *Elementary Forms of the Religious Life,* 418.

Chapter 8: "To Be Beautiful, Human, and Christian"

1. Sr. Mary Corita Kent, "Art and Beauty in the Life of the Sister," in *The Changing Sister,* ed. Sr. Mary Charles Borromeo Muckenhern (Notre Dame, Ind.: Fides, 1965). Reprinted in *Sister Corita,* ed. Corita Kent and Harvey Cox (Philadelphia: Pilgrim Press, 1968), 15.
2. Dan L. Thrapp, "Order of Nuns Here Plans to Modernize Dress and Ideas," *Los Angeles Times,* October 18, 1967, 1; "Reforms Planned by Nuns on Coast," *New York Times,* October 27, 1967, 27. Harvey Cox, "Corita: Celebration and Creativity," in *Sister Corita,* 17.
3. "California Order Tests Liberal Rules That Would Let Sisters Pick Their Jobs," *National Catholic Reporter* 4 (October 25, 1967): 7. "Criticism of Nuns' Innovations Is Widened by McIntyre Paper," *New York Times,* March 25, 1968, 29.
4. Thrapp, "Order of Nuns Here," 1; "Decree on the Appropriate Renewal of Religious Life" (*Perfectae Caritatis*), 466–85, in *The Documents of Vatican II,* ed. Walter Abbott, S.J. (New York: Herder and Herder, 1966). See especially part 3: "The manner of living, praying and working should be suitably adapted to the physical and psychological conditions of today's religious, and also, to the extent required by the nature of each community, to the needs of the apostolate, the requirements of a given culture, the social and economic circumstances anywhere" (469).
5. John Gregory Dunne, "Angels of LA," *New York Review of Books* 45 (May 28, 1998): 17. In reviewing Monsignor Francis J. Weber's recent life of McIntyre, *His Eminence of Los Angeles,* Dunne has noted that McIntyre, much like his fellow American bishops, came of Irish-born, working-class parents. Unlike other American bishops, McIntyre worked in a Wall Street brokerage house before entering New York's Dunwoodie Seminary (18).
6. "Told to Quit Schools, L.A. Nuns Say," *National Catholic Reporter* 4 (January 17, 1968): 1. "New L.A. Lay Association Sides with Nuns in Dispute," *National Catholic Reporter* 4 (January 24, 1968): 5.
7. Mary Augusta Neal, S.N.D., *Catholic Sisters in Transition: From the 1960s to the 1980s* (Wilmington, Del.: Michael Glazier, 1984), 18, 20. Mary

Ewens, O.P., "Women in the Convent," in *American Catholic Women: A Historical Exploration,* ed. Karen Kennelly, C.S.J. (New York: Macmillan, 1989), 25, 32–35. Mary Ewens, *The Role of the Nun in Nineteenth Century America* (New York: Ayer, 1978), is arguably the best single study of religious women in the field.

8. Corita Kent, *Damn Everything but the Circus: A Lot of Things Put Together by Corita Kent* (New York: Holt, Rinehart and Winston, 1970), jacket leaf.

9. "LA to Keep Schools; Woos 'Approved' Nuns," *National Catholic Reporter* 4 (January 31, 1968): 1; "Vatican Rules against IHM Nuns on Changes Opposed by McIntyre," *National Catholic Reporter* 4 (March 13, 1968): 1; "IHM Nuns Put Off Compliance; Other Sisters Organize Support," *National Catholic Reporter* 4 (March 20, 1968): 1; "Rome Official Says Case Still Open," *National Catholic Reporter* (March 20, 1968): 6; "3000 Sisters Support IHMs," *National Catholic Reporter* 4 (March 27, 1968): 1, 6; "U.S. Top Crust Protests IHM Decision to Pope," *National Catholic Reporter* 4 (April 17, 1968): 7; "25,556 Sign Appeals Backing IHM Nuns," *National Catholic Reporter* 4 (May 8, 1968): 7.

10. "Congregation of Religious Hits 'Groundless' IHM Criticism," *National Catholic Reporter* 4 (May 1, 1968): 3; "IHM Nuns Vote 10 to 1 to Join Renewal Group," *National Catholic Reporter* 4 (June 26, 1968): 1, 7.

11. Max Weber, *On Charisma and Institution Building,* ed. S. N. Eisenstadt (Chicago: University of Chicago Press, 1968), 48. See also Max Weber, *Theory of Social and Economic Organization,* trans. and ed. Talcott Parsons (New York: Oxford University Press, 1947), 329.

12. Weber, *On Charisma and Institution Building,* 19, 21.

13. Ibid., 54.

14. "Decree on the Appropriate Renewal of Religious Life," no. 2, 468.

15. "Canon law" refers to the official guidelines of the Roman Church. In the twentieth century there have been two major revisions of church law: in 1917 and again in 1984, when canon law was revised in light of the reforms of the Second Vatican Council. Canon 487 of the older (1917) code defined the "religious state" as "the firmly established manner of living in community, by which the faithful undertake to observe not only the ordinary precepts, but also the evangelical counsels, by means of the vows of obedience, poverty, and chastity." For a magisterial commentary on that code, see C. A. Bachofen, C. Aug., *A Commentary on the New Code of Canon Law,* 8 vols. (St. Louis: Herder, 1918–31). On American nuns see Mary Ewens, "Women in the Convent," 21, 24.

16. Ewens, "Women in the Convent," 24–25.

17. Ibid., 24–25.

18. Ibid., 26, 32–33.

19. Ibid., 39. See also Mary Schneider, "The Transformation of American Women Religious: The Sister Formation Movement as Catalyst, 1954–64," *Working Paper Series* 17, no. 1 (Spring 1986), Cushwa Center for the Study of American Catholicism, University of Notre Dame, Notre Dame, Ind.

20. Ewens, "Women in Convent," 39–40. Rosemary Rader, "Catholic Fem-

inism: Its Impact on U.S. Catholic Women," chapter 7 in *American Catholic Women*, ed. Kennelly, 185–86.

21. Rader, "Catholic Feminism," 185; Ewens, "Women in the Convent," 40–41.

22. Rader, "Catholic Feminism," 185.

23. "Decree on the Appropriate Renewal of Religious Life," in *Documents of Vatican II*, ed. Abbott, no. 17, 478; emphasis added.

24. Ibid., no. 20, 479–80.

25. "Order of Nuns Here Plans to Modernize," *Los Angeles Times*, October 18, 1967, 1, 8.

26. "Told to Quit Schools, L.A. Nuns Say," *National Catholic Reporter*, January 17, 1968, 1, 7.

27. Ibid., 1, 7. "Archdiocese Silent on Report Nun Teachers Will be Fired," *Los Angeles Times*, November 7, 1967, Part II (Editorial Section), 1; "Nuns Dispute with Cardinal Explained by Head of Order," *Los Angeles Times*, November 11, 1967, 1, 14; "McIntyre Looks to Rome in Nun Dispute," *Los Angeles Times*, November 18, 1967, 3.

28. "New L.A. Lay Association Sides with Nuns in Dispute," *National Catholic Reporter* 4 (January 24, 1968): 5.

29. "13 Jesuits Praise L.A. Nuns' Renewal," *National Catholic Reporter* 4 (January 31, 1968): 10.

30. "Nuns Appeal to Pope to Press Liberal Practices," *New York Times*, March 12, 1968, 37; "Fighting Nuns," *Newsweek* 91 (April 1, 1968): 100; "What to Wear?" *Newsweek* 91 (February 16, 1968): 73; "Vatican Is Entering Dispute Over Nuns on Coast," *New York Times*, April 17, 1968, 53. "Answer to Petition," *New York Times*, April 17, 1968, 53.

31. "Vatican Rules against IHM Nuns on Changes Opposed by McIntyre," *National Catholic Reporter* 4 (March 13, 1968): 1, 12; "IHM Nuns Put Off Compliance; Other Sisters Organize Support," *National Catholic Reporter* 4 (March 20, 1968): 1, 6.

32. "IHM Split Authorized, Sisters to Pick Group," *National Catholic Reporter* 4 (June 19, 1968): 3. "Ultimatum to Nuns," *Newsweek* 91 (June 21, 1968): 61. "3000 Sisters Support IHMs," *National Catholic Reporter* 4 (March 27, 1968): 1, 12.

33. "Whatever Happened to the IHMs?" *National Catholic Reporter* 7 (April 7, 1971): 1, 8.

34. Ibid., 8.

35. Quote of Margaret Rose Welch, in "Whatever Happened?" *National Catholic Reporter*, 8.

36. Sister Corita Kent, "Art and Beauty in the Life of the Sister," 15.

37. Neal, *Catholic Sisters in Transition*, 18, 21, 24.

38. Weber, *On Charisma and Institution Building*, 39.

39. Ibid., 61.

Chapter 9: Thomism and the T-Formation in 1966

1. Mike Celizic, *The Biggest Game of Them All: Notre Dame, Michigan State, and the Fall of '66* (New York: Simon and Schuster, 1992), 24. The two

works having most influence on my understanding of the University of Notre Dame and its place in American Catholic higher education are Philip Gleason, *Contending with Modernity: Catholic Higher Education in the Twentieth Century* (New York: Oxford University Press, 1995), and Theodore Hesburgh, *God, Country, Notre Dame* (New York: Doubleday, 1990).

2. Murray Sperber, *Shake Down the Thunder: The Creation of Notre Dame Football* (New York: Henry Holt, 1993), 436.

3. Celizic, *Biggest Game of Them All*, 286. Moose Krause with Stephen Singular, *Notre Dame's Greatest Coaches: Rockne, Leahy, Parseghian, and Holtz* (New York: Pocket Books: 1993), 5–6. "The Greening of the Fighting Irish," *Sports Illustrated* 33 (December 14, 1970): 76–78.

4. Arthur Daley, "No Decision" in "Sports of the Times," 3, *New York Times*, November 20, 1966.

5. Celizic, *Biggest Game of Them All*, 286–87, 295.

6. "Notre Dame–Michigan State Play to 10–10 Tie," *New York Times*, November 20, 1966, 1, 3. In the same issue see "No Decision" in the "Sports of the Times" column by Arthur Daley, 2. See also "Prestige Upheld Despite Deadlock," by Allison Danzig, *New York Times*, November 21, 1966, 66, and (in the same issue), "Without an R.S.V.P.," by Arthur Daly, 66. Celizic, *Biggest Game of Them All*, 295; Krause and Singular, *Notre Dame's Greatest Coaches*, 5–6.

7. Sperber, *Shake Down the Thunder*, 80.

8. It is generally agreed by Notre Dame aficionados that the "Victory March" was composed by Michael Shea, an alumnus who would go on to become the organist at St. Patrick's Cathedral in New York City. Sperber, *Shake Down the Thunder*, xix, 16, 21. See also Krause and Singular, *Notre Dame's Greatest Coaches*, 3ff.

9. Gleason, *Contending with Modernity*, 100. Harry A. Stuhldreher, *Knute Rockne, Man Builder* (Philadelphia: Macrae-Smith, 1931), 114, 139–40.

10. This entire paragraph is based on Sperber, *Shake Down the Thunder*, xxi.

11. William Brashler, "Ara in the Afternoon," *Notre Dame Magazine* 13 (Winter 1984): 38–41. Ralph Martin, "Letter from a Catholic College Graduate to the President," *Ave Maria* 103 (April 16, 1966): 7–10; see also David J. O'Brien, *From the Heart of the American Church: Catholic Higher Education and American Culture* (Maryknoll, N.Y.: Orbis, 1994), 50ff.

12. Martin, "Letter to the President," 7.

13. Ibid., 8. On the "New Notre Dame," see Andrew M. Greeley, *From Backwater to Mainstream: A Profile of Catholic Higher Education* (New York: McGraw-Hill, 1969), 21–22; "Hustler for Quality," *Time* 67 (May 7, 1956): 77–78; "God and Man at Notre Dame," cover story in *Time* 79 (February 9, 1962): 48–50; Robert F. Griffin, "Facing Life without Father," *Notre Dame Magazine* 14 (Spring 1985): 11; John Underwood, "A Shining Example," in *Spoiled Sport: A Fan's Notes on the Troubles of Spectator Sports* (Boston: Little, Brown, 1984), 235–71.

14. On Hesburgh's use of the athletic tradition (and revenues) for academic purposes, see "An Interview with Father Hesburgh," *Notre Dame Magazine* 6 (June 1977): 22; George N. Schuster, "The Hesburgh Years: A Personal Remem-

brance," *Notre Dame Magazine* 1 (June 1972): 19–20. Martin, "Letter to the President," 9.

15. "Our First Great Catholic University?" *Harpers* 234 (May 1967): 41–49. "God and Man at Notre Dame," 48–49; Richard Conklin, "The Hesburgh Years: The Challenge of Change," *Notre Dame Magazine* 1 (June 1972): 13–17. "Profile of a College Class," *America* 118 (March 9, 1968): 313–17.

16. Harold Abramson, "Religion," in *The Harvard Encyclopedia of American Ethnic Groups,* ed. Stephan Thernstrom (Cambridge, Mass.: Harvard University Press, 1980), 870. Andrew Greeley, *The American Catholic: A Social Portrait* (New York: Basic Books, 1979), 9. See also Richard Schermerhorn, *Comparative Ethnic Relations: A Framework for Theory and Research* (New York: Random House, 1969); Milton Gordon, *Assimilation in American Life* (New York: Oxford University Press, 1964); Nathan Glazer, "Ethnic Groups in America," in *Freedom and Control in Modern Society,* ed. Monroe Berger et al. (New York: Van Nostrand, 1954), 158–72. For an insightful glimpse of some of the issues in the history of the debate over the term "ethnicity," see Nathan Glazer and Daniel Patrick Moynihan, eds., *Ethnicity: Theory and Practice* (Cambridge: Harvard University Press, 1975), especially Talcott Parsons's important essay, "Some Theoretical Considerations on the Nature and Trends of Change of Ethnicity," 53–83, and Andrew Greeley and William McCready, "The Transmission of Cultural Heritages: The Case of the Irish and the Italians," 209–35.

17. Philip Gleason, "American Identity and Americanization," *The Harvard Encyclopedia of American Ethnic Groups,* 55; Richard Schermerhorn, *Comparative Ethnic Relations: A Framework for Theory and Research* (New York: Random House, 1969), 123. One of the best recent explorations of the much-debated meanings of the term "ethnicity" can be found in Richard Jenkins, *Rethinking Ethnicity: Arguments and Explorations* (London: Sage, 1997). See also John Hutchinson and Anthony D. Smith, eds. *Ethnicity* (New York: Oxford University Press, 1996); and Eugeen Roosens, *Creating Ethnicity: The Process of Ethnogenesis* (Newbury Park, Calif.: Sage Publications, 1989).

18. Greeley, *American Catholic,* 19, 21.

19. Andrew Greeley, *The Catholic Myth: The Behavior and Beliefs of American Catholics* (New York: Macmillan, 1990), 44–48; Greeley, "Denomination and Political Values: A Cross-National Analysis," *Sociology and Social Research* 54, 485–502.

20. Thomas Stritch, *My Notre Dame: Memories and Reflections of Sixty Years* (Notre Dame, Ind.: University of Notre Dame Press, 1991), 23, 40.

21. Stritch, *My Notre Dame,* 70. Theodore Hesburgh, *God, Country, Notre Dame,* 46–47; Thomas Stritch, "Seven Hesburgh Predecessors," *Notre Dame Magazine* 16 (Spring 1987): 22–26.

22. Colleen McDannell, *Material Christianity: Religion and Popular Culture in America* (New Haven: Yale University Press, 1995), 155. A. J. Hope, *Notre Dame: One Hundred Years* (Notre Dame, Ind.: University of Notre Dame Press, 1943), 1–3. Edward Sorin, *Chronicles of Notre Dame du Lac,* trans. John M. Toohey, ed. James T. Connelly (Notre Dame, Ind.: University of Notre Dame Press, 1992), 270ff.

23. McDannell, *Material Christianity*, 154–60; Robert Leader, "How the Landscape Has Changed," *Notre Dame Magazine* (Spring 1984): 22–25. Joseph P. Chinnici, *Living Stones: The History and Structure of Catholic Spiritual Life in the United States* (New York: Macmillan, 1989), chapter 7.

24. Stuhldreher, *Knute Rockne*, 221.

25. Stritch, *My Notre Dame*, 26.

26. Thomas T. McAvoy, *Father O'Hara of Notre Dame: The Cardinal Archbishop of Philadelphia* (Notre Dame, Ind.: University of Notre Dame Press, 1967), chapters 4 and 5. Stritch, *My Notre Dame*, 27, 205–6. Thomas Stritch, "Seven Hesburgh Predecessors," 22–26.

27. Stritch, *My Notre Dame*, 28–29.

28. James F. Armstrong, *Onward to Victory: A Chronicle of the Alumni of the University of Notre Dame, 1842–1973* (Notre Dame, Ind.: University of Notre Dame Press, 1974), 346–53; Hutchins quoted in William Cunningham, *General Education and the Liberal College* (St. Louis: B. Herder, 1953), 3–5. Gleason, *Contending with Modernity*, 218–19, 246–47.

29. Conklin, "Hesburgh Years," 13, 16.

30. Theodore Hesburgh, "Looking Back at Newman," *America*, March 3, 1963, 721. Gleason, *Contending with Modernity*, 295; "The Curriculum of a Catholic Liberal Arts College: A Report on the College of Arts and Letters of the University of Notre Dame" (Notre Dame, Ind.: mimeo, 1953).

31. "God and Man at Notre Dame," 48.

32. "Notre Dame's President Hesburgh," *Time* 79 (February 9, 1962): 51.

33. Krause and Singular, *Notre Dame's Greatest Coaches*, 64.

34. John C. Lungren, Jr., *Hesburgh of Notre Dame: Priest, Educator, Public Servant* (Kansas City, Mo.: Sheed and Ward, 1987), 22.

35. Arthur Daley, "Overheard in the Huddle," "Sports of the Times," *New York Times*, November 23, 1953; "Coach Evashevski Turns Poetic over Game, Charges Iowa Was 'Gypped' at Notre Dame," *New York Times*, November 25, 1953, 29; "Complaint by Iowa Stirs Notre Dame," *New York Times*, November 26, 1953, 53; "Leahy Will Miss Notre Dame Game," *New York Times*, November 28, 1953, 19; "Young Coach, Old Winning Ways," *Life* 37 (October 4, 1954): 23–27.

36. Lungren, *Hesburgh of Notre Dame*, 21–22, 37; Krause and Singular, *Notre Dame's Greatest Coaches*, 4. For a typical sports page write-up of Leahy's last triumphant season, see Arthur Daley's column, "Sports of the Times": "Monday Morning Quarterback," November 23, 1953, *New York Times*, 34.

37. Krause and Singular, *Notre Dame's Greatest Coaches*, 30, 118–19.

38. Celizic, *The Biggest Game of Them All*, 31. Kenneth Woodward, "Lessons of the Master," *Notre Dame Magazine* (Spring 1984): 14–21.

39. Celizic, *The Biggest Game of Them All*, 31. "Hesburgh of Notre Dame," *New York Times Magazine* (May 11, 1969): 56–67; "The Mellowing of a President," *Time* 97 (February 15, 1971): 67; "Hesburgh of Notre Dame," *Nation* 214 (March 6, 1972): 300–302; "Prince of Priests," *Time* 104 (May 7, 1977): 74–75.

40. Celizic, *The Biggest Game of Them All*, 127, 128. The question of academic quality versus religious identity was one that interviewers would continue

to ask Hesburgh until his retirement: in 1977, on the twenty-fifth anniversary of his presidency, an interviewer in *Notre Dame Magazine* asked the president: "Has the pursuit of academic excellence, which is at the heart of your presidency, cost Notre Dame in terms of the life of the place? What about those 'old' alumni who talked about the value of the potential Notre Dame students who might be very attracted to the values and traditions of Notre Dame but who have been refused admission because of higher requirements?" Hesburgh began his answer by dryly noting that "your question assumes that only dumb kids are attracted to values and tradition" ("An Interview with Father Hesburgh," *Notre Dame Magazine* 6 [June 1977]: 22).

41. Martin, "Letter to the President," *Ave Maria*, 8.

42. Ibid., 8, 9.

43. "A Reply," *Ave Maria* 103 (April 16, 1966): 11–15, 12. On Hesburgh's great admiration for Newman and his own debt to Newman's "idea of a university," see Hesburgh, "Looking Back at Newman," *America*, March 3, 1963, 721.

44. "A Reply," *Ave Maria*, 14.

45. Ibid., 12.

46. "An Interview with Father Hesburgh," 23; Griffin, "Facing Life without Father," 21.

47. Greeley, *The American Catholic*, 9.

48. The classic statement of the "melting pot" idea of immigrant and ethnic assimilation into an undifferentiated "mainstream" culture was (and is) Israel Zangwill's play, *The Melting Pot: A Drama in Four Acts* (New York: Macmillan, 1925). Greeley, *American Catholic*, 12, 15, 16.

49. Greeley, *American Catholic*, 19–20, 21. On this point of ethnicity's perdurance in American society, see Philip Gleason, "Ethnicity Recessive and Resurgent, 1924–1979," in *Harvard Encyclopedia of American Ethnic Groups*, 47–55; and William C. McCready, ed. *Culture, Ethnicity, and Identity: Current Issues in Research* (New York: Academic Press, 1983). For a somewhat different (and more critical) evaluation of the threat of ethnicity in the modern world, see Manning Nash, *The Cauldron of Ethnicity in the Modern World* (Chicago: University of Chicago Press, 1989).

50. Greeley, *American Catholic*, 28–29.

Conclusion: Magnalia Christi Americana

1. The title of this chapter is taken from the first work of "historical theology" written in America, Cotton Mather's *Magnalia Christi Americana, or The Ecclesiastical History of New-England, from Its First Planting, in the Year 1620, unto the Year of Our Lord 1698.* The best modern edition of this work, whose Latin title means "The Mighty Works of Christ in America," is edited by Raymond Cunningham (New York: Frederick Ungar, 1970). For the text of John Winthrop's "Modell of Christian Charitie," see *The Puritans in America: A Narrative Anthology,* ed. Alan Heimert and Andrew Delbanco (Cambridge, Mass.: Harvard University Press, 1985), 81–92. The Winthrop quote is from p. 91 of the Heimert/Delbanco edition.

2. For a fine sketch of the "doxological history" mentioned in this paragraph see Catherine Albanese, "Public Protestantism: Historical Dominance and the One Religion of the United States," chapter 12 (pp. 396–429), and "Civil Religion: Millennial Politics and History," chapter 13 (pp. 432–62) in *America: Religions and Religion* (Belmont, Calif.: Wadsworth, 1992).

3. On this style of writing American religious history, see Gerald Brauer, "Changing Perspectives on Religion in America," in *Reinterpretation in American Church History,* ed. Gerald Brauer (Chicago: University of Chicago Press, 1968), 1–28. The major texts in this "doxological" style of American religious history include: Robert Baird, *Religion in America* (New York: Harper & Brothers, 1856; originally published in Scotland in 1843); Philip Schaff, *America: A Sketch of the Political, Social, and Religious Character of the United States in North America* (New York: Charles Scribner, 1855); Daniel Dorchester, *Christianity in the United States* (New York: Phillips & Hunt, 1888). William Warren Sweet, founder of the great "University of Chicago" school of American religious history, used Frederick Jackson Turner's magisterial "frontier hypothesis" to refocus the emphasis on the American frontier. This entire genre came under criticism by Sidney Ahlstrom in his *Religious History of the American People* (New Haven, Conn.: Yale University Press, 1972), who offered an entirely new, "post-Protestant" style of American religious history. Woodrow Wilson's quote is found on the frontispiece of Ernest Lee Tuveson's *Redeemer Nation: The Idea of America's Millennial Role* (Chicago: University of Chicago Press, 1968).

4. It is only fairly recently that scholars of American religious history have turned their attention to the crucial role of missions in understanding America's millennial self-identity. The classic multivolume study of American (and European) foreign missions is Kenneth Scott Latourette, *A History of the Expansion of Christianity,* 7 vols. (New York: Harper and Brothers, 1937–45). An excellent collection of essays analyzing the relation of foreign mission ideology to American millennial impulses (among many other impulses) is John K. Fairbank, ed., *The Missionary Enterprise in China and America* (Cambridge, Mass.: Harvard University Press, 1974). The best interpretive study of American mission ideology and its relationship to American cultural identity is undoubtedly William R. Hutchison, *Errand to the World: American Protestant Thought and Foreign Missions* (Chicago: University of Chicago Press, 1987). See especially chapter 4: "A Moral Equivalent for Imperialism," 91–124.

5. For an especially perceptive essay by Niebuhr, drawing out and "problematizing" America's foreign policy ideology in relation to Christian principles, see Reinhold Niebuhr, "The Children of Light and the Children of Darkness," in *The Essential Reinhold Niebuhr,* ed. Robert McAfee Brown (New Haven, Conn.: Yale University Press, 1986), 160–81, originally delivered as the West Lectures at Stanford University in 1944.

6. Niebuhr's earlier classic reflection on the dichotomy between individual altruism and group selfishness was *Moral Man and Immoral Society* (New York: Charles Scribner's Sons, 1932), especially xi–xii of the Introduction. Quote is from *The Irony of American History* (New York: Charles Scribner's Sons, 1952), 147.

7. "Eschatology" is a theological term (and discipline) referring to the study

of those realities "beyond history" — heaven and hell, death and redemption. To term a hope "eschatological" thus means to look for its fulfillment beyond history, in God's redemption at the "end of history."

8. On the congeries of institutions and families that constituted the "Protestant Establishment" in the U.S. and its mid-century challenges, see William R. Hutchison, *Between the Times: The Travail of the Protestant Establishment in America, 1900–1960* (New York: Cambridge University Press, 1989), 3–13. The most accessible older account of this establishment is Digby Baltzell, *The Protestant Establishment: Aristocracy and Caste in America* (New York: Random House, 1966). Robert Wuthnow, *The Restructuring of American Religion* (Princeton, N.J.: Princeton University Press, 1988). See especially chapter 3.

9. On Christian Realism, see George Hammer, *Christian Realism in American Theology: A Study of Reinhold Niebuhr, W. M. Horton, and H. P. Van Dusen* (Uppsala, Sweden: Appelbergs Boktryckeriaktiebolag, 1940). On the "post-Protestant era in American religious history," see Sidney Ahlstrom, *A Religious History of the American People,* Introduction. Wuthnow, *The Restructuring of American Religion,* 35ff.

10. John Courtney Murray's brilliant intellectual "end run," arguing that Catholics were in the best position to understand the natural law language and intentions of America's founding documents, was offered in *We Hold These Truths: Catholic Reflections on the American Proposition* (New York: Sheed and Ward, 1960).

11. McAvoy brilliantly outlined this tension between Catholicism's doctrinal unity and ethnic pluralism in *The Formation of the American Catholic Minority, 1820–1860* (Philadelphia: Fortress Press, 1967), first published in *Review of Politics* 10 (1948): 13–34.

Index